MY SHANGHAI

MY SHANGHAI

Recipes and Stories from a City on the Water

BETTY LIU

HARPER DESIGN
An Imprint of HarperCollins Publishers

To my mom, my dad, and Alex's mom and dad.
You taught me about my roots and how to cook.
And to Alex, who is my everything.

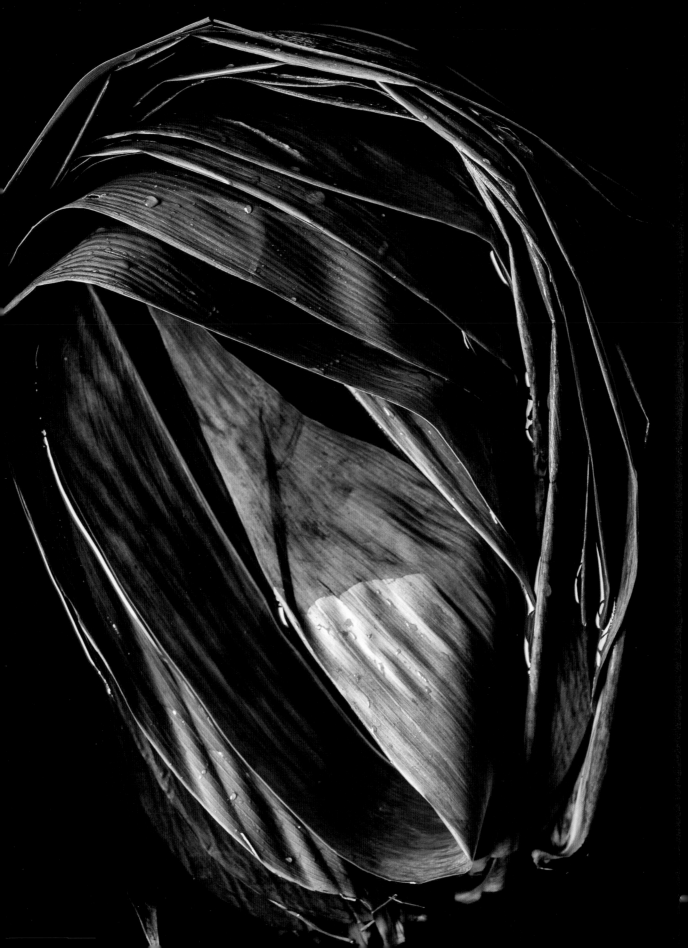

CONTENTS

INTRODUCTION

I first had the seed of an idea to write this book one afternoon as I watched my mom wrapping 粽子 *zongzi*, glutinous rice dumplings in bamboo leaves. I was just starting to learn how to cook, teaching myself with a combination of calls to my mother, Google searches, and old-fashioned trial and error.

My mom cooks from instinct and muscle memory rather than laboring over a recipe. No careful measuring with teaspoons or cups for her—she makes additions and adjustments by paying attention to her senses. All throughout cooking, she tastes and tests, adjusting to build up layers of flavor. That afternoon, as she instructed me to "add enough soy sauce," "cook until it's done," and "add about a throw of sugar"—instructions that made it obvious to me that I lacked her culinary instincts—I scribbled away on my notepad, guessing at quantities and noting the steps, ready to test it out for myself and develop a written recipe so that I would be able to reproduce this dish on my own in the future. There were no words to describe how my mom folded two sheets of long bamboo leaves into a pyramidal dumpling, so I recorded it with my phone, something to dissect and describe later.

These *zongzi* were subsequently frozen, tucked neatly into plastic bags, wrapped in cold packs, and hidden away in my check-in luggage. My mom isn't prone to overt expressions of sentiment, but the love was all there, in the food that went with me across the country.

My family is from 上海 Shanghai, a fertile land crisscrossed by rivers and streams. Shanghai sits in the Yangtze River Delta, a city on the water. The river runs through the city in an intricate weave of streams and runoffs, providing a variety of fresh produce and seafood. Once a fishing village, Shanghai transformed into a major commercial center when it became an official international port in the 1840s. Shanghai attracted merchants, traders, and travelers, soon adopting the name "Paris of the East." Domestically, it became the city of opportunity, and people from all over China flocked there, bringing their regional cuisines with them. Today, Shanghai is a modern metropolis, rife with international communities and influences. Yet pockets of old Shanghai still exist, and authentic Shanghai cuisine, which is referred to as 本帮菜 *ben bang cai*, "local cuisine," persists within this rich food culture. Visitors can find dishes like 生煎包 *sheng jian bao*, "pan-fried pork dumplings"; 小笼包 *xiao long bao*, "soup dumplings"; 红烧肉 *hong shao rou*, "red-braised pork belly"; and 葱油拌面 *cong you ban mian*, "scallion oil noodles," at bustling family-owned joints tucked away amid busy streets and on the menus of high-end restaurants atop gleaming skyscrapers.

My parents grew up in this bustling city during the Cultural Revolution. They spent most of their young lives in poverty. Food came directly from what grew on the land, which, luckily, was fertile and plentiful. Cooking wasn't fancy. There were no expensive kitchen appliances. Instead, they ate and cooked simply, as had been the norm for centuries. When my parents moved to Oregon for graduate school, they brought their culinary traditions with them: They foraged along the coast for wild mussels and crabs. They planted bamboo and dug up the young shoots in the winter. They cooked with what was in season. This is the home-style Shanghai food that I ate growing up.

It was only when I moved across the country to St. Louis for college that I realized how much I had taken my parents' food for granted. The very first dish I ever tried to make was born out of a desperate nostalgia for my mother's cooking. In the communal kitchen of my college dorm, I tried my hand at many Chinese Americans' gateway dish: tomato and egg stir-fry.

It was a disaster—the eggs stuck to the wok and the tomatoes turned it all to mush. I rued the fact that I had never tried to learn how to cook before I went to college. I begged my mom for cooking lessons. At first, my mom was a bit confused—how do you teach someone how to cook? When my mom was growing up, she lived in a complex with four or five other families, sharing a central communal kitchen. Families cooked together, shared the same pans and knives, exchanged recipes, and celebrated holidays together. She picked up the basics just by watching, helping out, and taking on every role in that kitchen. She learned by doing.

So, I did what she had done growing up—I observed. While home on college breaks, I would make my way to the kitchen, looking to see what was simmering on the stove and peppering my mom with a million questions (in fact, this hasn't changed—I still call her to ask questions as I'm cooking). I watched how she mixed spices and paired ingredients. I learned how to make small, simple dishes. Eventually, I learned how to make one of my favorites, Mom's Shanghai Red-Braised Pork Belly (page 93). With its fragrant caramelized pork; thick, glistening sauce; and tofu knots to soak it all up, this dish is legend in our family. It was a moment of personal triumph.

A little later, I studied abroad and worked in Shanghai. By this time, Shanghai had become the world's largest city, filled with cuisines from all over the globe. I knew to look for signs that said 本帮菜 *ben bang cai*. I ate my way through the city, sampling Shanghai's famous dumplings, seeking out the vendors with the best spices, and trying family-run restaurants with my cousins, fellow students, and coworkers. This experience informed my cooking and showed me the similarities and differences between home and restaurant cooking.

My Shanghai is an homage to my family's cooking—home-style cooking from the Shanghai region and surrounding areas—and a written record of recipes that had previously been passed down orally.

These recipes are my family's tradition. This book is not meant to freeze a culinary snapshot from decades ago or set strict guidelines about what is "authentic" or not. Home cooking is just that: food cooked at home, and thus open to adjustments according to your individual tastes. Instead of looking at these as rigid recipes, I hope you'll think of them as a starting point to begin developing your own traditions and making the food truly yours.

THE LAND OF FISH AND RICE

鱼米之乡 | yú mǐ zhī xiāng

China is a vast country with various geographies, terrains, and climates. As culinary preferences stem from the ingredients available from the land, it is not surprising that cuisines across China vary immensely. When I visit China, I take great joy in discovering and trying other regions' cuisines: 四川 Sichuan's mouth-numbingly spicy, bold flavors; 湖南 Hunan's fiercely sharp spice; 北京 Beijing's dumplings and bread; 云南 Yunnan's refreshing vegetables; 西安 Xi'An's warm, spicy lamb-forward dishes; and 广东 Guangdong's herby, medicinal stews. But despite my love for this vast spread of regional cuisines, I keep coming back to the food I grew up with, the food that brings me the most comfort: 江南 Jiangnan cuisine.

Geographically, China is bisected by the Yangtze River, 长江 Chang Jiang, "long river," which flows from Sichuan in western China all the way to 上海 Shanghai and into the East China Sea.

The Jiangnan region encompasses the lower Yangtze area, south of the long river. This includes the city of Shanghai, as well as the bordering coastal provinces 浙江 Zhejiang and 江苏 Jiangsu and part of 安徽 Anhui. The more well-known cities in this region are Shanghai, 南京 Nanjing, 苏州 Suzhou, 杭州 Hangzhou, and 无锡 Wuxi.

My family has roots in this beautiful region: My mom's whole family is from Shanghai. My dad grew up in Shanghai, but his ancestors are from Sichuan (this is where I get my penchant for spicy food). My husband, Alex, also has roots in the Jiangnan region. My mother-in-law is from Suzhou and Wuxi, and my father-in-law is from Nanjing. Over the years, I've eaten at their tables and frequented these cities, and slowly, I began to understand and appreciate the nuances in the cuisine, even within the overarching region.

Jiangnan is crisscrossed by small streams, ponds, and lakes, providing abundant aquatic products and yielding bountiful, fertile land. Because of this, Jiangnan is poetically called 鱼米之乡 *yu mi zhi xiang*, "Land of Fish and Rice," an homage to its rich aquatic and agricultural offerings. The fresh, seasonal, and local food from this region has long been held in high regard, seen as refined and elevated. It includes two of China's Eight Great Cuisines: Jiangsu and Zhejiang, which have similar qualities because of their proximity and shared produce and cooking philosophies (the others are Sichuan, Hunan, Cantonese, Fujian, Anhui, and Shandong). Jiangnan cuisine is also called 江浙菜 *Jiang-Zhe cai*, "Jiang-Zhe cuisine," which combines the first characters in Jiangsu and Zhejiang, intertwining these culinary histories even in name.

The first time I heard Jiangnan referred to as *yu mi zhi xiang* was as my family and I sped along a small road by 太湖 Taihu, "Lake Tai," with a beautiful golden field of rice swaying gently with the breeze on one side and the stunning expanse of the lake on the other. My dad told me, "There's a reason we call this region the 'Land of Fish and Rice.'" I thought back on the gorgeous, entirely local meal we'd just had: steamed, radiantly fragrant white fish; boiled tiny freshwater shrimp with vinegar; garlic fried eel; lightly pickled 芦根 *lu gen*, "water bamboo"; chives with egg; a light and pure broth with 莼菜 *chun cai*, a slippery water plant found only in this region; and white rice, rounded off with tangerines freshly plucked from the restaurant's tree.

THE FLAVORS OF JIANGNAN

江南风味 | Jiāng nán fēng wèi

The core tenets of Jiangnan cuisine are fresh ingredients and seasonality.

Compared with other regions of China, Jiangnan cuisine is the least strongly flavored, yet I would never call it bland. Instead of a complex blend of flavor profiles, the cuisine is straightforward, focusing on the ingredients and drawing on a few aromatics, subtle spices, and three core seasonings: soy sauce, cooking wine, and vinegar.

This cuisine adores its vegetables, highlighting aquatic plants, wild vegetables from the mountains, and classic greens, but it also uses pork, poultry, and seafood for protein. You'll get a mix of flavors: sweet, salty, vinegary, with depth added by a touch of umami or the aid of fermented elements. It's all about complementing foods and elevating their 本味 *ben wei*, "natural flavors." The flavors are not meant to overwhelm the main ingredient but enrich and deepen the natural flavors. We use the essential fresh aromatics of ginger and scallion; dried spices such as star anise and cinnamon bark; and umami bits, like rehydrated shiitake mushrooms, wind-cured salt pork, and snow vegetable, to give dishes a 咸味 *xian wei*, "salty flavor," and add depth. Much attention is paid to the other senses, particularly vision, touch, and smell, to create a complex, multidimensional sensory experience.

To coax out that pure, deep flavor, some dishes take a bit of time to prepare and cook, such as Suzhou Pork Belly Noodle Soup (page 130), which simmers on the stove for hours after a lengthy curing process. A look at the ingredients shows that the pork belly is only lightly flavored with aromatics, both fresh and dry, cooking wine, and a touch of soy sauce. Like all good food, it's all about layering. Layering—from the initial prep to seasoning while cooking and the final garnish—builds up the flavors seamlessly. It's no wonder that this is one of the most famous dishes in Suzhou, beloved for its pure flavor and delightfully melty texture.

JIANGSU CUISINE

There are subtle provincial differences under the umbrella of Jiang-Zhe cuisine. The province of Jiangsu, which notably includes Suzhou, Wuxi, and Nanjing, is sometimes called the "Land of Water" (with Suzhou often hailed as the "Venice of the East") because of the streams and canals that crisscross the landscape. The abundant and fertile freshwater lakes, 阳澄湖 Yangcheng Hu and Tai Hu, provide a variety of aquatic delicacies, from plants such as *lu gen*; 茭白 *jiao bai*, "wild rice stem"; *chun cai*; and 莲藕 *lian ou*, "lotus root," to various types of fish, tiny freshwater shrimp, soft-shell turtle, hairy crab, and eel. Even within the cuisine of this province, there are differences. You can find seasoned yet refreshing cuisine from Suzhou, richly sweet yet balanced dishes from Wuxi, and exquisite duck-centered dishes from Nanjing.

Suzhou is only twenty minutes by high-speed train from Shanghai (so close, in fact, that the two cities' dialects, Suzhounese and Shanghainese, can be understood by both cities' residents), and the two cuisines are very similar.

ZHEJIANG CUISINE

The province of Zhejiang, with its epic mountainous landscape, bamboo forests, and stunning lakes, encompasses Hangzhou, 湖州 Huzhou, 绍兴 Shaoxing, and 宁波 Ningbo. The region is known for its bamboo shoots, prominent use of seafood, and renowned 龙井茶 *long jing cha*, "dragon well tea." 浙菜 *Zhe cai*, "Zhe cuisine," is aromatic, fresh, and known for elevated, rich dishes. A lot of Zhe dishes' names are incredibly beautiful and poetic and tend to have an associated historical story. This region's cuisine includes fermented, funky flavors from Shaoxing, salty seafood dishes and rice cakes from Ningbo, and rich, fresh presentations from Hangzhou.

SHANGHAI CUISINE

Shanghai cuisine is hard to describe. To call it sweet is too simple and doesn't even get close to the heart of the cuisine. Yet, that is how Shanghainese food is commonly labeled. It's a real culinary nexus because it not only sits between the two aforementioned provinces, it is also a major metropolitan city, with a large population of Chinese people who are not truly Shanghainese, as well as foreigners who have made their home in Shanghai. Despite, or perhaps due to, the lightning-quick pace of development, Shanghainese traditions are lovingly preserved, most notably seen in the persistence and prevalence of *ben bang cai*, a source of comfort for those who have witnessed the rapid cosmopolitan changes to the city. Shanghai used to be a small fishing village, situated advantageously on the Yangtze River Delta with numerous webs of canals and rivers flowing through the land. The city's name translates to "over the sea." Because of its opportune landscape, Shanghai is now a transportation hub, a place of exchange and commerce. If you visit Shanghai, a plethora of international cuisines awaits you, but hidden within this rich international tapestry are its authentic culinary traditions.

Shanghai food is 清淡爽 *qing dan shuang*, "light and refreshing." The food has purity, with plenty of depth in flavor, and is bright and well rounded, with a foundation in 江南风味 *jiang nan feng wei*, the flavors from the two neighboring provinces mentioned above. The light and fresh sweetness of Jiangsu shows up in dishes such as the humble Blanched Water Spinach (page 222), while the refined saltiness of Zhejiang is represented by dishes such as Rice-Encrusted Pork Ribs (page 60). The cuisine is deeply seasonal and is really centered on the ingredients. Naturally, drawing from a land of rice and fish, the cuisine is rich in fresh vegetables and seafood, utilizing techniques such as steaming, braising, and saucing. Oftentimes, the ingredients will speak for themselves, enhanced by a few seasonings. 口感 *kou gan*, "mouthfeel," is as important as flavor in this cuisine.

Shanghai cooking is most famous for 红烧 *hong shao*, "red braise" or "red cooking," food glazed in a luxurious sauce of soy sauce, wine, and sugar.

The recipes and flavor profiles in my book are more typical of Jiangsu cuisine than Zhejiang, simply because this is the way my family cooks, but Shanghai's culinary borders are blurred, drawing deeply from its neighbors.

SEASONALITY

Out of all the cuisines in China, Jiangnan cuisine is the most rooted in seasonality. The calendar year is told not through dates on a piece of paper but by what's sold in the markets, the holidays that are celebrated, and the traditions practiced. If we look at the agricultural calendar, paying attention to the micro-changes in climate, there are, in fact, twenty-four seasons.

Thus, I chose to divide this book into seasons. When I told my dad of my plan to do so, he was not surprised—how else would you do it?

The way we interact with the seasons is at the heart of Shanghai cuisine. Seasonality is what makes this cuisine radiant: using what's in season ensures you're using the produce with the best flavors. What is on a dinner table is dictated by what is available in the market.

This focus on seasonality extends beyond what's available to include the body's needs in each season. For example, foods are categorized as either "hot" or "cold," but these categories do not refer to the temperature of the food; instead they refer to the food's effect on the body. In the hot summer season, the high temperatures inflame the body, and "hot" foods are avoided because they're considered inflammatory and are incongruent with the body's needs that season; in the winter, it is the reverse. Food is seen as akin to medicine, a way to help the body through the seasons, influencing both energy and health.

When I was growing up, my family ate specific things at different times of the year. In the winter, my mother always said, the body craves warm, thick stews to bolster energy and compensate for the cold outside. She prepared nutritious foods using citruses, pumpkins, yams, winter bamboo, and turnips, all abundant during that time of year, to nourish our bodies. In summer, chilled dishes were ubiquitous before meals, and we ate "cold" dishes to cool down the body, such as mung bean soup, watermelon, cucumber, and bitter melon.

Even tea is seasonal. In the spring and summer, mellow, delicate green tea is consumed, particularly because the prized young green tea leaves are picked around the time of 清明 Qing Ming Festival. When the climate grows colder, the Chinese put away green tea (or more likely, have brewed it all up) and take out black tea, 红茶 *hong cha*, or, fermented teas, such as 普洱 *pu er* tea.

FOOD AS A LANGUAGE OF LOVE AND WELCOME

Food is deeply entwined with pride, respect, and welcome in Chinese culture. It's a method for treating the body, but also for showing love and generosity. It's a well-known custom to be stuffed with food when visiting relatives or extended family, especially grandparents. My husband jokes that he was chubby as a child because his grandfather always, *always* had delicious pork belly and other goodies on the kitchen table for him. Eating is a communal event. Meals aren't meant to be divvied up into individual portions or carefully doled out over multiple courses. Instead, dishes are served family style, with numerous plates of delicacies, including a large pot of fluffy white rice, placed in the middle of the table for all to partake. It's a way to welcome everyone into the meal. In fact, my father made a circular wood tabletop with a center rotating piece so that we could comfortably hold and serve up to fifteen people.

A typical Jiangnan meal is balanced, both visually and in terms of the menu, meant to keep dinner guests fulfilled but not uncomfortably stuffed. No matter if you are serving two people or ten, there are core components that make up the meal. Usually, every dinner guest starts with a heaping bowl of white rice and a pair of chopsticks. Then a steaming bowl of soup is served from a large clay pot (or cast-iron Dutch oven, for me). A spread of main dishes sits in the middle of the table, within reach of all participants. The content of these dishes is where balance is achieved: a luxurious, rich red-braised pork belly is usually served with a *qing dan* greens dish. A tangy dish, such as snow vegetable, would be served with something more mellow and warm, such as soupy napa cabbage and pork. The colors, main ingredients, and soupiness of the dishes are balanced and not repeated too frequently. In a restaurant, the meal will start with cold dishes, then move on to hot, soupy, starchy dishes like rice or noodles, and end with dessert and fruit. At home, there's less formal order. Usually, all the dishes are served at once, with rice eaten alongside. Soup is often eaten near the end, spooned into a rice bowl to soak the leftover rice, so that the rice absorbs the flavors of the soup and is deliciously plump, then slurped up.

COOKING TECHNIQUES

红烧 *hóng shāo*, "red braising": The hallmark cooking method of Shanghai cuisine, red braising involves slowly braising food in a magical combination of soy sauces, wine, sugar, and, sometimes, dried aromatic spices until the food is mouth-meltingly tender and luscious. It's one of my favorite ways to prepare pork belly, and it is truly versatile, as the red-braise flavor will change subtly when used with different proteins. The syrupy sauce is superb over a bed of white rice, too. See Mom's Shanghai Red-Braised Pork Belly (page 93), Red-Braised Fish (page 79), and red-braised Lion's Head Meatballs (page 133).

炸 *zhà*, "deep-fry": This technique is used to crisp up protein and create an external layer that holds the interior in. It's used most notably with fish (see Shanghai "Smoked" Fish, page 203) and spareribs (see Sweet-and-Sour Ribs, page 208). I like to deep-fry in my wok, as the tapered base means I can use less oil if I fry in small batches. As always, be very careful when deep-frying and remember that oil and water do not mix. The Shanghainese do something unique: they sometimes deep-fry their food twice. Once to set shape and a second time to caramelize and set flavor, as in Oil-Exploded Shrimp (page 163).

炒 *chǎo*, "stir-fry": A classic technique associated with Chinese cooking, stir-frying involves frying food in a small amount of oil over high heat to quickly sear the food, stirring continuously to dislodge stuck food and ensure all of the food makes equal contact with the wok and seasonings. Flowering Chives and Pork Slivers (page 156) is one of my favorite stir-fry dishes to make, as it can be slapped together in less

than half an hour and illustrates this method perfectly. Some tips to keep in mind:

Prepare all of your ingredients ahead of time. Have all of your ingredients chopped, sauces mixed, and everything laid out. Try to have your ingredients at room temperature, as anything cold will bring down the temperature in the wok.

Know every step. Things move quickly in a stir-fry, and there's usually no time to consult a recipe (unless there's a simmering step).

Don't cook too much at once. The size of your wok determines how much to make at a time. I cook with a bigger wok because I want both the space to properly stir-fry and the flexibility to make dishes that serve more than two people.

Heat up your wok properly. A carbon-steel wok is the most traditional, and it's my choice of wok, as it heats up quickly and effectively.

But don't overheat. After adding the oil, swirl to coat the wok and then immediately add the aromatics to *bao xiang*, as described below. Letting the oil get too hot may cause the aromatics to burn, which is why we often add oil after the wok has heated.

爆香 *bào xiāng*, "explode into fragrance": This technique involves flash-frying aromatics in hot oil to release their fragrance.

煎 *jiān*, "pan-fry": In this method, food is shallow-fried, or sautéed, in a small amount of oil for a long period, usually untouched, to create a nice crust.

蒸 *zhēng*, "steam": One of the healthiest cooking methods is to steam food, an incredibly clean

and pure way to cook that preserves all the natural flavors.

卤 *lǔ*, "simmer in spiced stock": This technique involves simmering in a spiced, flavored stock. See Spiced Braised Beef Shank (page 212) and Soy-Braised Duck Legs (page 219).

焖 *mèn*, "stew and smother": The best way to learn this method is to make Suzhou Pork Belly Noodle Soup (page 130). You stew the pork belly for hours over the smallest flame, lid on to create a tight seal and smother the meat, until it is so tender (more tender than in a red braise) it can be placed, cold from the fridge, in a hot bowl of soup and immediately take in the heat and become melty soft.

白灼 *bái zhuó*, "white boiled": Boiling or blanching vegetables creates a light, fresh dish. See Blanched Water Spinach (page 222) for a sublime example, and then use the same method to cook cabbage, lettuce, asparagus, or any other greens.

煮 *zhǔ*, "boiled" or "poached": A simple boil or poach. Scallion Oil–Poached Chicken (page 179) uses this method to slowly cook poultry so that you get tender, juicy chicken. A quick shock in an ice bath crisps up the skin—not in a fried chicken sort of way; instead it makes the skin 脆 *cui*, "more brittle."

炖 *dùn*, "long simmer": A long simmer coaxes out flavor from ingredients. It's about depth. Clear-simmered Lion's Head Meatballs (page 133) and Winter Melon, Bamboo, and Pork Rib Soup (page 65) are classic examples of 炖汤 *dun tang*, an umbrella term for any long-simmered soup.

风干 *fēng gān*, "wind dried": This is a method for preserving meat in the winter, when the air is less humid and cool enough to dry salted meat

safely. See Wind-Cured Salt Pork (page 268) to make this at home.

收汁 *shōu zhī* or 收干 *shōu gān*, "reduction": This is a method for reducing sauce, uncovered, over high flame, to create the characteristic Shanghainese thick, glistening sauce.

勾芡 *gōu qiàn*, "thickening with starch": In some recipes, such as Hairy Crab Tofu (page 45), the ingredients might not generate enough natural gelatin and the sauce needs a little help to thicken up. Dissolving a bit of cornstarch in water and adding it to your sauce will do the trick.

炒糖色 *chǎo táng sè*, "fry with sugar to color": In this technique, meat is fried in sugar melted in oil. It's utilized in dishes such as Mom's Shanghai Red-Braised Pork Belly (page 93) and Sweet-and-Sour Ribs (page 208) to add color and a caramelly sweetness.

手工剁肉 *shǒu gōng duò ròu*, "hand-minced meat": This is the secret to super-tender Lion's Head Meatballs (page 133). Mincing meat by hand not only gives you control over the size of the mince, but also ensures the type and quality of the meat in your dish (see page 270).

滚刀 *gǔn dāo*, "rolling knife": This method of cutting food is meant to transform a cylindrical stem (such as one of bamboo, carrot, or celtuce) into a geometric shape with multiple surfaces to absorb sauce. Begin by cutting one end at an angle. Roll the stem a quarter and cut at an angle again. If the resultant piece is too thick, cut it in half lengthwise.

小包酥 *xiǎo bāo sū*, "small bun paste": A method for assembling pastry utilizing two types of dough—an oil paste and a water dough— to create lamination and flaky layers. This is demonstrated photographically in Suzhou-Style Mooncakes (page 73).

A SHANGHAINESE PANTRY

As any Shanghainese cook will tell you, your food is only as good as your ingredients. The Chinese home-cooking pantry staples are light soy sauce, dark soy sauce, Shaoxing cooking wine, white rice, black vinegar, sesame oil, ground white pepper, salt, rock sugar, ginger, scallion, dried shiitake mushrooms, and star anise. If you start with these, you can make most home-style dishes, and then add to your pantry as you make more complex dishes.

Many of these ingredients are available in any supermarket, such as scallions or shiitake mushrooms, but others may require a trip to your local Asian supermarket. If there's no Asian supermarket near you, you can also try Amazon.

As for protein, pork is one of the main proteins in this region, as is poultry: chicken, of course, but also duck and goose. Duck, in particular, is prized in Jiangnan—with so many streams, ponds, lakes, and rivers, ducks thrive in this region. Similarly, seafood and freshwater aquatic life are abundant and eaten with vigor: freshwater fish (such as white fish native to Tai Hu or "knife" fish, tiny with the sweetest flesh but a million impossibly thin bones), shrimp, eels, crab, and even crawfish. Tofu is prominent in Buddhist vegetarian cuisine, with certain dishes adopted by the surrounding community (like the "Duck" Tofu Rolls, page 82).

Foreign imports have become household staples, too, such as tomato. Tomatoes are used most famously in the classic home-style dish Tomato and Egg Stir-Fry (page 207) or as a simple appetizer in Wuxi, where they sprinkle ripe tomatoes with sugar and eat them fresh.

FRESH AROMATICS

Scallion and ginger are cardinal aromatics used in almost every dish. My kitchen will always have a few knobs of ginger and stalks of scallion waiting to be used. Fresh aromatics are used in almost every step of cooking: in the preparation, to dispel any fishiness or porkiness, and in the cooking, to impart their fragrance and enrich the dish. Scallion and ginger are the mirepoix of the East, often combined and cooked to create a flavor base before adding the other ingredients.

香葱 *xiāng cōng*, "scallions": These small green onions are prized not only for their slightly peppery taste when eaten raw, but also for their toasty aroma when cooked. They can help flavor a stock or soup or power an entire dish when slowly rendered in a nutty oil (Scallion Oil Noodles, page 167).

生姜 *sheng jiāng*, "fresh ginger": Ginger root is used in almost every dish, one of the essential ingredients in Jiangnan cooking. It complements meat, poultry, and shellfish particularly well. Ginger is prized in Chinese culture for its warming and cleansing qualities.

蒜 *suàn*, "garlic": Young green garlic is valued for its sharp, pungent flavor. *Suan* refers to both green and cloves of garlic, and I will note in recipes which one is used.

香菜 *xiāng cài*, "cilantro": A delightful herb used mostly as a garnish.

韭菜 *jiǔ cài*, "garlic chives": These flat, long, sharp green leaves hold a pungent flavor that becomes fragrant when cooked.

韭黄 *jiǔ huáng,* "yellow chives": These chives are grown away from sunlight and therefore are a delicate pale yellow. Their flavor is also subtler than their green counterparts, and I love to use them when frying rice cakes or noodles. You can find these in Asian supermarkets.

韭菜花 *jiǔ cài huā,* "flowering chives": These are really the flowering stems of garlic chives, typically sold in a separate bundle with unopened yellow flowers at the tips. Their stems are round (versus the flat leaves of chives) and thus have a juicy crunch that the leaves lack. They have a similar flavor to garlic chives with an additional touch of sweetness. With minimal additional seasoning, these stems will carry a dish.

FATS

For normal cooking, the Shanghainese use a neutral cooking oil with a high smoke point, such as rapeseed oil. When I'm cooking at home for myself, I use a high-quality olive oil.

猪油 *zhū yóu,* "pork lard": This is the not-so-secret treasure of Chinese cooking and the linchpin of aroma in Jiangnan cooking (see recipe, page 271). A dollop of it in noodle soup, a scallion pancake, or black sesame sticky rice balls will add an indescribable 香 *xiang,* "fragrance," one that you won't be able to pinpoint but will definitely notice if it is omitted.

You can ask your butcher for pork fat. I usually go up to the meat counter at Chinese grocery stores and ask for 猪肥 *zhu fei,* and I'll receive a bag of pork fat. This fat is what I render into pork lard.

鸡油 *jī yóu,* "chicken fat": When I make chicken soup, the fat that rises after refrigerating the stock for a bit is this golden-yellow chicken fat. I scoop it up and freeze it, ready to take out and use whenever I need a boost of umami.

麻油 *má yóu,* "sesame oil": Sesame oil is strong and fragrant—a little goes a long way. It's usually added at the end of a dish for a little bit of fragrance.

红油 *hóng yóu,* "red chili oil": Every single breakfast wonton, soup dumpling, congee, tofu flower, or soy milk joint will have the same condiments available, whether set to the side for you to help yourself or in little jars at each table: soy sauce, vinegars, and chili oil (see recipe, page 273).

STARCHES

白米饭 *bái mǐ fàn,* "white rice": White rice is an absolute staple in Chinese home cooking. Use it to make cooked rice, soupy rice, congee, or fried rice. Usually, Chinese people eat medium- or long-grain rice, as the rice grains will fluff and separate, yet cling to one another other slightly. (This is how you can eat rice with chopsticks!)

Rice is *the* staple food in Southern China. A typical meal in a Chinese home begins and ends with the bowl of white rice. It's the bowl you hold on to as you navigate the crowd of savory dishes in the center of the table. Well-cooked rice (not too soggy or too dry) takes on the flavor of whatever you put on it. I love to take a piece of red-braised pork, for example, glistening with its inky glaze, and let it rest on my rice before eating it. That gorgeous sauce leaves behind an imprint on the pristine rice, and the subsequent bite of rice is simply divine, full of porky flavor. At the end of a meal, when all the dishes are gone, that bit of leftover rice isn't thrown away, nor is it eaten plain. I ladle some steaming soup into my bowl to finish my meal in a satisfying way: a slurp of soup and loose grains of rice.

There are rice paddy fields all across Southern China. Like any crop, rice goes through seasonal cycles. The fields flood in the spring, giving the paddies that characteristic silver sheen, and become home to numerous aquatic life, such as paddy eels. The rice grows until autumn arrives, when the paddies become golden yellow and dry, ready for scything, and harvesting.

The "traditional" way to cook rice in my family is with a rice cooker. It's easy and fast and cooks rice amazingly well. You can also cook it on a stovetop, the true traditional way. I've included several ways to enjoy rice, including Congee (page 275) and Fried Rice (page 276).

糯米 *nuò mǐ* "glutinous white rice": Also called sticky rice (you'll see me using these terms interchangeably in this book), this rice is a short-grain rice. It sticks together in clumps when cooked and has a wonderful texture.

年糕 *nián gāo*, "rice cake": Ningbo in Zhejiang province is renowned as the birthplace of rice cakes. Rice is milled with water to create a super-fine flour, which is then drained until a certain amount is left to create a long log, and then sliced on the diagonal to make ovals. They're a treat traditionally eaten during the New Year, and the characters literally translate to "year cake." These can be steamed, stir-fried (as in Shanghai Stir-Fried Rice Cake, page 109), eaten in soup, or even eaten sweet.

米粉 *mǐ fěn* "rice flour": Long-grain rice is ground to make rice flour (not to be confused with glutinous rice flour).

水磨糯米粉 *shuǐ mó nuò mǐ fěn*, "water-ground glutinous rice flour": You can find glutinous rice flour in Asian supermarkets. Look for the bags of glutinous rice flour with green lettering.

红曲米 *hóng qū mǐ*, "red yeast rice": Grains of rice are inoculated with yeast, creating a deep red color that acts as a natural food dye. You can use just a little bit in braises, for example, to impart a bright red color.

生粉 *shēng fěn*, "cornstarch": Used primarily in a slurry with water to thicken sauces or in fillings. Potato starch can also be used as a substitute.

小麦淀粉 *xiǎo mài diàn fěn*, "wheat starch": Often used with rice and glutinous rice flour (like in Qing Tuan, page 159) to create an incredibly soft, sticky wrapper.

面 *miàn*, "noodles": There are many kinds of noodles you can buy at the supermarket. In this book, a thin, long, egg-free fresh noodle is appropriate. The 真味 Twin Marquis brand is a pretty reliable one, and it's sold in the fresh noodle refrigerated section in most Asian supermarkets.

馄饨皮 *Hún tún pí*, "wonton wrappers": The wonton wrappers sold in the United States are smaller than traditional Shanghai ones,

but they work! Buy the square, eggless wonton wrappers for Shanghainese wontons.

油面筋 *yóu miàn jīn*, "fried dough puff": This is also called a fried gluten ball. Raw, *you mian jin* looks almost like a doughnut, puffed up, golden yellow, hollow, and light. When cooked, it shrinks and becomes a sponge, soaking up all the flavors.

烤麸 *kǎo fū*, "wheat gluten": This is a delicious, elastic, sponge-like food and can be bought dried or frozen. If dried, it will need to be rehydrated. If frozen, it will need to be boiled before using. It's full of protein and used in Buddhist vegetarian cuisine, but it's also famously used in Shanghainese Four Happiness Wheat Gluten (page 189), where the wheat gluten cubes are marinated in an aromatic sauce that perfuses them with flavor.

SEASONINGS

盐 *yán*, "salt": You can use any kind of salt you want, unless otherwise specified in the recipe (for example, using coarse sea salt when curing meat). So much of home cooking is seasoning to your preference, so always start with less and then add more.

糖 *táng*, "sugar": Shanghainese cooking is often hailed as sweet, but the dishes aren't really meant to be simply sweet. Sugar is never the main flavor and is instead used to round out salty flavors and add balance to a dish. Rock sugar is traditionally used in Shanghainese cooking, but when I'm seasoning stir-fries or other home-style dishes, I just use white cane sugar.

冰糖 *bīng táng*, "rock sugar": Rock sugar is a crystallized raw sugar that is often used in Chinese cooking. Compared with its white sugar counterpart, rock sugar is milder and less sweet, with more caramelly tones, and becomes more treacly when dissolved. It's used in braises and sauces because it also gives an extra gleam to the liquid.

酱油 *jiàng yóu*, "soy sauce": In Shanghai, soy sauce (as opposed to salt) is the main seasoning, used to add an umami-savory touch to dishes. The cuisine of Jiangnan is famous for its use of soy sauce. Soy sauce comes in two main varieties: 生抽 *sheng chou*, "light soy sauce," and 老抽 *lao chou*, "dark soy sauce." Light soy sauce is thinner and has more flavor, used for giving a dish "umami saltiness." Dark soy sauce is more syrupy and molasses-like. It's less salty and is great for adding color. Pearl River Bridge and Lee Kum Kee make good "premium" soy sauces, though my parents have always used Kimlan's soy sauce, and that's what sits in my pantry.

镇江香醋 *Zhènjiāng xiāng cù*, "black vinegar": Also called Chinkiang vinegar (the Cantonese pronunciation of Zhenjiang, a city in Jiangsu province) or *xiang cu*, "fragrant vinegar," this aged black vinegar is made from glutinous rice.

It's my favorite vinegar to use in cooking and has a rich, tart, sweet flavor. This black vinegar is available in Western supermarkets these days. I would highly recommend stocking this in your pantry.

大红浙醋 *dà hóng zhè cù*, "red rice vinegar": This is the counterpart to Jiangsu black vinegar from the neighboring Zhejiang province. This vinegar is made from red rice yeast for that classic rosy-red color.

白米醋 *bái mǐ cù*, "rice vinegar": This is the more widely known, mild, fruity rice vinegar that I use to balance out black vinegar in my sweet-and-sour dishes, as well as in my pickles (Soy-Pickled Radish, page 53).

绍兴黄酒 *Shàoxīng huáng jiǔ*, "Shaoxing cooking wine": Also called 黄酒 *huang jiu* or 料酒 *liao jiu*, this is a type of yellow rice wine with a dark amber hue, famously from the city Shaoxing (where fermentation is prized and the local cuisine is full of funky, fermented foods, like 梅干菜 *mei gan cai*, "dried and pickled mustard greens"). It's a heady, fragrant wine that serves as the main ingredient in dishes like Drunken Chicken (page 225). It's used in cooking to help dispel the fishiness of seafood and the meatiness of pork. This wine has a stunning fragrance. When using it as a main flavoring, try to find 花雕酒 *hua diao jiu*, a finer quality Shaoxing wine that can also be drunk. This is also readily available in Western supermarkets, but if you can't find it, you can try to use a pale dry sherry or sake as a substitute.

白酒 *bái jiǔ*, "white liquor": This is famously known as "the celebratory drink." It's served in tiny goblets and meant to be drunk quickly (干掉 *gan diao*, essentially "bottom's up"). *Bai jiu* is taken out and served at celebrations, group dinners, or business meetings. It's a sign of respect. In cooking, *bai jiu* lends a special fragrance, and because of its high alcohol content, it's used to preserve meats (as in Wind-Cured Salt Pork, page 268).

酒酿 *jiǔ niàng*, "sweet, fermented glutinous rice wine": Sweet Rice Wine and Rice Ball Soup (page 116) is one of my favorite desserts, utilizing sweet, tangy, fragrant, and slightly boozy fermented rice as a soup base. It's made with 酒曲 *jiu qu*, a wine yeast ball that ferments the glutinous rice. It's sold in jars in any Asian grocery store.

STOCKS

A tenet in Shanghainese cooking is quality ingredients. Nowhere is this more relevant than in stock. Stock is used not only for soup but also as a flavor kick in stir-fries and braises. I make 鸡汤 *ji tang*, "chicken stock," and 高汤 *gao tang*, "high stock" (see page 277), on a regular basis, and then freeze them in batches for future use.

DRY AROMATICS

白胡椒 *bái hú jiāo*, "white pepper": On every Shanghainese table sit little dishes of salt, ground white pepper, fragrant vinegar, and maybe a jar of chili oil.

花椒 *huā jiāo*, "Sichuan red peppercorns": While Shanghai cuisine isn't known for spiciness, it does know how to coax out flavors in a dish, and these red peppercorns are integral to complement certain meat and poultry dishes. They are used in both Father-in-Law's Nanjing Saltwater Duck (page 211) and Wind-Cured Salt Pork (page 268), where the peppercorn (actually, the husk of the berry versus the whole peppercorn) contributes not spiciness but fragrance. It's one of the five ingredients in five-spice powder (along with star anise, cassia bark, fennel seed, and clove). When you open a box or bag for the first time, a distinct aroma should waft up—heavenly.

青花椒 *qīng huā jiāo*, "green peppercorn": This peppercorn is more about the fragrance and "mouth-numbing" than heat and is lovely to add to chili oil.

辣椒碎 *là jiāo suì*, "crushed red peppers": I use these to make my Red Chili Oil (page 273). I buy mine directly from China, but you can find them online (I recommend those from Mala Market or Spicy Element).

SPICES

八角 *bā jiǎo*, "star anise": One of the most important spices in Jiangnan cooking, star anise is a warming spice, wonderful in slow cooking.

桂皮 *guì pí*, "cassia bark": Called "Chinese cinnamon," cassia bark is more bark-like than a cinnamon stick, with a thick texture, and it is less potent and sharp than cinnamon, with an almost smoky flavor, perfectly suited for braising, for stewing, and in marinades.

丁香 *dīng xiāng*, "clove": This spice is sharp and pungent, with a sweet aroma that permeates the whole dish. Use it sparsely, as it can easily overwhelm a dish.

茴香籽 *huí xiāng zǐ*, "fennel seeds": This tasty, aromatic spice is used in five-spice powder.

草果 *cǎo guǒ*, "black cardamom pods": This is one of my favorite spices for braising, and a must-use when making Spiced Braised Beef Shank (page 212). Crack slightly with a mortar and pestle or the flat side of a cleaver before using.

香叶 *xiāng yè*, "bay leaves": Familiar in Western cooking as well, these are used for aroma and fragrance.

芝麻 *zhī ma*, "sesame seeds": Black and white sesame seeds are essential in Shanghainese

cooking, whether as a garnish, for their nutty flavor in rice balls, or for extra fragrance. I like to buy them raw and toast them myself on the stovetop.

DRIED AND PRESERVED FOODS

The Shanghainese have a special love for funky, fermented foods. An addition of just a bit of anything fermented can transform the flavor of a dish, adding rich umami and depth. I've included the recipes to make Wind-Cured Salt Pork (page 268) and Snow Vegetable (page 272), two cardinal preserved dishes in Shanghainese cooking, but these and other fermented and preserved foods can easily be found at your local Asian grocery store.

咸肉 *xián ròu*, "salt pork": This traditional winter staple can easily be made at home and adds umami to any dish. I always keep some salt pork belly in my freezer, ready to be sliced off and added to my stir-fries or stews (or used in chunks, as in Double Pork Soup, page 102).

雪菜 *xuě cài*, "snow vegetable": Pickled mustard greens that are tangy and rich with umami. They can be easily salted and pickled at home (see recipe, page 272) and will transform soups or stir-fries.

When choosing your mustard greens, look for fresh ones with minimal yellowing leaves. Short, small mustard greens are better for flavor, as the longer ones can be bitter.

梅干菜 *méi gān cài*, "salted and dried fermented greens": Aged, dried fermented greens are funky and have a pungent, tangy flavor that is the star in Sun-Dried and Preserved Greens with Steamed Pork Belly (page 198). It's the renowned fermented green of Shaoxing in Zhejiang province. The mustard greens are first salted, then dried in the sun (getting darker and darker in the process). Packs of dried *mei gan cai* can be found in your local Asian grocery store.

Be sure to look for one that is from 绍兴 Shaoxing, for there is another variety from the Hakka that is sweeter and more moist. Rinse thoroughly with water to get rid of any grit before using.

榨菜 *zhà cài*, "pickled vegetables": The perfect accompaniment to congee, these pickled mustard stalks come in little packets and are easily found in Asian grocery stores. They're crisp, juicy, and refreshingly tangy. They can also be used in stir-fries or to top soups. Wu Jiang brand has some particularly aromatic ones.

鲞 *xiǎng* or 咸鱼 *xián yú*, "salt fish": The seafood counterpart to salt pork, salt fish is beloved in Jiangsu and Zhejiang provinces, where seafood and freshwater creatures are abundant. If you go to any lakeside market (or even city market), you'll find bags of dried fish, ready to be used in cooking for that 鲜咸 *xian xian*, "fresh and salty flavor." You can find it in Asian supermarkets, particularly salted yellow croaker. Soak in cold water overnight before using.

干贝 *gān bèi*, "dried scallops": These are little gems of flavor. If I have some on hand, I love to throw a handful into my High Stock (page 277) for an extra umami kick.

咸蛋 *xián dàn*, "salted duck egg": With a brilliantly golden yolk surrounded by salty white, you'll find this served with breakfast congee and wrapped into *zongzi* and other treats.

皮蛋 *pí dàn*, "thousand-year egg": One of the more controversial Chinese foods, thousand-year egg is funky and delicious, fermented to become a gray-blue-green food.

豆腐乳 *dòu fu rǔ*, "fermented tofu": I've had to work to convince people unfamiliar with this food to try it. "It's a bit like cheese," I say. On first glance, it looks like giant, creamy tofu floating in brine. Cubes of tofu are allowed to "rot" and get moldy, then the containers are sealed and they ferment. There are red (spicy) and white versions, and they're most commonly eaten with congee (see recipe, page 275).

豆豉 *dòu chǐ*, "fermented black beans": These soybeans fermented with salt and spices pack a punch. They are used in moderation.

虾米 *xiā mǐ*, "dried shrimp 'rice'": Plump dried shrimp, also referred to as 开洋 *kai yang*, "open ocean," comes in many sizes. They're like little flavor-bombs that can instantly elevate a dish. *Xia mi* are the size of corn kernels and are rehydrated before cooking, providing not only shrimp but also a flavorful stock.

虾皮 *xiā pí*, "dried shrimp 'skins'": These are as small as sesame seeds and are meant to be used as a dried aromatic—briefly fried for a garnish or topping.

花菇 *hua gu*, "shiitake mushrooms": These are a must-have in a Shanghainese pantry. Dried shiitake mushrooms hold a fountain of umami flavor and yield both soft caps as well as a flavorful stock. There are multiple grades of quality, and one of the best is the 花菇 *hua gu*, "flower mushrooms," called such because of the floral pattern on the cap. If you're browsing for dried mushrooms, try to find some from Japan, as those are usually of high quality.

木耳 *mù ěr*, "wood-ear mushrooms": One time in Wuxi, Alex's uncle pointed out a small stump and told me, "This is *mu er*." And so it was: a little cluster of thin, wavy, ruffled wood-ear mushrooms. These slippery black mushrooms with an almost crispy texture are delightful. They shrink when dried, so don't be alarmed when you rehydrate a lot more than you expect.

银耳 *yín ěr*, "silver mushrooms": Called "silver" because of their shimmery pale color, these mushrooms are prized for their healing properties and often used in soups.

金针 *jīn zhēn*, "dried lily flowers": Also called "golden needles," these are used in Four Happiness Wheat Gluten (page 189) and contribute a fruity, floral aroma. They will need to be rehydrated.

红枣 *hóng zǎo*, "red dates": Used in dessert soups, these are healthy and thought to 补身 *bu shen*, "fix the body."

莲子 *lián zǐ*, "lotus seeds": These are great in porridges and soups and famous for being a filling in sweet mooncakes.

百合 *bǎi hé*, "lily bulbs": Used in congees and soups (like Mung Bean Soup with Lily Bulb, page 194), these are also considered medicinal and healthy for the body.

荷叶 *hé yè*, "lotus leaves": Use these to make Rice-Encrusted Pork Ribs (page 60), which are steamed inside large, aromatic lotus leaves. They can be found fresh in China, but in the United States, you can usually only find them dried.

粽叶 *zòng yè*, "zongzi leaf": This is the leaf of a type of water bamboo (see photograph, page 29) found near lakes and ponds that is used to wrap *zongzi* (see Shanghai-Style Pork Zongzi, page 183).

桂花 *guì huā*, "osmanthus": A famous flower in Jiangnan. It has a lovely sweet aroma that is so delicious when paired with sticky rice balls (see Sweet Rice Wine and Rice Ball Soup, page 116) or lotus root (see Sweet Osmanthus-Stuffed Lotus Root, page 49).

LEGUMES

红豆 *hóng dòu*, "adzuki (red) beans": Dried adzuki beans are used to make red bean paste, one of the core fillings for desserts (as in Pumpkin Rice Cakes, page 39)

绿豆 *lǜ dòu*, "mung beans": Also called green beans, mung beans are commonly used in Shanghainese cooking, usually in dessert form. I use these every summer to make Mung Bean Soup with Lily Bulb (page 194). You can also turn that soup into mung bean popsicles or add the beans to congee.

SOYBEAN PRODUCTS

Soybean products in the East are akin to dairy products in the West. This is something my dad often said. And after pondering it for a bit, I realized he was entirely correct. Soybean is milled into soy milk, which is the basis for making tofu and a whole slew of other products.

黄豆 *huáng dòu*, "soybeans": These are essentially aged, sun-dried edamame, and they're the foundation for all soy products, including soy sauce, soy milk, and tofu.

豆腐皮 *dòu fu pí*, "tofu skin": This is tofu pressed into thin sheets, resembling skin. It's prepackaged and can come either fresh or dried. If dried, it needs to be rehydrated before using. It becomes the "skin" for dishes like "Duck" Tofu Rolls (page 82).

豆花 *dòu huā*, "tofu flower": The ultimate breakfast tofu, tofu flower refers to just-set tofu, softer and with even less body than silken tofu. In Southern China, tofu flower is served warm and topped with seasonings and scallions.

嫩豆腐 *nèn dòu fu*, "soft 'silken' tofu": There are various types of tofu—silken, soft, firm, extra-firm—and they differ based on the amount of water pressed from the tofu. Silken tofu isn't pressed and is extremely soft and custard-like. It will break easily with a touch and works wonderfully in Chilled Thousand-Year Egg with Tofu (page 215). Soft tofu is my favorite tofu to work with. It's not as soft as silken tofu, but not as hard as firm tofu. It has enough body (while keeping its silkiness) that it's perfect to use in braises, such as Hairy Crab Tofu (page 45) or Sichuan mala tofu. Find it at Asian supermarkets. The Vitasoy brand is my favorite for soft tofu, though pay attention to the character 嫩 *nen*, "soft, tender," as sometimes the English label will still call it "silken." House Foods also has a good soft tofu, and it will specify "soft" in English.

豆腐干 *dòu fu gān*, "seasoned tofu": Seasoned tofu blocks usually come in squares, either in a light brine or with a five-spice seasoning. They are wonderful in stir-fries, as fillings for vegetable buns, or even as an afternoon snack.

百叶结 *bǎi yè jié*, "tofu knots": Thin sheets of tofu "skin" are tied into little knots, easily thrown into braises or soups.

OTHER

芝麻糊 *zhī ma hú*, "sesame paste": A rich paste made from toasted sesame seeds with a deep, nutty flavor that works wonderfully in sauces.

KITCHEN EQUIPMENT

锅 *guō*, "wok": The wok is one of the most important tools in a Chinese kitchen. It's not only the best pan for stir-fry (because it heats rapidly), it can also be used to boil noodles, deep-fry, steam, and braise. It has a dome-like shape with a narrow base and high, sloped edges. This shape makes it very functional for flipping and turning food quickly without much effort, but it also makes it ideal for deep-frying, as you can use less oil to cover a large area. (Never fill oil more than halfway up the wok.)

A traditional wok is hand-hammered from uncoated carbon steel, with a rounded bottom. I'm partial to carbon-steel woks with handles (either two curved "ears" or a handle that sticks out) because they're light and heat up quickly, but they do require some care and seasoning (as with cast-iron pans), to strengthen them over time. Stainless-steel woks are nice, low-maintenance alternatives to carbon steel—they are nonreactive, light, and you don't need to season them.

Rounded woks are meant for gas burners. A lot of gas ranges will have a large burner that produces a larger flame—required for Chinese cooking. However, if your gas burner isn't big enough to comfortably sit your round-bottomed wok, I recommend getting a wok ring to sit on the burner and keep it in place (or a flat-bottomed wok). Safety is the most important thing, after all, and a wok that slips and slides is a recipe for disaster.

I would highly recommend not buying a nonstick wok, as the high heat is unsuitable for most nonstick coatings. A properly heated wok will become nonstick, in a similar principle to cast-iron cooking.

CARE OF YOUR WOK

Despite the maintenance involved, I prefer to cook with a carbon-steel wok. Over time, with proper care, a shiny patina will form that protects the wok and creates a nonstick surface.

THE FIRST USE: The first season is important. Scrub with hot water and soap to remove any residual oil from its shaping process. Rinse and dry the wok thoroughly, then heat over low heat to dry completely. If you have wooden handles on your wok, wrap them with aluminum foil to prevent them from burning. Turn the flame up to high. As you heat up the wok, the remaining grease and impurities will start to burn off, and the carbon steel will become darker. Cover your hands with a towel or oven mitts and tilt the wok so that every part of it is heated. Be sure to have your exhaust fan on and windows open, as it may give off a smell.

Let the wok cool. Once cool enough to handle, use a little bit of soap to gently wash and scrub to remove any remaining impurities. Dry with a paper towel and place back on the stovetop. Heat over medium heat to cook off any remaining moisture. Once dried, turn the flame down to medium-low and add a tablespoon of neutral cooking oil. Throw in a knob of ginger and move it around with a wok spatula or chopsticks to spread the oil around the surface of the wok. Stir-fry the ginger for fifteen minutes. This allows the patina to build up. Turn off the heat, remove the ginger, then use a folded-up paper towel held by chopsticks or a spatula to wipe off the wok. Repeat this process once more for a perfectly seasoned wok.

DAILY MAINTENANCE: After making lighter dishes, I rinse my wok with water and scrub lightly, without any soap. For heavier dishes, such as meat braises, I follow the advice of Grace Young, dubbed the "Poet Laureate of the Wok," and let the wok it soak in hot water for five minutes, then wash with a sponge. If that doesn't do the trick, I will use some soap to cut through the grease. After every wash, dry completely on the stove over low heat before putting it away. (Never put your wok away moist! Always dry it completely.) If I had to use soap, or if I used the wok to boil or steam (thus cooking off the patina), I reseason it by rubbing the interior surface with oil (using a knob of fresh ginger) and heating it on medium-high for five minutes, then wiping out the oil with a paper towel.

锅盖 *guō gài*, "wok lid": A wok lid is a must. A good wok lid will fit a bit below the rim of the wok.

锅铲 *guō chǎn*, "wok spatula": A metal spatula is critical in stir-fry, especially when dealing with sticky rice or breaking up ground meat. A wok spatula should have a slight curve and a large surface area in order to handle a large amount of food in one motion.

竹锅刷 *zhú guō shuā*, "wok brush": Made of bristly, firm split bamboo stalks, a wok brush is ideal for cleaning a hot wok, as the wood will not melt as plastic would. When washing with hot water, you can use a wok brush to scrub and clean the wok.

砂锅 *shā guō*, "clay pot": Clay pots are a common find on the dinner table, usually holding hearty, warming soups, stews, or braises. They are often glazed on the inside but may not be on the outside. Clay pots retain heat well and are ideal for keeping food warm. They're also wonderful for cooking rice (like Celtuce-Leaf Rice, page 168), as the heat and cooking method create a crusty layer on the bottom of the pot. Using a cast-iron pot is a good substitute—I often use my Staub rice pan in lieu of a clay pot for rice.

蒸笼 *zhēng lóng*, "steamer": There are two types of steamers: layered bamboo and metal. I prefer bamboo steamers for ease of use—I like that I can place it on top of boiling water in a wok without swapping for a different pan—and for their fragrance. Be sure to let the bamboo baskets air dry after using, otherwise mold can develop. Metal steamers are ideal for steaming larger items but are also more likely to gather condensation on their lids, which can then drip into your food.

Food will stick to your steamer without a lining, so you should line your steamer basket with napa cabbage, cheesecloth, parchment paper, or oiled bamboo steamer liners. Make sure the bamboo steamer basket bottom never touches the water, and be careful of the hot steam when lifting your steamer out of the wok! I always protect my hands with oven mitts or dish towels, or use retriever tongs.

电饭锅 *diàn fàn guō*, "rice cooker": Electric rice cookers are a fixture in most Chinese households. I often wash and start rice before prepping a meal, knowing that it will cook and be kept warm until served. It's a great investment. Some rice cookers can make sticky rice, brown rice, or congee, as well, which is handy.

擀面杖 *gǎn miàn zhàng*, "Chinese rolling pin": Chinese rolling pins are small, light, and usually made of bamboo. Sometimes, they have tapered ends. They are usually a foot long and one inch in diameter. Use these to roll out skins for dumplings, soup dumplings, scallion pancakes, and steamed buns.

竹姜末 *zhú jiāng mò*, "grater": A bamboo or metal grater is a great tool for creating a fine ginger pulp or extracting juice.

筷子 *kuài zi*, "cooking chopsticks": Long cooking chopsticks are indispensable, and I use them for separating food, turning food, and, most important, tasting as I cook.

笊篱 *zhào li*, "metal strainer": A metal strainer is wonderful for both straining and deep-frying. I use a generic "spider" strainer with a thin wire netting—it's great for removing dumplings and wontons from their cooking water. I also have a larger metal strainer with a polka-dot pattern, like a giant, flat slotted spoon. This is great for deep-frying, and I will often place food (like shrimp) in the large spoon and dip it into the heated oil and leave it in the wok. I can then use the spoon to gently "shake" the food, keeping it from sticking.

菜刀 *cài dāo*, "vegetable cleaver": This is the first knife my dad taught me to use, and it's the one I probably use the most, as I usually cook more vegetables than meat. Any sharp knife will do, but a vegetable cleaver is light and straight, with a proper amount of flat surface to smack aromatics like ginger or scallion and scoop up chopped vegetables to throw into a pot. This cleaver is ideal for slicing, dicing, mincing, and chopping. It can also be used for boneless pieces of meat, but for meat with bones or heavier meats, you should use a meat cleaver.

切刀 *qiē dāo*, "meat cleaver": Meat cleavers are serious tools, and I recommend using them only if you have some experience with cooking. They are a bit larger and much heavier than vegetable cleavers, as their weight helps chop through bones. I mostly use mine to mince pork or chop through cooked poultry bones.

厨房剪刀 *chú fáng jiǎn dāo*, "kitchen shears": Another essential kitchen tool, a good pair of kitchen shears can aid with so many things: trimming seafood, cutting meat, cutting vegetables, and snipping tendons.

Candy (or oil) thermometer: I use my candy thermometer every time I deep-fry to ensure the right temperature is reached and maintained.

Mortar and pestle: I use these quite often in my kitchen, most frequently to crush rock sugar, but also to grind spices or mash aromatics into a paste.

秋

qiū

AUTUMN

When autumn arrives in the southern provinces, it's not the change in foliage that is anticipated, it's the new crop of food. The cooling foods of summer yield to warming, nourishing foods in preparation for winter. In early fall, winter melon is ripe and ready to be cooked, and okra, taro, and yams are abundant. Aquatic plants thrive and are ready to be harvested. Water chestnuts are native to northern Jiangsu, and in times of famine, people turned to the land and foraged water chestnuts as a hearty addition to their meals. Later in the season, golden fields of rice are a breathtaking vision, swaying gently with the wind. Early in autumn, osmanthus flowers bloom and fall, blanketing the ground with golden-yellow flurries. Of course, this is also the season of the hairy crab—no matter where you turn in the southern provinces, eye-catching signs and roadside hawkers announce their top-grade, authentic 大闸蟹 *da zha xie* from the famous Yang Cheng Lake—the perfect gift for your loved ones.

PUMPKIN RICE CAKES

南瓜饼 | *nán guā bǐng* | *Makes 20*

My mom has been making pumpkin rice cakes stuffed with gooey, warm red bean paste for as long as I can remember. She sometimes deviates from tradition and uses sweet potato in place of pumpkin, which is what I prefer to use. These cakes are very simple to make: Pumpkin (or sweet potato) and glutinous rice flour are combined to make an easy dough that is then stuffed with red bean paste and pan-fried on the stove to create a crispy golden exterior and a soft, gooey interior.

1 pound (455 g) pumpkin or
    sweet potato
1 tablespoon granulated sugar,
    or to taste
2 teaspoons pork lard
    (store-bought or homemade,
    page 271), softened butter,
    or neutral cooking oil, such as
    canola or grapeseed oil
1½ to 2 cups (240 to 320 g)
    water-ground glutinous
    rice flour
about 7 ounces (200 g)
    red bean paste (store-bought
    or homemade, page 159)
white sesame seeds
neutral cooking oil, such as
    canola or grapeseed oil

1. Peel and seed the pumpkin (or peel the sweet potato). Cut it into rough chunks and steam until fork-tender, 15 to 20 minutes. Let cool completely.

2. Mash or blend the pumpkin into a puree. Add the sugar, adjusting to taste depending on the sweetness of the pumpkin (you're looking for a mild sweetness). Stir in the lard. Add 1½ cups (240 g) of the rice flour and mix with a wooden spatula (or your hands) until a well-combined dough forms. It should be Play-Doh-like in consistency. If the dough sticks to your hands, add 1 to 2 tablespoons of additional flour, a little at a time, until the right consistency is achieved. Wrap the dough in plastic and let it rest at room temperature for 30 minutes.

3. Meanwhile, form the red bean paste into 20 balls, using about 2 teaspoons (10 g) of paste each, and set aside.

4. To shape the rice cakes, divide the dough in two, keeping one half under plastic wrap so it does not dry out.

5. Pinch off about 2 tablespoons of dough and roll it between your palm and a flat surface to form a sphere. Cupping the sphere with your left palm, use your right thumb (or the reverse, if you are left-handed) to create an indentation in the center, then pinch at the edges to create a deep bowl shape.

6. Place a ball of red bean paste into this bowl, then wrap your right hand around the pumpkin-dough bowl and squeeze while traveling up the bowl, drawing up the sides of the bowl and slowly pinching the opening closed (see photographs, page 115). Roll between your palms to form a sphere that encloses the red bean paste.

7. Roll the ball in a shallow bowl of sesame seeds. Press to flatten slightly into a disc.

8. Repeat steps 5 through 7 with the remaining dough, making approximately 20 discs in all.

9. Heat about 2 tablespoons cooking oil in a flat-bottomed skillet over low. Working in batches, gently arrange the discs in the skillet in a single layer. Cook until the rice cakes have browned on one side, then flip and brown on the other side, about 4 minutes per side. The cakes will become very soft and warm through.

10. Serve immediately. Refrigerate any leftover rice cakes and reheat them in a skillet before serving.

CRAZY FOR HAIRY CRABS

大闸蟹 | dà zhá xiè

"Beware all the fake hairy crabs out there," my parents warned me as I prepared for a trip to Shanghai late one October. In autumn in Shanghai, one cannot escape the fervor for hairy crabs. Throughout the markets, signs boast of hairy crabs from 阳澄湖 Yang Cheng Lake. Here and there, as if to prove a point, crabs cooked and broken in half revealed golden, creamy innards—this is what costs a premium. Every vendor I talked to sincerely impressed upon me their authenticity and brandished their certificate of authenticity to prove it.

It's not that "fake" crabs aren't real crabs; they just aren't farmed from Yang Cheng Lake, a freshwater lake northeast of Suzhou. This lake is famous for its aquatic offerings, including softshell turtle, shrimp, and hairy crab.

大闸蟹 *da zha xie*, "hairy crabs," also known as mitten crabs, are burrowers native to East Asia, particularly in the Jiangsu region. They're known as hairy or mitten crabs because of the "hair" on their legs and claws, as if they were wearing mittens. These crustaceans are prized for their clean, sweet flesh and golden-yellow creamy innards and roe.

To add to the sense of exclusivity, these crabs are available only for a short time every year: the ninth and tenth lunar calendar months, approximately late October to December. The crabs fill out and become extra flavorful when the weather gets cold.

On one trip, we had the opportunity to visit a crab farm in Yang Cheng Lake.

Longtime crab farmers Mr. and Mrs. Zhou brought us to the middle of the lake, which was peppered with small, single-room "houses" standing precariously on spindly legs, surrounded by an organized netted grid. Mr. Zhou brought up a rounded net, not dissimilar to the nets I've seen used to snare shrimp and eel, and a whole clump of crabs were lifted out of the lake, their distinctive yellow-tipped claws brilliant against the dark blue netting.

He pointed out the characteristics that make them true Yang Cheng Lake crabs: the white belly straight out of the water, a result of the cleanliness of the freshwater lake; the bright yellow tips of their legs; the stiff golden-yellow hair on the legs; and the green back (versus brown), also due to the clean water. Less visible on the surface but clear when cooked are their energy and strength from climbing the hard floor of the lake (versus the softer, muddier floors of other lakes).

The classic way to eat hairy crab is steamed, with a shallow bowl of fragrant vinegar accented with shreds of ginger for dipping. Eating them this way perfectly illustrates the culinary philosophy of the region: a great ingredient doesn't need much else to accompany it. The flavor is entirely from the crab.

HAIRY CRAB TOFU

蟹粉豆腐 | xiè fěn dòu fu | *Makes 2 to 4 servings*

Part of the experience of eating hairy crab, which is traditionally steamed in the simplest of ways, is to spend a good amount of time picking it apart, getting at the delicious 黄 *huang*, "yellow," sometimes referred to as "crab butter," as well as the sweet, delicate flesh. The Shanghainese also love to dunk raw crab in white liquor, creating nectar-like drunken crab.

While I love steamed crab, I have a weakness for crab roe tofu. Sweet crab flesh is stir-fried in pork lard with the crabs' juices and umami *huang*, simmered in stock, and then used to flavor soft tofu. It's warming and thick, with a symphony of flavors, and is magical over rice.

NOTE: Soft tofu is the second-softest tofu, with the softest being silken. Soft tofu has the best texture for this kind of dish (silken tofu will break too easily). The best place to find this tofu is at an Asian supermarket.

salt
1 (12-ounce/340-g) brick soft
    tofu, cut into 1-inch cubes
4 or 5 in-season crabs (Shanghai
    hairy crabs, if you can get
    them, or blue crabs)
1 tablespoon pork lard
    (store-bought or homemade,
    page 271)
2 teaspoons minced fresh ginger
1 tablespoon Shaoxing wine
1 tablespoon granulated sugar
1 tablespoon light soy sauce
1 cup (240 ml) High Stock
    (page 277) or chicken, pork,
    or vegetable stock
1 tablespoon cornstarch
    dissolved in 2 tablespoons
    water
½ teaspoon ground white pepper
2 scallions, thinly sliced
cooked white rice, for serving

1. Bring a pot of water with a pinch of salt to a boil over high. Add the tofu and cook for 1 minute, without letting the water return to a boil. Gently remove the tofu with a slotted spoon. Set aside.

2. In the same or a separate steaming pot, bring 1 inch (2.5 cm) of water to a boil over high. Place the crabs in the pot and cook, covered, for 5 to 6 minutes, until the shells are orange in color. Remove with tongs and set aside to cool.

3. When the crabs are cool enough to handle, break open the shells, catching any roe and crab juice in a bowl. In another bowl, separate the crabmeat, discarding the shells. Be sure not to include the lungs. (To remove the meat from the legs, snip an opening in each leg, then use a rolling pin to squeeze out the meat.)

4. Heat a well-seasoned wok over high until smoking. Add the lard and let it melt. Reduce the heat to medium and add the ginger. Stir-fry until fragrant.

5. Add the crabmeat along with any roe and cook for 2 to 3 minutes to release their flavor.

6. Pour in the wine and stir-fry quickly as it reduces. Add the sugar and light soy sauce. Pour in the stock and the reserved crab juice and bring to a boil over high.

7. Gently add the reserved tofu and return the mixture to a boil. Then reduce the heat to low, cover, and let simmer for 5 to 10 minutes to thicken. Avoid stirring too much, as this will break up the soft tofu—instead gently shake the wok or gently fold the ingredients with the back of a spatula.

8. Stream in the cornstarch slurry, stir gently to combine, and continue to simmer, thickening the mixture to your preference. Add the white pepper and season with salt. Sprinkle with the scallions and serve with white rice.

PIG TROTTER SOYBEAN SOUP

猪蹄黄豆汤 | *zhū tí huáng dòu tāng* | *Makes 4 servings*

It's a well-known fact in the Chinese community that pigs' feet make the best stock. Pork trotters and hocks, among the cheapest, most unwanted parts of a pig, are full of fat and meat. In the fall of 2017, I made pork trotter soup weekly. Why? Because I was on my surgery rotation in medical school, and instead of practicing my suturing skills on banana skins or chicken thighs, I bought two trotters for about two dollars, practiced, then made pork trotter and soybean soup. Including the skin adds some natural gelatin to give it a thicker, heartier texture.

This is a perfect dish by itself as a main, but it can also act as a flavorful base to hold noodles or wontons or be used in stir-fry in lieu of water. Pork stock of any kind (not just pigs' feet) has a meaty, rich flavor that will enhance any dish you use it in, even if it's just a tablespoon. Just make a lot and freeze it so you always have some on hand.

Be sure to ask your butcher to chop the bones into several parts (say, 2-inch/5-centimeter segments) to expose the bone marrow and release flavor more readily. I buy pork hocks in addition to the trotters. Hock meat can be a bit tougher, but with long and slow cooking, the meat becomes fall-off-the-bone tender, and the stock has a richer, meatier "ham" taste.

NOTE: An important step in this process is draining the stock after the first boil and removing any blood or brown foam—this keeps the stock "clean."

½ cup (95 g) dried soybeans
2 pigs' feet (about 3 pounds/
   1.4 kg), including hocks
5 slices fresh ginger
3 tablespoons Shaoxing wine
6 scallions, roughly chopped
about 1 teaspoon salt
about 1 tablespoon ground white
   pepper, plus more for serving

1. Soak the soybeans in warm water for 1 hour.

2. Using tweezers, pull any remaining hairs out of the skin of the pigs' feet, then wash the trotters under cold water.

3. Bring a big pot of water, enough to submerge the pigs' feet, to a boil over high, then carefully add the pigs' feet, 1 slice of the ginger, and 1 tablespoon of the wine. Blanch for 15 minutes. Remove the trotters with tongs, discard the water and ginger, and rinse the pot. If any foam clings to the trotters, rinse them.

4. Transfer the soybeans with their soaking water to the clean pot. Add the pigs' feet and fill the pot with water until it reaches about 1 inch (2.5 cm) above the feet. Add the remaining 4 slices of ginger, 2 tablespoons of wine, and most of the scallions, reserving some for serving.

5. Cover the pot and bring to a boil over high. Reduce the heat to low and simmer for at least 2 hours.

6. The soup should be creamy and semitransparent. The meat on the pork trotters should be fork-tender and easily fall off the bones, and the soybeans should be soft. Add the salt and white pepper, adjusting the quantities to taste. Pork trotters will render a fair amount of fat—skim off the excess fat and discard. Alternatively, refrigerate the soup until the top layer of fat solidifies, then remove it and discard before reheating the soup.

7. Serve the soup with additional white pepper and the reserved scallions.

SWEET OSMANTHUS-STUFFED LOTUS ROOT

桂花糖藕 | guì huā táng ǒu | *Makes 4 servings*

桂花 *gui hua*, "osmanthus," petals blanket the ground in bright yellow every autumn. I keep a jar of dried osmanthus blooms in my pantry and use them in my Sticky Rice Balls (page 113), Sweet Rice Wine and Rice Ball Soup (page 116), and this sticky, floral-scented delicacy well-known to people familiar with Shanghai cuisine.

This dish utilizes the plump 莲藕 *lian ou*, "lotus root," that grows anywhere there's a pond or lake in Jiangsu and Zhejiang provinces. Short-grain glutinous rice is stuffed into the holes of the lotus root, then the whole thing is capped to hold in the rice, cooked, sliced thinly, and coated in osmanthus-infused sweet syrup. Some people will dip it in granulated sugar or sprinkle sugar on it for an extra-sweet treat.

NOTE: You will need toothpicks or bamboo skewers to secure the rice filling in the lotus root. You may need to cut off part of the skewers to fit in your pan.

1 segment fresh lotus root with the joints attached (about ½ pound/225 g)

⅓ cup (65 g) glutinous (sweet) rice, soaked for at least 3 hours or overnight

2 tablespoons rock sugar, crushed coarsely with a mortar and pestle

3 tablespoons dark brown sugar

1 tablespoon dried osmanthus petals, 桂花 *gui hua*

½ cup (65 g) dried red dates (optional)

1. Peel the lotus root. Slice off ½ inch (12 mm) at one end, reserving the piece for later. Rinse the revealed holes thoroughly with water and use a chopstick to clear the holes of any grit.

2. Stuff as much sweet glutinous rice as you can in the holes— a chopstick can help get the rice all the way into the lotus root. Place the reserved piece over the exposed end of the lotus root and use toothpicks or a bamboo skewer to fix it in place.

3. Place the lotus root in the bottom of a pot large enough to fit the root comfortably. Add enough water to cover the root by at least 1 inch (2.5 cm). Bring to a boil over high, then reduce the heat to low and simmer for 1 hour, slightly covered. The color of the cooking water will start to turn pink.

4. Add the rock sugar, brown sugar, and dried osmanthus to the pot along with the dates, if using. Simmer for another hour. When fork-tender, remove the lotus root and set it aside to cool; keep the cooking water in the pot.

5. When the root is cool enough to handle, remove the cap and discard it with the skewers. Cut the root into ¼- to ½-inch (6- to 12-mm) slices.

6. Return the cooking water to a boil over high and reduce it to a syrup-like consistency. Spoon the syrup over the lotus root slices. Serve at room temperature or refrigerate for a few hours and serve cold.

MOUNTAIN YAM PEARL MEATBALLS

糯米肉丸 | nuò mǐ ròu wán | *Makes about 12 meatballs*

山药 *shan yao*, "mountain yam," is one of my favorite autumnal root vegetables. It has white flesh that has long been used in traditional Chinese medicine. It's a delightful addition in soups and can be used in the same way you would a potato. But I also love to steam it into a puree and incorporate it into meatballs. Mountain yam tenderizes the meat and binds it together, creating incredibly fragrant and soft meatballs. In this dish they are called "pearl meatballs" because they are rolled in grains of sweet glutinous rice that take on a silver sheen when steamed, evoking pearls. Because of that, they are usually served for special or celebratory occasions.

½ segment (3½ ounces/100 g) mountain yam

¼ cup (50 g) glutinous (sweet) rice, soaked overnight

7 ounces (200 g) ground pork or hand-minced pork (page 270)

1 tablespoon minced scallion

1 teaspoon minced fresh ginger

1 tablespoon Shaoxing wine

1 tablespoon light soy sauce

½ teaspoon kosher salt

½ teaspoon ground white pepper

½ teaspoon cornstarch

1 teaspoon granulated sugar

1 teaspoon toasted sesame oil

3 fresh water chestnuts, peeled and diced, or canned water chestnuts (optional)

napa cabbage leaves, for lining the steamer basket

1. Peel the yam and cut it into ½-inch (1.25-cm) slices. In a bamboo steamer set over 2 inches (5 cm) of simmering water, steam the yam over high for 20 minutes or until soft. Let cool.

2. Drain the glutinous rice and place it in a shallow bowl.

3. In a large bowl, combine the pork with the scallion, ginger, wine, soy sauce, salt, white pepper, cornstarch, sugar, sesame oil, and the water chestnuts, if using. Stir in one direction (see page 133, step 1) until well combined. Mash the cooled yam, then add it to the meat mixture, stirring in the same direction.

4. Line the steamer basket with napa cabbage leaves, and add more water to the steamer.

5. To shape the meatballs, place 1 heaping tablespoon of the mixture in the palm of one hand and slap it from one hand to the other, turning the ball between slaps. This forms the meatball while getting rid of any excess air. Gently reshape between your palms to form a ball. Roll the meatball in the glutinous rice, coating it all over. Place it on the bed of napa cabbage. Repeat with the rest of the meat mixture.

6. Steam the meatballs over high for 20 minutes, then transfer to a platter and serve with rice or over noodles.

SOY-PICKLED RADISH

酱萝卜 | jiàng luó bo | *Makes 4 to 6 servings*

This crisp, tangy, juicy pickle is meant to 开胃 *kai wei*, "open your appetite," but I find myself sneaking bites throughout the meal, or even outside of meals. The initial cycles of salting and sugaring get rid of the spicy, bitter taste of daikon and leave behind its deep, floral notes. It's delightful as part of a pickle spread with breakfast congee—in fact, sometimes I'll have plain congee with only these soy-pickled radishes. It's hard to resist touching the daikon for two days, but the resulting pickle is worth it: savory yet sweet, tangy, and crispy.

Choose a radish that is white and firm, without any holes. You don't have to peel it, as the skin crisps up beautifully and holds the discs together, but if there are any bruises or "hairs" growing out, you can peel off a little bit.

1 fresh, firm small daikon (about 2½ inches/6 cm in diameter, 9 inches/23 cm long)

2 teaspoons salt, plus more as needed to cover radish

2 teaspoons plus 2 tablespoons granulated sugar

⅓ cup (80 ml) light soy sauce

½ cup (120 ml) boiled water, cooled to room temperature

2 tablespoons red or white rice vinegar

1 tablespoon black vinegar

1. Wash the radish thoroughly. Cut off and discard both ends and slice the daikon into ¼-inch (6-mm) slices.

2. In a nonreactive container, toss the radish with 1 teaspoon of the salt. Let sit for 30 minutes.

3. Rinse and drain the radish. Toss the radish with 1 teaspoon of the sugar and let sit for another 30 minutes.

4. Rinse and drain the radish. Repeat step 2 with the remaining teaspoon salt.

5. Rinse and drain the radish. Repeat step 3 with the remaining teaspoon sugar.

6. Rinse and drain a final time, squeezing the daikon slightly to wring out any excess water. These cycles of salt and sugar will help rid the radish of its bitter, spicy taste.

7. Place the radish in a clean, nonreactive container. Combine the soy sauce, water, 2 tablespoons sugar, rice vinegar, and black vinegar, stirring to dissolve the sugar. Pour the brine over the radish slices and seal the container. Let them pickle in the fridge for at least 2 days before enjoying. Pickles will keep (and become stronger in flavor) in the fridge for a month.

WOOD-EAR MUSHROOM AND MOUNTAIN YAM STIR-FRY

木耳炒山药 | mù ěr chǎo shān yāo | *Makes 2 to 4 servings*

When a 江浙菜 *Jiang-Zhe cai,* menu is put together, color is considered: you won't find a table full of just greens or browns. Instead, a green dish balances out a red-braised dish; a white dish sits next to a brown one. Stir-fries can be monochromatic (think winter bok choy or snow pea shoots), but in this case, because the main ingredient is a plain white, 四色 *si se,* "four colors," is the goal: the white flesh of mountain yam, vibrant orange of carrot, dark brown of wood-ear mushrooms, and green of scallion. I sometimes toss in snap peas for even more green. In truth, you can add whatever you want; it's a universal stir-fry formula.

When choosing mountain yam, look for thick, straight, dense sticks. They should have a smooth surface without any obvious spots or bruising. Look at the end, where the flesh is revealed—if it's white, it's fresh; if it's black or yellow, avoid it.

NOTE: The mountain yam and carrot can be sliced to form aesthetically pleasing parallelograms. To do this, first cut the root vegetable lengthwise. Then place one long piece cut side down. Slice into 2-inch (5-cm) segments on a diagonal. Then, with your knife perpendicular to the slanted cut edges, cut into thin (about ¼-inch/5-mm) slices.

1½ segments (10½ ounces/ 300 g) mountain yam

white vinegar, for soaking the yam

1 medium (2½ ounces/75 g) carrot

kosher salt

2 tablespoons neutral cooking oil, such as canola or grapeseed oil

2 scallions, finely chopped, white and green parts kept separate

8 to 10 dried wood-ear mushrooms, soaked in warm water for at least 30 minutes

¼ cup (60 ml) High Stock (page 277), if needed

ground white pepper

1. Peel the mountain yam. Submerge it in a bowl of cold water with a splash of white vinegar. This step gets rid of the intrinsic stickiness of the yam and prevents discoloring. Let sit for 10 minutes.

2. Rinse the yam and dry it thoroughly. Slice the yam and carrot into thin slices (see Note).

3. Bring a pot of salted water to a boil over high. Add the mountain yam and carrot slices and bring back to a boil. Once the water boils, drain and rinse the root vegetables.

4. Heat a well-seasoned wok over medium-high. When hot, add the oil and swirl to coat. Add the white parts of the scallions and stir-fry until fragrant. Increase the heat to high, add the mountain yam, carrot, and mushrooms, and stir-fry until the mountain yam starts to turn translucent, about 3 minutes. If the wok becomes too dry, pour in ⅛ cup of the stock (up to the full ¼ cup, if needed) and continue to stir-fry, letting the stock reduce.

5. Sprinkle with the green parts of the scallions, season with salt and white pepper, and serve.

YANG CHUN NOODLES

阳春面 | *yáng chūn miàn* | *Makes 2 servings*

These noodles are often called a "poor man's soup" and were traditionally sold for just 10 yuan. 阳春 *yang chun* refers to the tenth month of the Chinese calendar. My father-in-law told me that this is his favorite bowl of noodles. "They're truly special," he said. Their flavor comes from very humble ingredients, so they must be of the highest quality. Light and dark soy sauce with a dollop of fragrant pork lard sits in a bowl, awaiting just-cooked noodles. Fresh, piping-hot High Stock (page 277), made from chicken, pork, and often ham, is ladled over the noodles, gently dispersing the soy sauce and melting the lard. Right before serving, thin slices of scallion and green garlic are scattered for the aromatic crunch they provide the dish. Together, they make an incredibly fragrant and special bowl of noodles.

1 teaspoon dark soy sauce

2½ teaspoons light soy sauce

½ teaspoon sesame oil

2 tablespoons pork lard (store-bought or homemade, page 271)

10½ ounces (300 g) fresh Shanghai thin noodles

about 3 cups (720 ml) High Stock (page 277), heated

ground white pepper

1 scallion, thinly sliced

1 stalk green garlic, thinly sliced

1. In a small bowl, whisk together the dark and light soy sauces and the sesame oil. Divide between two soup bowls and add 1 tablespoon of lard to each bowl.

2. Bring a large pot of water to a boil over high. Cook the noodles until al dente, 3 to 5 minutes. Drain and divide the noodles between the bowls.

3. Ladle enough hot stock into each bowl to reach the top of the noodles.

4. Top each bowl with a pinch of white pepper, sliced scallion, and green garlic, and serve.

RICE-ENCRUSTED PORK RIBS

荷叶粉蒸排骨 | hé yè fěn zhēng pái gǔ | *Makes 4 servings*

These gems, usually served in individual portions in small steamers, start popping up in towering stacks in the summer and fall, when the lotus leaves are gorgeous and ready for picking. All around the region, you'll find ponds and lakes with majestic, undulating fields of lotus leaves—a ubiquitous part of the landscape. In the West, it's harder to find fresh lotus leaves, so I buy them dried and rehydrate them.

These lotus-fragrant ribs are considered a delicacy, a more refined dish not only because of that extra layer of fragrance from the lotus leaves, but also because of the special marinade that gives the ribs depth. It's a celebratory, effortlessly impressive dish for special occasions. Thinly sliced pork belly can also be used, but there's something about bone-in pork spareribs that suits the fragrance and flavors of the dish so perfectly.

I make my own spiced rice powder for this dish. However, the word *powder* is misleading: it's a coarse, crushed rice, giving the resulting steamed product some body. The coating of crushed rice absorbs the flavors of the meat and any oil and keeps the ribs juicy and tender, creating great balance. You can buy premade spiced rice powder in Asian supermarkets, but by making it myself, I can control which dried aromatics I use and how coarse the rice is. At its simplest, a good spiced rice powder contains star anise and cassia, but I've come to love the addition of warming peppercorns, fennel seeds, and cardamom. One of my favorite parts is eating the extra clumps of cooked spiced rice that fall off the ribs.

In Jiangsu, 腐乳 *fu ru*, "fermented, briny tofu," is used for the marinade, but if you don't have that on hand, you can omit it and use white miso instead (the final result will be different, but still delicious), or do what the Sichuanese do and use 豆瓣酱 *dou ban jiang*, "fermented broad bean paste."

This dish is poetically described as 肥而不腻, 粉肉酥烂, 荷叶清香, 诱人食欲 *fei er bu ni, fen rou su lan, he ye qing xiang, you ren shi yu*, meaning "fatty yet without grease, meltingly tender, fragrant from lotus leaf, seductively appetizing."

NOTES: You can steam individual servings of this dish in small, stacked bamboo steamers, but I find it easiest to steam the ribs all at once in a large steamer. You can ask your butcher to cut the ribs in half lengthwise for you, leaving you with two long strips of spareribs, each roughly 2 inches (5 cm) wide.

(See recipe page 62.)

1½ pounds (680 g) pork spareribs or pork belly
3 tablespoons light soy sauce
1 tablespoon dark soy sauce
3 tablespoons white fermented
  tofu, 豆腐乳 dou fu ru
  (optional)
pinch of ground white pepper
2 tablespoons Shaoxing wine
2 tablespoons granulated sugar
2 teaspoons minced fresh ginger
2 large dried lotus leaves
¾ cup (175 g) white rice
⅓ cup (60 g) glutinous
  (sweet) rice
½ teaspoon whole Sichuan
  peppercorns
¼ teaspoon white peppercorns
2 whole star anise
1 teaspoon fennel seeds
3-inch (7.5-cm) piece of cassia
  bark or cinnamon stick
1 black cardamom pod
1 small (7 ounces/200 g) sweet
  potato or pumpkin, peeled and
  cut into 1-inch (2.5-cm) chunks
1 scallion, sliced on the diagonal

1. Rinse the spareribs and cut between the bones into 1½-inch (4-cm) chunks. If using pork belly, cut the meat into ¼-inch (6-mm) slices. Pat dry.

2. In a large bowl, stir together the light and dark soy sauces, fermented tofu (if using), white pepper, wine, sugar, and ginger. Add the spareribs to the bowl and toss to coat them with the marinade. Let sit for 30 minutes.

3. Meanwhile, bring a pot of water to a boil over high. Add the dried lotus leaves and boil for 2 to 3 minutes, until the leaves are supple. Remove the leaves and place them in a large bowl of cold water until cool enough to handle.

4. Lotus leaves come folded in half. When ready to assemble, take a reconstituted lotus leaf out of the cool water, pat dry, remove the root, then cut along the fold to form two pieces. Lay one piece, shiny side up, over a heatproof shallow bowl that will fit in your steamer. The leaf should spill over the edges of the bowl. If you're steaming all the ribs at once in a big bowl, add the other half of the leaf perpendicular to the first so the leaves spill over the bowl on all four sides. Cut the remaining lotus leaf into large chunks and set aside two pieces (if you have extra pieces of lotus leaf, discard them).

5. In a dry, well-seasoned wok over medium heat, combine the white and sweet glutinous rice with the Sichuan and white peppercorns, star anise, fennel seeds, cassia bark, and cardamom. Toast for 10 to 15 minutes, stirring constantly to prevent the rice and spices from burning, until the rice is golden and aromatic. Let cool, then grind in a food processor or mortar and pestle until a coarse meal forms.

6. Stir the rice meal into the bowl with the marinating pork until well combined. There should be a small pool of liquid from the marinade in the bowl. If not, add a tablespoon of water. Add the reserved lotus leaf bits and let sit for 10 minutes.

7. Layer sweet potato along the bottom of the lotus leaf–lined bowl. Carefully scoop the sparerib mixture over the sweet potatoes. Loosely fold the lotus leaves over the top, leaving an opening in the middle to let steam out.

8. Steam for 1½ to 2 hours over 2 inches (5 cm) of simmering water over medium, until the pork is tender and the sweet potato is soft. Check the steamer periodically to make sure the water has not evaporated, and add more water as needed.

9. Unfold the lotus leaves to reveal the fragrant, cooked ribs. Discard the bits of lotus leaf mixed within the ribs, sprinkle with the scallion, then serve in the lotus leaf–lined bowl. Alternatively, place a large plate over the bowl and flip the spiced rice-encrusted ribs onto the plate, removing and discarding the lotus leaves. Sprinkle with the scallions and serve.

SNOW VEGETABLE, EDAMAME, AND TOFU SKIN

雪菜毛豆炒百叶 | xuě cài máo dòu chǎo bǎi yè | *Makes 4 servings*

This dish is the embodiment of Shanghai cuisine—a simple stir-fry with classic, tangy snow vegetable, juicy edamame, nutritious tofu, and minimal seasoning. Snow Vegetable (page 272) contributes the bulk of the flavor, adding that sour, yet savory, crunch. I love to make this for a casual weeknight meal for two or as a side when feeding others. It doesn't look like much, but the umami punch from the pickled vegetable makes this dish perfect for scooping over white rice or noodles. A delicious variation on this recipe is using just snow vegetable and edamame (omitting the tofu skin) as a topping for soup noodles.

1 cup (3½ ounces/100 g) snow vegetable (store-bought or homemade, page 272)

kosher salt

1½ cups fresh or frozen shelled edamame

2 tablespoons neutral cooking oil, such as canola or grapeseed oil

1 scallion, finely chopped

2 teaspoons finely chopped fresh ginger

¼ cup (50 g) tofu skin strips, 百叶 *bai ye*

1 teaspoon Shaoxing wine

1 teaspoon granulated sugar

1 teaspoon sesame oil

ground white pepper

1. If using store-bought snow vegetable, rinse the greens briefly in cold water to remove excess salt. If using homemade snow vegetable, skip this step and just wring out any excess liquid. Finely dice.

2. Bring a pot of salted water to a boil over high. Boil the fresh edamame until tender, 4 to 5 minutes, then drain, reserving 2 tablespoons of the cooking water. If using frozen edamame, simply blanch quickly to defrost.

3. Heat a well-seasoned wok over medium-high. When hot, add the oil and swirl to coat. Add the scallion and ginger and cook until they explode into fragrance, 爆香 *bao xiang*, about 30 seconds. Add the snow vegetable and stir-fry until fragrant. Add the edamame and tofu skin strips and briefly stir-fry until hot. Stir in the reserved cooking water, wine, and sugar. Cover the wok and steam for 2 minutes to meld the tangy flavor of the snow vegetable with the edamame and tofu skin.

4. Drizzle in the sesame oil, season with salt and white pepper, and serve.

WINTER MELON, BAMBOO, AND PORK RIB SOUP

冬瓜排骨汤 | dōng guā pái gǔ tāng | *Makes 4 servings*

排骨汤 *pai gu tang*, "pork rib soup," is a familiar soup to anyone who grew up in a Chinese household. It's a nourishing soup, perfect for easing the transition from summer to fall. Chunks of winter melon are a classic addition, and they cook down into soft, translucent squares. If you're looking for a soup to ladle over your rice, this is the one.

This recipe isn't meant to be complicated and doesn't need to be followed exactly. Instead, use it as a base for a nourishing, comforting soup. I sometimes like to add in a few slices of salt pork to punch up the umami flavor, but lotus root and mountain yam are also delightful, healthy additions.

NOTE: 扁尖 *bian jian* refers to "flat-tip bamboo." You can find it dried as 笋干 *sun gan*, use frozen bamboo shoot tips, or find fresh bamboo and cut it into chunks.

NOTE: If you're using dried bamboo shoots, see below for instructions on how to rehydrate them.

1 pound (455 g) pork ribs with bone
4 slices fresh ginger
2 scallions, cut into 2-inch (5-cm) segments
1 tablespoon Shaoxing wine
5¼ ounces (150 g) fresh or dried bamboo shoots (see Note)
½ wedge (1 pound/455 g) winter melon, peeled, deseeded, and sliced into ½-inch (1.25-cm) pieces
kosher salt
ground white pepper

1. Place the pork ribs in a pot, add enough water to cover, and bring to a boil over high. Cook for 3 minutes, then drain and rinse. Rinse the pot.

2. Crush the ginger and scallions with the flat side of a cleaver to loosen the fibers.

3. Return the ribs to the clean pot and cover them with fresh water. Add the ginger, scallions, and wine. If you're using rehydrated dried bamboo, add that, too. Bring to a boil over medium-high, then reduce the heat to low and simmer, covered, for 2 hours, or until the ribs are fork-tender.

4. If you're using fresh bamboo, add it and the winter melon slices to the pot. Simmer for another 20 minutes over low, until the winter melon is translucent and soft. Season with salt and white pepper. Serve hot, making sure each serving includes some winter melon, bamboo, and a few pieces of pork.

HOW TO PREPARE DRIED BAMBOO FOR COOKING
Dried bamboo (or any preserved bamboo) can have a funky smell. The cycles of soaking and simmering get rid of that funky smell while preserving the desired fragrance from the dried bamboo.

1. Soak the dried bamboo shoots in water for 2 days, changing the water daily. Drain and squeeze out excess water.

2. Place the bamboo in a pot and add enough water to cover. Bring to a boil over high, then reduce to low and simmer for 1 hour. Drain and rinse. Return the bamboo to the pot, cover with fresh water, and simmer for another hour. Drain and rinse again. At this point, the bamboo is ready to use and will keep for 2 days in the fridge or 1 month in the freezer if wrapped well in plastic. Cut off and discard any tough parts before using.

CHESTNUT CHICKEN

板栗烧鸡 | bǎn lì shāo jī | *Makes 4 servings*

In autumn, young, tender chestnuts appear in the markets, and the tantalizing smell of roasting chestnuts fills the air. There is an old folk saying, 八月的梨枣, 九月的山楂, 十月的板栗笑哈哈 *ba yue de li zao, jiu yue de shan zha, shi yue de ban li xiao ha ha,* "August's pears and dates, September's hawthorn, and October's chestnuts all laugh."

I wish I could try chestnuts, but I'm unfortunately allergic to tree nuts. My husband loves nuts, though, and I just couldn't omit this classic, warming , savory-sweet Shanghai autumn dish. I often make this without chestnuts, too. My husband and his family were the ultimate taste testers for this book, and they all say that the nutty, sweet flavor of chestnuts complements the chicken well.

12 fresh chestnuts (or frozen, vacuum-packed, or canned peeled chestnuts)

8 dried shiitake mushrooms, rehydrated in hot water to cover for 1 hour

1 to 1½ pounds (455 to 680 g) chicken thighs or legs, bone in, skin on, cut into 1½-inch (4-cm) chunks

3 tablespoons light soy sauce

2 tablespoons pork lard (store-bought or homemade, page 271) or neutral cooking oil, such as canola or grapeseed oil

3 scallions—2 chopped into 2-inch (5-cm) segments and 1 finely chopped

3 cloves garlic, smashed

2 thin slices fresh ginger

3 tablespoons Shaoxing wine

1 tablespoon dark soy sauce

½ teaspoon kosher salt

2 tablespoons rock sugar, crushed coarsely with a mortar and pestle

2 whole star anise

1 (3-inch/7.5-cm) piece cassia bark

1 teaspoon Sichuan peppercorns (optional)

pinch of ground white pepper

1 teaspoon sesame oil

1. Bring a pot of water to a boil over high. For fresh chestnuts, slice off their bases, boil for 3 to 5 minutes, then remove the pot from the heat. Working with 4 or 5 chestnuts at a time, remove the chestnuts with a slotted spoon and carefully place them on a clean kitchen towel. Taking care not to burn yourself, rub until the skins fall off and a pale yellow nut is revealed. Dry thoroughly. If using peeled frozen chestnuts, add them to the pot and boil for 4 minutes. Vacuum-packed or canned chestnuts don't need any prep.

2. Drain the soaked mushrooms, reserving the soaking liquid (run it through a sieve to remove any grit). Remove the stalks and discard. Quarter the mushroom caps.

3. Toss the chicken with the light soy sauce and let sit for 10 minutes.

4. Heat the lard in a well-seasoned wok over medium and fry the chestnuts until golden on all sides. Remove the chestnuts to a plate and set aside.

5. Add the scallion segments, garlic, and ginger and stir-fry over medium-high until fragrant. Add the mushrooms and cook, stir-frying occasionally, until the mushrooms are deeply browned and the liquid has seeped out, about 10 minutes.

6. Add the chicken pieces in a single layer and fry until they are golden. Flip and fry until golden on all sides.

7. Transfer the contents of the wok to a clay pot, if using. You can also continue the braise directly in the wok. Add the wine, dark soy sauce, salt, and sugar, then stir in the chestnuts until everything is well combined.

8. Pour in enough water and the reserved shiitake soaking water to cover three-fourths of the chicken. Add the star anise, cassia bark, and Sichuan peppercorns, if using. Bring to a boil over high, then reduce the heat to low and simmer partially covered for 20 minutes.

9. Remove the lid and return the chicken to a boil over high and reduce the liquid by one-third or until thickened to your liking. Season with the white pepper. Just before serving, drizzle with the sesame oil and sprinkle with the finely chopped scallion.

THE MID-AUTUMN FESTIVAL

中秋节 | zhōng qiū jié

床前明月光 / *chuang qian ming yue guang* / bright moonlight before my bed
疑是地上霜 / *yi shi di shang shuang* / there is frost on the ground
举头望明月 / *ju tou wang ming yue* / I lift my head to gaze at the bright moon
低头思故乡 / *di tou si gu xiang* / I lower my head, nostalgic for my home

"Quiet Night Thought" (静夜思), a famous poem by Chinese poet Li Bai, is likely one of the most memorized poems among Asian Americans, including myself. From elementary school to high school, I attended Sunday Chinese school, where I learned not only how to read and write Chinese, but also various aspects of Chinese culture as a way to preserve and pass down traditions.

The Mid-Autumn Festival, which falls on the fifteenth day of the eighth month of the Chinese calendar, celebrates the full moon and is considered a time of good fortune, full of well-wishing and celebration. The star of this holiday is the mooncake, a round treat that is filled with anything from lotus paste and salted yolks to fragrant pork, encased in a lard-rich pastry dough.

Mooncakes are not meant solely for personal pleasure. They're for sharing and gifting. They're meant to be a symbol of family, reunion, love, and celebration. Giving one is akin to the Western tradition of sending a Christmas card. The act is a blessing, a gesture of well-wishes and prosperity for the next year. I look forward to the yearly care package from my mother-in-law, sent with love.

The Mid-Autumn Festival is also referred to as the Family Reunion Festival and the Harvest Festival, as it takes place at the end of the harvest season. After a meal celebrating the harvest, the family heads outside to view the beautiful full moon. Traditionally, a mooncake is divided into the same number of pieces as there are family members, counting even those who are far away.

Mooncakes come in so many different forms, with fillings such as sweet red bean paste, jujube, nuts and seeds, and salted meat, and can be encased in lard dough, snow skin, or pastry skin.

The shape, however, is consistently round in homage to the full moon. The calligraphy on the outside is a source of pride and tradition. It can refer to the name of a particular baker, with heirloom molds passed from generation to generation. Or it can be a word such as *harmony, happiness,* or *wealth,* words intended to offer blessings and well-wishes from the giver to the receiver.

As Li Bai's poem suggests, in Chinese tradition the full moon brings on nostalgia for family and the home. The act of moon gazing is rooted in reunion and family, but these days, the nuclear family is often dispersed across the world, and physically reuniting for this act may be harder to do in reality. In my family, my parents are on the West Coast, my sister in Chicago, my brother in the Pacific Northwest, and my husband and I are on the East Coast. Our extended families all remain in China. It's been years since I celebrated this holiday with my family in person, but every year, my husband and I receive our care package from his mother, we send out some of our own, and I make my mom's savory mooncakes. We sit down, just the two of us, for a simple meal, and we call our families. No matter how far we are physically, the family bond is strong, and through the common act of gifting, receiving, and eating mooncakes, we celebrate this holiday together.

SUZHOU-STYLE MOONCAKES

苏式鲜肉月饼　|　sū shì xiān ròu yuè bǐng　|　*Makes 16 mooncakes*

There are many varieties of mooncake, but my favorite by far is the recipe that hails from the city of Suzhou, which neighbors Shanghai. The Shanghainese have adopted this for their own, and you'll find it labeled as such. This mooncake is stuffed with fragrant pork and encased by a shatteringly flaky lard crust. After the first time I had one as a child, Suzhou-style mooncakes were the only ones I would eat. When we went back to China, even if it was summer and nowhere near the Mid-Autumn Festival, we scoured pastry shops and bakeries in search of these, usually to no avail. Taking pity on me, my mom began to make them at home.

This method of making dough, 小包酥 *xiao bao su,* "small bun paste," yields an incredibly flaky pastry, with layers shedding off at the slightest touch. This method of lamination is well-known across Asia and involves layering two types of dough—oil paste and water dough—to create extra-thin layers. You can make the filling and dough in advance, chilling them in the fridge before assembling and cooking. Let the dough sit for an hour at room temperature before shaping.

NOTE: You can substitute an equal amount of softened butter (ideally high-fat butter) for the lard with a similar result, but using lard adds more fragrance.

MEAT FILLING
½ pound (225 g) ground pork
3 tablespoons Ginger-Scallion Water (see page 257)
½ teaspoon salt
½ teaspoon minced fresh ginger
1 tablespoon cornstarch
1 tablespoon light soy sauce
1½ teaspoons dark soy sauce
1 tablespoon granulated sugar
pinch of ground white pepper
½ teaspoon sesame oil
1 tablespoon Shaoxing wine

OIL PASTE, 油酥面皮 *you su mian pi*
1 cup plus 3 tablespoons (150 g) all-purpose flour
½ cup (110 g) pork lard (store-bought or homemade, page 271) or softened unsalted butter

WATER DOUGH
1⅔ cups plus 1 tablespoon (225 g) all-purpose flour
2 tablespoons (23 g) granulated sugar

(continued)

1. **MAKE THE MEAT FILLING:** In a medium bowl, mix together all the meat filling ingredients. Wet your hands slightly to prevent sticking, then divide the meat mixture into 16 balls (about ¾ ounce/21 g each) on a baking sheet. Cover lightly with plastic wrap and refrigerate so the meatballs firm up as you prep the other ingredients.

2. **MAKE THE OIL PASTE:** Mix together the flour and lard with a silicone spatula or your hands until they form a dough. The oil paste should just hold together—it will be dry and flaky but still oily. Shape into 16 small balls on another baking sheet and cover lightly with plastic wrap.

3. **MAKE THE WATER DOUGH:** In a large heatproof bowl, mix together the flour, sugar, salt, and lard until just combined. Stream in the water and mix to form a dough. Start with a silicone spatula, and when cool enough to handle use your hands to knead the dough until it is very smooth with no lumps, adding additional water or flour as needed to obtain the desired consistency (the dough should be tacky but not sticky). Divide the dough into 16 balls on another baking sheet and cover lightly with plastic wrap.

4. Let both doughs rest for 20 minutes. Then assemble and bake the mooncakes as described.

HOW TO ASSEMBLE AND BAKE MOONCAKES

1. Preheat the oven to 400°F (205°C).

2. Place a ball of the water dough in one palm and use your other palm to press it into a flat disc. Take a ball of the oil paste and place that in the center (do not flatten it). Bring the sides *(continued)*

pinch of kosher salt

3 tablespoons (45 g) pork lard (store-bought or homemade, page 271) or softened unsalted butter

½ cup (120 ml) boiling water

EGG WASH

1 egg, whisked with a splash of water

of the water dough up and around the oil paste ball so that the oil paste is nestled within the water dough.

3. With a rolling pin, roll this ball of dough into a flat, long, thin oval. Then start at one end and roll the dough up onto itself into a spiral shaped like a log. Set aside under a layer of plastic wrap.

4. Repeat with the remaining balls of dough, making sure to keep the finished logs under plastic wrap to prevent them from drying out. Let the logs rest for 10 minutes.

5. With a rolling pin, roll each log again into a long oval, then roll again into a log.

6. Take one log and press a chopstick or your finger crosswise down the middle so that the two edges bend upward. Now flatten this semicircle with your palm so that you see two spirals. Using a rolling pin, roll the dough into a thin circle.

7. Place one of the balls of meat inside the circle. Pleat the dough around the meat and pinch to close.

8. Pinch off any excess dough. Flip the ball over, gently press with your palm to flatten it slightly, and set it aside, covering it loosely with plastic wrap to prevent it from drying out. Repeat with all of the logs of dough and balls of meat.

9. Brush the mooncakes with the egg wash and bake for 25 to 30 minutes, until golden brown. Let cool slightly, then serve hot. Mooncakes will keep for 3 to 5 days refrigerated, covered, or for several months frozen.

SUGARY "CRAB-SHELL" PASTRIES 蟹壳黄 | xie ke huang | *Makes 16 mooncakes*

The method for making these is the same as making Suzhou-Style Mooncakes (page 73), only with a sweet filling.

SUGARY OIL PASTE

3 tablespoons (45 g) pork lard (store-bought or homemade, page 271) or softened unsalted butter

½ cup (100 g) granulated sugar

2 tablespoons dried osmanthus petals, 桂花 gui hua

WATER DOUGH (see ingredients and recipe, page 73)

EGG WASH

1 egg, whisked with a splash of water

white sesame seeds

1. **MAKE THE SUGARY OIL PASTE:** Pound the lard, sugar, and osmanthus petals in a mortar and pestle to crush the petals and combine the ingredients into a paste. Chill the paste in the fridge for 15 minutes, then shape into 16 balls on a baking sheet and cover lightly with plastic wrap.

2. **MAKE THE WATER DOUGH:** In a large heatproof bowl, mix together the flour, sugar, salt, and lard until just combined. Stream in the water and mix to form a dough. Start with a spatula, and when cool enough to handle use your hands to knead the dough until it is very smooth with no lumps, adding additional water or flour as needed to obtain the desired consistency (the dough should be tacky but not sticky). Divide the dough into 16 balls on a baking sheet and cover lightly with plastic wrap.

3. To prepare the mooncakes, see How to Assemble and Bake Mooncakes (above and opposite). Brush the cakes with the egg wash, sprinkle with the sesame seeds, and bake as directed.

DOUBLE-MUSHROOM NOODLE SOUP

双菇面 | shuāng gū miàn | *Makes 2 servings*

During one visit to Suzhou to see my husband's grandparents, they suggested, "Why not go up 灵岩山 Ling Yan Mountain to eat some temple noodles?" 素面 *su mian*, "vegetarian noodles," are often mentioned in relation to temples. That's because there's a whole subset of Chinese cuisine that exists only in Buddhist monasteries, where no meat products are used.

After a short hike, we reached 灵岩山寺 Ling Yan Shan Si, the Ling Yan temple, which is worth a visit by itself. It's a historic monastery with stunning gardens and a pagoda. Right outside the temple is a nondescript sign: "素面馆" (vegetarian noodle shop). Five options are offered on the menu, and all of them feature mushrooms. My favorite was 双菇冬笋 *shuang gu dong sun*, "double mushroom and winter bamboo shoots," heady with the umami flavor of mushroom and the crispness of bamboo. The noodles were freshly cooked and chewy. This is my version of that dish.

2 cups boiling water

10 dried shiitake mushrooms

10 button, wood-ear, or oyster mushrooms

about 2 cups (5 ounces/140 g) sprouted soybeans

3 ounces (80 g) dried bamboo shoots (optional; for instructions on hydrating, see page 65)

1 teaspoon kosher salt, plus more as needed

5 thin slices fresh ginger

1 cup (135 g) fresh winter bamboo, peeled and blanched from 1 medium winter bamboo shoot

2 tablespoons neutral cooking oil, such as canola or grapeseed oil

4 cloves garlic, thinly sliced

3 scallions—2 thinly sliced and 1 chopped

1 tablespoon granulated sugar

¼ cup light soy sauce

handful of wheat gluten (6 to 8 pieces)

2 tablespoons black vinegar

ground white pepper

1 tablespoon sesame oil

10½ ounces (300 g) fresh Shanghai thin noodles

a few cilantro stems

1. Pour the boiling water over the dried shiitakes to cover, and let them soak for 1 hour, until the caps are soft. Drain the mushrooms and retain the stock. If there is any dirt or grit in the stock, strain it through a fine-mesh sieve. Remove the shiitake stems and set aside. Cut the shiitake caps in half and set aside. Slice the button (or other) mushrooms and set aside.

2. In a saucepan, combine the reserved stock and shiitake stems with the soybean sprouts, hydrated bamboo shoots, 1 teaspoon salt, and ginger. Bring to a boil over high, then reduce to low and simmer for 1 hour.

3. Slice the fresh winter bamboo into ⅛-inch (3-mm) slices. Place in the simmering stock and let cook for 2 minutes, then remove to a bowl with a slotted spoon. Reserve.

4. Heat a well-seasoned wok over medium-high. When hot, add the oil and swirl to coat. Add the garlic and thinly sliced scallions and stir-fry until fragrant and starting to turn golden brown, 3 to 4 minutes. Add the shiitake, the button mushrooms, and the drained bamboo, and cook, undisturbed and stirring occasionally, until the mushrooms are deeply browned and their liquid released. Add the sugar and 2 tablespoons of the soy sauce and stir-fry. Add the wheat gluten, then add 4 to 5 cups (960 ml to 1.2 L) of your mushroom-sprout stock, another tablespoon of soy sauce, and the vinegar. Bring it to a boil, then simmer until the flavors have melded, 15 to 20 minutes. Season to taste with salt and white pepper.

5. Divide the sesame oil and remaining 1 tablespoon soy sauce between two bowls.

6. In a separate pot, cook the noodles according to package directions until al dente. Divide the noodles between the bowls. Ladle in the mushroom stock, making sure to get mushrooms and sprouts, dividing it evenly. Season with additional white pepper to taste. Top with the chopped scallions and cilantro.

WINTER MELON AND EDAMAME

开洋冬瓜毛豆 | kāi yáng dōng guā máo dòu | *Makes 2 to 4 servings*

Soft, translucent squares of winter melon sprinkled with vibrant green edamame spooned up over rice is a combination of taste and textures I will always associate with home. Winter melon is a type of gourd that is commonly used in Asian cuisine. The melons can be huge—I've seen ones that are twenty pounds. Luckily, most Asian supermarkets sell wedges of this melon, with one wedge large enough for several dishes. This is one of my favorite ways to use this ingredient, but I also love it in Winter Melon, Bamboo, and Pork Rib Soup (page 65), where it melts into the soup and soaks up all the flavor.

1 tablespoon dried shrimp
  虾米 *xiā mǐ*
1 tablespoon Shaoxing wine
⅓ wedge (about 10½ ounces/
  300 g) winter melon
kosher salt
1 cup (185 g) fresh or frozen
  shelled edamame
2 tablespoons neutral cooking oil,
  such as canola or grapeseed
  oil
⅓ cup High Stock (page 277)
cooked white rice, for serving

1. Place the shrimp in a bowl with the wine and water to cover and let soak for 1 hour, until soft. Drain and set aside.

2. Remove the peel from the winter melon wedge. Cut the melon into 2-inch (5-cm) squares about ⅓ inch (8 mm) thick (you should have about 2 cups).

3. Bring a pot of salted water to a boil over high. Cook the fresh edamame for 4 to 5 minutes, until tender, and drain. If using frozen, simply blanch quickly to defrost.

4. In a well-seasoned wok, heat the oil over medium-high. Add the rehydrated shrimp and stir-fry until fragrant. Add the edamame and stir-fry until the beans turn vibrant green. Add the winter melon and continue to stir-fry to incorporate, about another minute.

5. Gently stream in the stock. Bring to a boil over high, then reduce the heat to medium-low and simmer, covered, until the melon becomes almost completely transparent and soft, 3 to 5 minutes.

6. Remove the lid and reduce the stock by half, or even more if you prefer less liquid in the final dish. Serve with white rice.

RED-BRAISED FISH

红烧鱼 | *hóng shāo yú* | *Servings will vary*

Red braising is the cooking method that Shanghai cuisine is known for, most notably red-braised pork belly (see Mom's Shanghai Red-Braised Pork Belly, page 93). When used with different kinds of protein, the braise takes on different flavors and textures. Here, the sauce takes on the natural flavor of the fish. It's a particularly fragrant way to enjoy fish, especially when accompanied by white rice.

1 tablespoon dark soy sauce

2 tablespoons light soy sauce

1 sea bass (or bream), scaled and gutted by your fishmonger

¼ cup (60 ml) Shaoxing wine, plus more for brushing the fish

4 scallions—3 cut into 2-inch (5-cm) segments and 1 thinly sliced

4 thin slices fresh ginger, plus one small peeled nub for the wok

2 to 3 tablespoons pork lard (store-bought or homemade, page 271) or neutral cooking oil, such as canola or grapeseed oil

2 tablespoons rock sugar, crushed coarsely with a mortar and pestle

1. Combine the dark and light soy sauces and pour the mixture into a shallow bowl or baking sheet large enough to fit the whole fish.

2. Rinse the fish and pat dry thoroughly with a paper towel. Use a sharp knife to cut three or four diagonal slits in the thickest part on both sides, reaching the bone.

3. Brush the Shaoxing wine over both sides of the fish, making sure it coats the inside of the diagonal slits as well as inside the belly. Stuff the belly with two-thirds of the scallion segments and 2 slices of the ginger.

4. Place the fish in the shallow bowl with the soy sauces. Let sit for 10 minutes. Flip and let the other side soak in the soy sauces for another 10 minutes. Discard the scallions and ginger, but reserve the marinade.

5. Rub the inside of a well-seasoned wok with the small peeled nub of ginger. Heat the pork lard in the wok over medium-high. When the lard is shimmering, gently slide in the fish. Fry the fish slowly until golden brown, 3 to 5 minutes. As you fry, tilt the wok and swish the lard so that every part of the fish touches the hot lard. This way you can keep the fish stationary while reaching every part. Wiggle the wok a little bit, and if the fish moves, it is ready to flip. If it's stuck to the wok, let it cook a bit more. Carefully flip the fish and repeat to brown the other side.

6. Push the fish to the side of the wok and then add the remaining 2 slices of ginger and the remaining scallion segments and stir-fry until fragrant.

7. Add the remaining ¼ cup (60 ml) wine, the reserved soy sauce marinade, and the rock sugar. If the liquid reaches halfway up the fish, cook as is. If not, add enough hot water to reach halfway up the fish.

8. Increase the heat to high and let the liquid come to a boil, then let it simmer and bubble on medium-low, cooking the fish while simultaneously reducing the sauce, 收干 *shou gan*. There is no need to flip the fish—instead, use a spoon to scoop the sauce up and over the top of the fish so it cooks as well. After about 3 minutes, the bubbles will change from large to fine. Continue to cook until the sauce is thickened to your preference, about 5 minutes more. *(continued)*

The fish is cooked when a poke with chopsticks causes the meat to easily flake off the bones. Gently slide the fish onto a serving dish.

9. If the sauce is still not thick enough for your liking, heat the sauce over high to cook it down further. Turn off the heat and spoon the sauce onto the fish. Sprinkle with the thinly sliced scallion and serve.

VARIATIONS

糖醋鱼 *tang cu yu*, Sweetened Vinegar Fish
2 tablespoons light soy sauce,
1½ teaspoons dark soy sauce, 2 tablespoons black vinegar, 1½ teaspoons rice vinegar, 2 tablespoons rock sugar, crushed coarsely with a mortar and pestle

Finish with a sprinkling of finely grated ginger instead of fresh scallions.

"DUCK" TOFU ROLLS

素鸭 | sù yā | *Makes 4 servings*

Jiangnan is peppered with temples and monasteries, and Buddhist temple cuisine. Buddhist monks and nuns abstain from meat, fish, and eggs (as well as other indulgences, such as alcohol and "strong-flavored" aromatics like garlic and onion) to keep their diets in line with their philosophies and beliefs. This dish, which was supposedly invented by a monk, uses tofu to mimic the appearance, taste, and texture of meat. The way the roll is sliced up mimics slices of chopped-up duck, with the crisped tofu skin paralleling crispy duck skin. The sauce used in this dish is reminiscent in flavor to that of Soy-Braised Duck Legs (page 219).

NOTE: You can insert toothpicks at the end to keep the layers in place if you feel like they will fall apart during cooking.

10 dried shiitake mushrooms
5¼ ounces (150 g) fresh or frozen winter bamboo shoots
1 medium carrot, peeled
2 tablespoons neutral cooking oil, such as canola or grapeseed oil, plus more for frying
1 teaspoon minced fresh ginger
1 scallion, finely chopped, white and green parts kept separate
3 tablespoons Shaoxing wine
2 tablespoons light soy sauce
1 teaspoon granulated sugar
½ teaspoon kosher salt
1½ teaspoons dark soy sauce
1 teaspoon sesame oil
1 tablespoon rock sugar, crushed coarsely with a mortar and pestle
6 sheets fresh or frozen dried tofu skin, 腐皮 *fu pi*
napa cabbage leaves (optional; for steaming)

1. Pour enough boiling water over the dried shiitakes to cover, and let them soak for 1 hour, until the mushroom caps are soft. Drain the mushrooms, retaining the stock. Strain the stock through a fine-mesh sieve to remove dirt or grit.

2. If using fresh winter bamboo, peel off the woody layers, cut crosswise into discs, and boil in water over high for 5 minutes. Otherwise simply defrost.

3. Cut the carrot into 3-inch (7.5-cm) segments, then julienne the segments. Julienne the bamboo and shiitake caps; discard the shiitake stems.

4. In a well-seasoned wok, heat 2 tablespoons of the cooking oil over medium-high. Add the ginger and white parts of the scallion and stir-fry until fragrant. Add the julienne of bamboo, carrot, and mushroom (together, called 三丝 *sansi*, "three ribbons") to the wok. Stir-fry to combine. Add 1 tablespoon of the wine, 1 tablespoon of the soy sauce, the granulated sugar, and salt, and stir-fry to incorporate. Adjust the seasoning to taste, then transfer the vegetables to a large bowl and set aside.

5. In a small bowl, whisk together ½ cup (120 ml) of the reserved mushroom stock with the remaining light soy sauce, remaining wine, dark soy sauce, sesame oil, and rock sugar. Pour the sauce into the wok and bring to a boil. Once it comes to a boil, remove from the heat and return the sauce to the bowl. Let cool completely.

6. Trim the hard outer rim of the tofu skin and discard it. Spread out a sheet of dried tofu skin on a flat surface. Brush a light layer of the sauce over the tofu skin. Lay another skin on top of that and brush it again. Repeat with one more skin, making a layer of 3 skins. Spoon half of the vegetable filling onto the bottom center of the sheet, about 3 inches (7.5 cm) from the bottom edge. Fold the two sides of the tofu skin over the filling and then roll the sheet up (see photographs on opposite page), like you would a burrito. Repeat to make one more roll with the 3 remaining tofu skins and the remaining vegetables. Cut the rolls in half if necessary to fit in your pan.

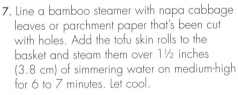

7. Line a bamboo steamer with napa cabbage leaves or parchment paper that's been cut with holes. Add the tofu skin rolls to the basket and steam them over 1½ inches (3.8 cm) of simmering water on medium-high for 6 to 7 minutes. Let cool.

8. When the rolls are cooled, heat the wok with enough oil to deep-fry (alternatively, you can pan-fry) to about 350°F (175°C), or when tiny bubbles appear around a chopstick inserted in the oil, then gently transfer the tofu skin rolls to the wok and deep-fry until golden brown and puffed on both sides, 3 to 5 minutes a side.

9. Let the tofu skin rolls cool slightly, then slice them into ½-inch (1.25-cm) segments and serve immediately with the leftover sauce poured over.

BEAN SPROUT STIR-FRY WITH CHICKEN AND GARLIC CHIVES

鸡肉炒豆芽 | jī ròu chǎo dòu yá | *Makes 4 servings*

This rustic, earthy dish is one of my favorites. It is perfectly balanced in all senses: the salty with a hint of sweet flavor from the chives; a crisp, juicy texture; a pleasing pale yellow with vibrant green color; and a fragrant aroma from the bean sprouts. (Buddhist vegetarian cuisine often utilizes bean sprouts to make an aromatic vegetarian stock.)

You can use either mung bean or soybean sprouts for this dish. Mung bean sprouts are more tender and crisp, and smaller. Soybean sprouts are larger. For this dish, I prefer mung bean sprouts, which you can usually find fresh in your local Asian grocery store. Before adding the sprouts to the finished dish, I first like to flash-fry them in hot oil to prevent them from losing water in the subsequent fry.

2 small boneless, skinless chicken thighs
2 tablespoons Shaoxing wine
2 tablespoons light soy sauce
1 teaspoon cornstarch
pinch of ground white pepper
about 3 cups (300 g) mung bean sprouts
3 tablespoons neutral cooking oil, such as canola or grapeseed oil
1½ teaspoons granulated sugar
about 1 cup (100 g) garlic chives, chopped into 1-inch (2.5-cm) segments
½ teaspoon salt, or to taste
¼ teaspoon sesame oil

1. Slice the chicken thighs into thin ¼-inch (6-mm) slivers and toss with 1 tablespoon of the Shaoxing wine, 1 tablespoon of the soy sauce, the cornstarch, and the white pepper. Set aside.

2. Rinse the mung bean sprouts and let them drain for 5 minutes.

3. Heat a well-seasoned wok over medium-high. When hot, add 1 tablespoon of the cooking oil and swirl to coat. Add the bean sprouts and quickly stir-fry for about 30 seconds. Remove the sprouts to a bowl and set aside.

4. Wipe down the wok with a paper towel. Heat the wok again over high, until smoke wisps up from the surface. Add the remaining 2 tablespoons of cooking oil and swirl the wok to distribute it. Add the chicken, let sit briefly to sear, then stir-fry until the color has changed.

5. Pour in the remaining wine and soy sauce, then return the bean sprouts to the wok. Sprinkle the contents of the wok with the sugar and stir to combine.

6. Add the chives and quickly stir-fry them. Season with the salt, adding more or less according to taste. Drizzle with the sesame oil.

冬

dōng

WINTER

Winter, *dōng*, is all about comfort, family, and time together. During this season, we celebrate the much-anticipated Lunar New Year, one of the biggest Chinese festivals with the most food traditions. Festivities start with a family reunion dinner on Lunar New Year's Eve and last until we eat 汤圆 *tang yuan*, "sticky rice balls," on the fifteenth day of the New Year to celebrate the first full moon.

Shanghai has a true winter. I refer to it as "true" because there is a discernible shift in temperature and a change in lifestyle as the Shanghainese adapt to the new season. Snow may or may not fall, but regardless of the precipitation, winter is cold. Life moves more slowly as we huddle indoors to escape the chill. But because of Shanghai's fertile land and network of small streams, winter fruits and vegetables are still plentiful and hearty.

I love winter because of all the comfort foods. This is the season of some of my favorite dishes: congee; long braises, where meat is braised for hours, until it's fall-off-the-bone tender; and piping-hot noodle and wonton soups that are served in the morning, afternoon, and night, spiced with copious amounts of white pepper for an extra kick.

This is also the period of preserving, utilizing the cool temperatures to control fermentation. Wind-dried salt pork, sausages, goose, duck, and fish are strung up to cure in the brisk air.

SHANGHAI BIG WONTONS

上海大馄饨 | *shàng hǎi dà hún tun* | *Makes 90 wontons*

Wontons can be deeply personal: from ratio of filling to wrapper, contents of the filling, and method of wrapping to the way of serving. My favorite way to eat wontons is in a steaming bowl of hearty, homemade broth, with generous amounts of white pepper, scallions, and garlic greens. In warmer weather, wontons are often served at room temperature in a vibrant chili oil and vinegar sauce.

One of my earliest memories of helping my mom in the kitchen involves wrapping these wontons. It is considerably easier to wrap wontons than pleat dumplings, especially for small, young hands with poor coordination. But my sister and I still needed practice. As my mom moved in a fluid arc of chopstick to pork mix to wrapper, fold, seal, and back to pork, rapidly filling up a tray of wontons, I recall slowly using a spoon to scoop the filling, dipping my finger in water to wet the perimeter of the wrapper, then carefully sealing it. Our tray was mostly empty, with a few wobbly, lopsided wontons in a variety of sizes, containing too much or too little filling (evidence of my sister's and my amateur attempts). Next to my mom's neat rows of wontons, which ones were ours was glaringly obvious.

These days, I make wontons regularly. There is always a giant bag of frozen wontons in my freezer. It's the food I turn to when I'm in need of the comfort of home away from home.

NOTE: To make shrimp-pork wontons, add equal amounts of raw, peeled, deveined, minced shrimp instead of greens.

PORK AND SHEPHERD'S PURSE FILLING

generous 1 pound (500 g) fresh or frozen shepherd's purse or other greens such as baby bok choy, napa cabbage, or Chinese celery

2 thin slices fresh ginger

2 scallions, roughly chopped

generous 1 pound (500 g) ground pork

1 teaspoon cornstarch

¼ cup (60 ml) light soy sauce

2 tablespoons Shaoxing wine

½ teaspoon kosher salt

1 teaspoon granulated sugar

½ teaspoon ground white pepper

1 teaspoon sesame oil

2 (14-ounce/398-g) packages eggless wonton wrappers

(continued)

1. **MAKE THE FILLING:** To prepare frozen shepherd's purse, thaw it in the fridge or in cold water on the counter. When using fresh or thawed shepherd's purse, rinse it under cold water, then wring it well, reserving some of the water in a bowl. Add enough water to make ½ cup (120 ml). Discard the root of each stalk, then chop it as finely as you can. In a blender or food processor, combine the ginger and scallions with the reserved water. Mix 2 tablespoons of this ginger-scallion water with the rest of the filling ingredients and stir with chopsticks in one direction (see page 133, step 1) until the mixture resembles a sticky paste. Cover and chill for 30 minutes.

2. Place about 2 teaspoons of filling in the center of a wonton wrapper. Trace water along the top edge of the wrapper. Bring the bottom half up to meet it and seal along the edges. Bring the two bottom corners together and seal them with a dab of water. (See page 91 for step-by-step photographs.) Continue to fill and seal the rest of the wonton wrappers following these instructions.

3. At this point, you can either cook the wontons immediately or freeze some or all of them for later. To freeze, line up the wontons on a baking sheet and put in the freezer. Once frozen, after about an hour, transfer the wontons to freezer-safe bags and return them to the freezer. They will keep for several months.

4. To cook the wontons, bring a pot of water to a boil over high. Add 10 to 15 wontons (depending on the size of your pot; do not overcrowd) and stir gently to prevent sticking. *(continued)*

WONTON SOUP BROTH

pork, chicken, or High Stock
  (page 277)
kosher salt
ground white pepper
1 scallion, chopped
2 tablespoons chopped fresh
  cilantro

CHILI OIL WONTON SAUCE

红油抄手 *hong you chao shou*
cilantro leaves
¼ cup (60 ml) chili oil with
  red pepper flakes (preferably
  homemade, page 273)
¼ cup (60 ml) light soy sauce
2 tablespoons black vinegar
2 teaspoons grated garlic
1 scallion, finely sliced crosswise
1 tablespoon granulated sugar

toasted white sesame seeds

Bring to a simmer, just before the water reaches a rolling boil, and keep at this temperature for about 7 minutes, depending on the size of your wontons. The wontons should float, and their skin will turn more translucent, but they should not turn mushy or fall apart. If your water comes to a boil before the wontons float, add ½ cup (120 ml) of cold water and let it come to a simmer again. (To cook frozen wontons, let them simmer for 10 to 12 minutes.) You can always cut open a wonton to check that the pork is cooked through.

5. **MAKE THE WONTON SOUP:** Heat the broth until it is piping hot, add salt to taste, and ladle into individual bowls. Remove the wontons from the boiling water with a slotted spoon and divide them among the bowls of broth. Serve immediately with white pepper, the scallions, and the cilantro.

6. **MAKE CHILI OIL WONTONS:** Remove the wontons from the boiling water with a slotted spoon and place in individual bowls. Place a few cilantro leaves in each bowl. In a separate small bowl, mix together the chili oil, soy sauce, vinegar, garlic, scallion slices, and sugar with 2 tablespoons of the boiling wonton cooking water and spoon it over the wontons. Toss to combine and serve immediately with a spoonful of toasted white sesame seeds.

MOM'S SHANGHAI RED-BRAISED PORK BELLY

上海红烧肉 | shàng hǎi hóng shāo ròu | *Makes 4 servings*

If there is one dish that represents Shanghai cuisine, this is the one. Perhaps my favorite recipe in this entire book, this recipe holds a dear place in my heart. My mom has been making red-braised pork belly for as long as I can remember. Whenever we gathered with family or friends, my mom made this recipe, the one that her mom taught her, and the one that I want to teach to my future children.

红烧 *hong shao*, "red cooking," is one of the most well-known cooking methods from Shanghai. A mix of dark and light soy sauce is a must to achieve the right flavor profile. There are many variations of this dish in Jiangnan: In Suzhou, where my husband's family is from, hard-boiled eggs are added to give extra dimension to the dish. In Shanghai, tofu knots are added. In Ningbo, salted yellow croaker is added for an extra umami kick. Some recipes will call for adding cornstarch, but I can tell you with certainty that this recipe should never need to be thickened with cornstarch. The gelatin from the pork belly's skin and the rock sugar will naturally thicken the sauce. Finishing the dish by cooking the braise down will produce a thick, gleaming sauce to coat the pork belly.

I've put three hours as the recommended braise time, but in truth, the longer the better. My husband's grandfather makes this dish as well, and he just lets it simmer over a small flame all day, filling the kitchen with the most tantalizing aroma.

NOTE: This is a very forgiving recipe. If it's too salty or sweet, add more sugar or soy sauce to compensate. In line with true Chinese cooking, taste the sauce as it simmers and adjust to your preference. Be wary of adding the tofu knots too early, as they can become overcooked and mushy.

1½ pounds (680 g) boneless pork belly, 五花肉 *wu hua rou*

2 tablespoons neutral cooking oil, such as canola or grapeseed oil

4 tablespoons (60 g) rock sugar—
2 tablespoons finely crushed with a mortar and pestle, 2 tablespoons left whole

3 tablespoons dark soy sauce

1 cup (240 ml) chicken stock or water

¼ cup (60 ml) light soy sauce

¼ cup (60 ml) Shaoxing wine

3 whole star anise

2 thin slices peeled fresh ginger

4 scallions—3 cut into 2-inch (5-cm) segments and 1 chopped

cooked white rice, for serving

1. Bring about 2 inches (5 cm) of water to a boil over high in a large pot. Add the pork belly and boil for 3 minutes. Add more water to cover the pork if necessary. This step removes impurities from the pork, making for a clearer dish. Drain and set aside. When cool enough to handle, cut the pork into 1½-inch (4-cm) cubes.

2. Heat the oil in a well-seasoned wok on low, until wisps of smoke curl up off the edges. Add the crushed rock sugar and stir until the sugar melts and dissolves.

3. Increase the heat to medium and, working in two batches if necessary, gently slide in the chunks of pork belly. Brown all sides of the pork. Any residual water on the pork will pop in the oil—don't be scared! A splatter screen can help keep the oil contained. Stir only occasionally, so that the pork can caramelize and brown. This step gives it a rich caramel flavor. Add the dark soy sauce and fry for an additional minute.

4. In the wok or in a separate Dutch oven (a clay pot works well for this), combine the browned pork with the stock, light soy sauce, Shaoxing wine, remaining rock sugar, star anise, *(continued)*

4 to 6 hard-boiled eggs,
peeled and slashed lengthwise
2 or 3 times for maximum
sauce absorption
8 frozen tofu knots (available at
Asian markets)

ginger, and scallion segments. The mixture should come three-quarters of the way up the side of the pile of pork. If not, add more stock or water.

5. Bring to a boil over high, then reduce the heat to the lowest setting and simmer, partially covered, for at least 3 hours, stirring occasionally to prevent sticking. The longer the pork simmers, the more tender and flavorful it will be; it's ready when it's soft enough to slip a chopstick in with ease, but you can go up to 2 hours longer to build the flavor even more. Add more stock or water as needed; the wok should never be dry. When there's approximately 2 hours of braising time left, add the hard-boiled eggs to the wok, if using. Twenty minutes before you're ready to serve, add the frozen tofu knots, if using.

6. When nearly ready to serve, remove the lid, increase the heat to high, and boil until the cooking liquid becomes a thick, dark, glistening sauce that covers the pork belly. If the pork belly has begun to break down (the lean meat is separating from the fatty portion), use a slotted spoon to remove the cubes before cooking down the sauce, and add the cubes of meat back in at the end.

7. Serve with white rice and the chopped scallions.

PORK BELLY BAO

红烧肉刈包 | *hóng shāo ròu guà bāo* | *Makes 8 to 12 buns*

My mom always made this dish when my friends came over. A few years ago, pork belly buns were a sensation that swept the country, showing up at every modern Asian restaurant, and with good reason: succulent, melty pork belly lovingly nestled in fluffy steamed buns with the contrasting texture of fresh slivers of scallion or thin slices of cucumber is an experience. For this recipe, my mom simply adjusted her famous red-braised pork belly and created this pork belly bun that still reigns over all other buns I've ever tasted. The deep flavor of the red braise permeates the whole piece of pork, so much so that no extra sauce is needed. I like mine simple—just a few slivers of fresh scallion are the perfect topping to complete the *bao* for me—but you can also top yours with crushed peanuts, thin slices of cucumber, or cilantro if you wish.

NOTE: The steamed *baos* are made using my go-to steamed bun-wrapper dough, shaped into 刈包 *gua bao*, "cut bun," which is folded over the filling kind of like a taco. I let these rise a bit longer for a slightly deeper flavor and fermentation. You can make more or less of them depending on how large you want them. This recipe makes 8 generous-sized *baos*, but I've stretched it to make 12 smaller ones as well. You can prep them beforehand—they will keep for a day in the fridge (steam for 3 minutes to reheat) or 4 to 6 weeks in the freezer (steam for 7 minutes to reheat).

1 recipe Mom's Shanghai Red-Braised Pork Belly (page 93; but see alterations described in step 1)

1 teaspoon active dry yeast

1 tablespoon granulated sugar

1 cup (240 ml) warm water

2¾ cups plus 1 tablespoon (350 g) all-purpose flour

1¼ cups (150 g) cake flour

2 teaspoons baking powder

1 teaspoon pork lard (store-bought or homemade, page 271) or vegetable oil, plus more for greasing the bowl

3 scallions, cut lengthwise into slivers then crosswise into 3-inch (7.5-cm) segments

1. **MAKE THE PORK BELLY:** Make Mom's Shanghai Red-Braised Pork Belly with these changes: After boiling the pork belly, instead of cutting the pieces into cubes, cut them into 2- x ½-inch (5-cm x 12-mm) slices. Proceed with the recipe to the point where the pork belly has simmered for 1½ to 2 hours.

2. Using a slotted spoon, carefully remove the pork belly slices from the braise and set them aside. Increase the heat to high and reduce the braising liquid until a thick and glistening sauce forms.

3. Heat a flat-bottomed pan over medium, then fry the pork belly slices in a single layer, flipping once to brown on both sides, 2 to 3 minutes a side. Pour the sauce through a sieve over the pork belly, so that the pork belly slices are covered in the sauce.

4. **MAKE THE BAO:** Make the dough by combining the yeast, sugar, and warm water.
   Let sit for 5 minutes to let the yeast bloom to ensure that it is active. Foamy bubbles should appear on the surface.

5. Combine both flours in a mixing bowl and make a well in the center. Sprinkle the baking powder around the outer edge of the flour so that it will be incorporated last. Gradually stream in the yeast mixture, using your other hand to mix with chopsticks. Once all the liquid is in and the dough is loosely mixed, add the lard.

6. Use your hands to knead for about 10 minutes, until the dough is soft, elastic, and so smooth it can be described as "three shines," 三光 *san guang*. This indicates that your hands, the dough, and the bowl should be "shiny," without anything sticking to *(continued)*

them. If you try to stretch the dough, it should offer some resistance and pull back. If the dough is too tight, wet your hands with water and keep kneading. Be careful of how much extra water you add—the more hydrated the dough, the heavier it will be. Alternatively, combine the dry ingredients in the bowl of a stand mixer with the dough hook and mix on low until combined. Slowly stream in the yeast mixture, then when the dough starts to come together add the lard. Increase the speed to medium and mix until smooth and elastic and the dough begins to pull away from the sides of the bowl, 5 to 7 minutes. The dough and bowl should be smooth and shiny—if not, add more flour gradually.

7. Place the dough in an oiled bowl. Let rise, covered with a dishcloth, for 60 to 90 minutes, until doubled in size.

8. Meanwhile, prepare 3 x 3-inch (7.5 x 7.5-cm) squares of parchment paper. You will need 24 squares.

9. To check the dough, pull the dough from the edge of the bowl. If you see a honeycomb of airy texture, the dough is ready. It should stretch easily without any elastic recoil. Punch down the dough and knead vigorously until smooth and shiny once more, 3 to 5 minutes. How vigorously you knead (which will get rid of the air bubbles from the rise) will dictate how smooth your resulting bun surface is.

10. On a surface lightly dusted with flour, roll the dough with your hands into a log. Divide it into two portions. Cover one portion with a kitchen towel so it doesn't dry out while you work with the other portion. Shape this portion into a longer log, then divide it into 6 equal portions. Place one portion, cut side down, on your board and use your palm to flatten it. Using a rolling pin, roll the dough to form an oval. Use a chopstick to mark the halfway point, and lightly fold one half over the other, being careful not to press down and sliding a sheet of parchment paper between the halves to prevent sticking. Place the *bao* on top of another square of parchment and put it in a steamer. Repeat with the remaining dough leaving 1½ inches (4 cm) between *baos*. Cover the steamer with the lid and let the *baos* rise for 15 minutes, until doubled in size.

11. To steam the *baos*, bring about 2 inches (5 cm) of cold water to a boil in your wok or the bottom of a steamer (make sure the water does not touch the bottom of the steamer basket) over high. Once the water boils, immediately reduce the heat to medium and steam for 15 minutes. Remove the lid. Press a fingertip into a *bao*: If the indentation bounces back, the *baos* are ready. If not, let them steam for another 3 minutes. At this point, you can refrigerate or freeze the *baos* for use later. If you're not eating them within a few days, freeze and use within 1 month. To reheat from the fridge, steam for 2 to 3 minutes. To reheat from frozen, steam for 7 to 8 minutes. Remember to remove all the parchment paper before consuming the *baos*.

12. **ASSEMBLE THE BAO:** nestle one or two pieces of pork belly with fresh slivers of scallion in each bun and serve.

LUNAR NEW YEAR

过春节 | guò chūn jié

As a child, Lunar New Year meant family gatherings, the hustle and bustle of preparations for a delicious feast, and 红包 *hong bao*, "red envelopes filled with monetary gifts." I didn't think about it much beyond that, but as I grew older, having spent some of these holidays away from family, I began to appreciate how much this holiday was rooted in togetherness.

The lunar calendar is based on the movement of the moon, a method of timekeeping used, in part, because of China's agrarian society. The start of a new cycle, the Lunar New Year is perhaps one of the most anticipated festivals in China. Preparation starts days before the new year and festivities extend halfway into the first month. The migration is phenomenal—more than three billion people make their way home to celebrate with their families.

The preparations for this holiday are some of my favorite memories from childhood: helping my mom with small tasks like washing vegetables, wrapping dumplings, and setting the table. The anticipation was an energy in and of itself: giddy and utterly exciting.

On New Year's Eve, guests are welcomed with cups of tea and fresh fruit. Places are set for those who cannot return home. Specific foods are served for their symbolism—anything to maximize prosperity. Fish, whose Chinese character, 鱼 *yu*, is a homophone for *surplus*, 余 *yu*, is served whole for fortune. Golden egg dumplings because they resemble gold ingots of a time past. Tatsoi, 塌棵菜 *ta ke cai* or *ta ku cai* in Chinese, in Shanghainese sounds phonetically similar to 脱苦 *tuo ku*, which means "warding off any bitterness for the new year." 年糕 *nian gao*, "sticky rice cake," is served because it contains the character for "year," and the second character, *gao*, is a homophone for "high." Together, "year high" symbolizes upward mobility in the coming year.

灶君 *Zao Jun*, the "stove god," oversees all household activities. According to tradition, he checks in on the twentieth day of the twelfth lunar month and assesses the household. For this reason, everything is left in place until then. When he departs on the twenty-third or twenty-fourth (depending on the region) to report to 玉皇 *Yu Huang*, the "Jade Emperor," families begin the pre–New Year ritual of cleansing the home, kicking up dust and shifting furniture. The purpose of cleaning is twofold: to sweep away any evil spirits lurking in forgotten corners and residual bad luck and to have a presentable, pristine house for the upcoming feast. The new year is ushered in with a fresh environment—a fresh start to a new cycle.

The coveted *hong bao* is not just a cute tradition to make kids happy, but a way to connect the older generation with the younger. Visiting the elderly is a sign of respect, and the red envelopes are a reward to the children, a reminder and encouragement to continue to respect their elders.

In the days after the New Year, the festivities continue. On the fifth day, the fortune god comes to town, and sweeping is avoided at this time, for fear that you could sweep out good luck. The fifteenth day of the new year is called 元宵 *Yuan Xiao*, "Lantern Festival." *Yuan Xiao* also refers to *tang yuan*, "sticky rice balls" (see recipe, pages 113–115), which are eaten as symbols of togetherness and unity. During this time, intricate lanterns are lit and sent off into the night sky, to help the gods see, followed by a last celebratory meal to end the New Year festivities.

At this point, half of the new month has passed in celebration. In the agricultural cycle, this is when the first rains of the new year will happen, and people ready themselves to go back to work to prepare the fields. Thus, another cycle begins.

DOUBLE PORK SOUP

腌笃鲜 | yān dǔ xiān | *Makes 4 servings*

One of the key characteristics of this soup is the purity of the broth—it should be clear enough to see to the bottom of the pot. Like much of Shanghai cuisine, on the surface it looks simple, almost rustic, but 腌笃鲜 *yan du xian* has a sophisticated flavor. A writer once noted that high stock is basically chicken and cured pork, but the actual king of broth is *yan du xian*. The direct translation of the name is "cured simmering fresh," and that's basically what it is. Salted and fresh pork are added to a succulent clear broth with crisp winter bamboo shoots, then the ingredients are simmered slowly. A clay pot is wonderful for this, as it holds heat very evenly, allowing the food to cook gently for a long period of time. (As with all clay-pot recipes, remember to be mindful of sudden temperature changes to avoid breaking the pot.)

Yan du xian, for me, will always be associated with New Year's celebrations and gatherings. It's a warm welcome.

NOTE: If your salt pork is too salty, remove some salt by soaking the pork in cold water for 2 to 3 hours, then rinsing it a few times with more cold water. If you can't find fresh winter bamboo, use frozen or vacuum-packed shoots.

1 pound (455 g) boneless pork belly, cut into 1-inch (2.5-cm) cubes

1 pound (455 g) salt pork (recipe for homemade on page 268), cut into 1-inch (2.5-cm) cubes (see Note)

10 cups (2.4 L) water, plus more as needed

4 slices fresh ginger

2 scallions, cut into 2-inch (5-cm) segments

2 tablespoons Shaoxing wine

1 pound (455 g) fresh winter bamboo shoots, woody layers removed, sliced using the 滚刀 *gun dao* "rolling knife" method (see page 20)

handful of frozen tofu knots (optional; available at Asian markets)

kosher salt

1 teaspoon ground white pepper

1. Bring about 2 inches (5 cm) of water to a boil in a pot over high. Add the pork belly and boil for 3 minutes, adding more water to cover the pork if necessary. This step removes impurities from the pork, making for a clearer dish. Drain.

2. Place the blanched pork belly and the salt pork in a clay pot or Dutch oven. Add the water and slowly bring to a boil over medium-high heat. Reduce the heat to low and bring to a simmer. Crush the ginger and scallion segments with the flat side of a cleaver to loosen the fibers, then add them along with the wine to the pot. Simmer, partially covered, over low for 1 hour, occasionally removing any scum that rises to the surface.

3. Add the bamboo, increase the heat to high, and bring to a boil. Then reduce the heat to low and simmer, partially covered, for another 1½ hours.

4. Add the tofu knots, if using, and simmer for another 20 minutes. Season with salt to taste and the white pepper. Serve piping hot.

GOLDEN EGG DUMPLINGS

蛋饺 | dàn jiǎo | *Makes about 36 dumplings*

These egg dumplings resemble the old currency of gold ingots, 元宝 *yuan bao*. For this reason, egg dumplings are considered lucky foods. But what I love most about them is the ritual of making them. They are labor-intensive, but the end result of meat encased in a lard-cooked egg is worth it. You can serve them as is or steeped in a hot, rich stock with vermicelli noodles and cabbage.

NOTE: You should use a steel ladle for this recipe, which is flatter than a soup ladle but still has a subtle curve. The end of the handle is usually wood to protect the holder when the ladle is heated.

NOTE: When you freeze these dumplings, the filling won't be fully cooked. They must be steamed or cooked in a broth before serving. If you have an electric stovetop, you can try to cook these dumplings using this hot ladle technique, but the heat won't be as evenly distributed as on a gas range, nor will it have the intensity of an open flame.

2 tablespoons Ginger-Scallion Water (page 257), plus 1 nub of ginger

2 tablespoons minced scallions

½ pound (225 g) ground pork

2 tablespoons light soy sauce

2 tablespoons Shaoxing wine

¾ tablespoon granulated sugar

½ teaspoon sesame oil

pinch of ground white pepper

neutral cooking oil, such as canola or grapeseed oil, or pork lard (store-bought or homemade, page 271)

5 large eggs, thoroughly beaten

3 cups (720 ml) pork, chicken, or High Stock (page 277), for 2 to 3 servings

1. In a medium bowl, combine the pork, soy sauce, wine, and sugar and, using chopsticks, stir in one direction (see page 133, step 1) until well combined. Stir in the sesame oil and white pepper. Add the ginger-scallion water and continue to stir until the mixture is completely incorporated and resembles a paste. Refrigerate.

2. Over an open flame, heat a metal ladle (see first Note). Use tongs or chopsticks to rub the nub of ginger on the ladle to prevent any sticking. Add ½ teaspoon of oil to the hot ladle. (If using lard, let it melt.)

3. Add 1 tablespoon of the beaten egg to the center of the ladle, and immediately but carefully swirl the ladle so that the egg coats the entire surface. Add 1 tablespoon of the meat mixture to the center, then gently use chopsticks to peel away the top half of the egg and place it over the bottom half, creating a half-moon shape. Use chopsticks to gently apply pressure along the open edge to seal. Set aside on a plate.

4. Continue to make the egg dumplings until you've used up the eggs and filling. You should be able to make about 36. At this point, you can freeze the dumplings for several months or proceed to step 5.

5. There are two ways to cook the dumplings:
STEAM: Steam the dumplings for 5 minutes (plus an additional 3 minutes if already frozen).
SIMMER: Bring the stock to a boil over high. Gently slide in the egg dumplings, reduce the heat to low, and simmer for 10 minutes. Serve hot with the stock.

STEAMED FISH

清蒸鱼 | qīng zhēng yú | *Servings will vary*

The word for "fish" in Chinese, 鱼 *yu*, is a homophone of *surplus,* 余 *yu.* The characters are different but phonetically indistinguishable. Chinese superstitions are often based on homophones: for example, the number eight, 八 *ba,* is a fortuitous number because it sounds like *success,* 发财 *fa cai.* Fish is a symbol of luck. 年年有余 *nian nian you yu* translates to "may you have a surplus every year."

This dish is meant to be eaten family style. It's often one of the first dishes to be picked clean. The cheek muscles and collar are the most highly coveted parts, as they are the most succulent and flavorful. The most tender meat is close to the bones.

Each family has their own way of cooking whole steamed fish. This recipe is my parents'. The fish is marinated with Shaoxing wine and salt, which takes away the "fishiness" and leaves only the wondrous, aromatic flavor.

1 (1- to 1½-pound/455- to 565-g) whole sea bass, scaled and gutted by your fishmonger (see Note)

3 tablespoons coarse sea salt

3 tablespoons Shaoxing wine

3 slices ginger, plus 1 slice julienned

5 scallions—2 cut into 2-inch (5-cm) segments and 3 left whole

⅓ cup (15 g) chopped fresh cilantro

OPTIONAL TOPPINGS

3 tablespoons vegetable oil

3 thin slices fresh ginger

2 tablespoons light soy sauce

1 teaspoon granulated sugar

1. Pat the fish dry with a paper towel. Use a sharp knife to cut three or four diagonal slits in the thickest part of the fish on both sides, reaching to the bone. Rub a thin layer of salt all over, and brush the wine over both sides, making sure to reach inside the slits and the belly. Place 3 ginger slices and the scallion segments into the belly of the fish. Let sit for 20 to 30 minutes.

2. Meanwhile, cut off the green parts of the 3 remaining scallions and reserve. Cut the white parts in half lengthwise. Lay the halves cut side up and slice the scallion into julienne. Place the julienned ginger, scallions, and cilantro into ice-cold water to keep fresh. This will also cause the scallion to curl for presentation.

3. Smash the reserved green parts of the scallions with the flat side of a cleaver to loosen the fibers and spread them across your steamer plate to become a bed for the fish.

4. Prepare a steamer pot or place a bamboo steamer in your wok. Place the prepared fish on top of the bed of green scallions and place the plate inside the steamer. Cover with the lid and steam for 10 minutes. Turn off the heat and let sit, covered, for another 3 minutes.

5. Remove the lid and check if the fish is done by gently probing inside one of the slits—the meat should be opaque down to the bone, but the bone will be translucent and the flesh should easily flake off.

6. Drain off excess water. Remove and discard the cooked scallions and ginger. Drain the cilantro, ginger, and scallions from the ice-water bath and garnish the fish.

7. Prepare the optional toppings (if using): Heat the vegetable oil and the slices of ginger in a small saucepan over high heat. Once the ginger begins to sizzle, remove from the heat and pour the oil over the fish and garnish, discarding the ginger. The oil will sizzle once it hits the fish, both crisping the skin and releasing fragrance from the aromatics.

8. Whisk the soy sauce and sugar together in a small saucepan and heat over medium-high so that it sizzles and bubbles for a minute. Remove from the heat and spoon the mixture over the crisped fish and garnish or serve it on the side. Serve the fish immediately.

BASIC WINTER GREENS STIR-FRY

清炒青菜 | qīng chǎo qīng cài | *Makes 2 servings*

Whether it's bok choy, choy sum, or Chinese water spinach, stir-fried greens are a staple dish. It's never served alone, as it's treated as a supplement to balance the protein dish. Stir-fried greens are such a background staple in Chinese cooking that they're not really mentioned in any special way.

This dish is *fast*—make sure to have all your ingredients ready and memorize these directions, because once you start cooking you won't have time to reference the next step. After doing this a few times, however, the motions will become ingrained, and you'll be able to whip up a stir-fry with any greens you have on hand without thinking about it.

There's a concept in Chinese cooking called 热锅冷油 *re guo leng you,* "hot wok, cold oil," meaning that the wok is heated first, then cold oil is added. This practice brings down the temperature of the wok quickly to a level that is suitable for aromatics. The oil is warmed by the heated wok as the aromatics cook, so that their flavors are released without burning them. Then, when the oil warms up sufficiently, you add the vegetables. The seconds after you add the vegetables are crucial—you must immediately begin to stir-fry, scooping from the bottom of the wok so that none of the aromatics burn at the high temperature the vegetables require to cook. Any stock added should be hot, to keep the wok at the right temperature.

The amount of time you cook the vegetables is up to individual preference. My husband likes them softer and more wilted, whereas I like them crisper, so experiment until you discover what you like.

NOTE: I use a good-quality olive oil that can withstand heat for my stir-fries, but if the taste is too strong, use a neutral cooking oil, such as canola or grapeseed oil.

1 pound (455 g) baby bok choy
2 tablespoons olive oil (see Note)
2 cloves garlic, thinly sliced
2 slices fresh ginger
1 teaspoon kosher salt
pinch of granulated sugar
½ teaspoon ground white pepper
2 tablespoons pork, chicken, or
  High Stock (page 277)

1. To prepare the bok choy, either remove the individual leaves and cut them into chunks, or slice each bok choy in half lengthwise but otherwise keep whole for a pleasing presentation. Trim off the tough base at the stem end and discard. Place the bok choy in a large bowl of cold water and gently shake to release any dirt. Rinse and soak one more time, then rinse and drain thoroughly, shaking to dry.

2. Heat a well-seasoned wok over medium-high. Add the oil and swirl to coat.

3. Immediately add the garlic and ginger and let them explode into fragrance, 爆香 *bao xiang,* stirring constantly.

4. Add the bok choy, increase the heat to high, and stir-fry, making sure to reach the bottom of the wok so that the aromatics are evenly distributed.

5. Add the salt, sugar, white pepper, and hot stock. Stir-fry for another 1 to 2 minutes and serve.

SHANGHAI STIR-FRIED RICE CAKE

上海炒年糕 | shàng hǎi chǎo nián gāo | *Makes 4 servings*

Rice cakes are handmade by pounding cooked rice into a powder, then mixing it with water and rolling it into a cake. In North America, it's hard to find fresh logs of rice cake. Instead, you can find dried or frozen sliced rice cake, which is what I prefer.

The beauty of this recipe is that, like most stir-fries, the variations are endless. This is one of my favorites, with pork, napa cabbage, and shiitake mushrooms, because I love the way the pork and shiitake elevate the umami-ness of the sauce. Other variations I enjoy are shepherd's purse with fresh bamboo shoots (even more reminiscent of Ningbo) and snow vegetable with pork slivers.

NOTE: If you can't find yellow chives, substitute stalks of scallion. Simply crush them with the flat side of a cleaver to loosen the fibers.

1½ teaspoons cornstarch

2 tablespoons plus 2 teaspoons Shaoxing wine

2 tablespoons plus 1½ teaspoons light soy sauce

½ pound (225 g) pork belly, loin, or shoulder

12 ounces (half a package) frozen rice cakes, thawed and rinsed

6 dried shiitake mushrooms, rehydrated in hot water to cover for 1 hour until soft

2 tablespoons neutral cooking oil, such as canola or grapeseed oil, plus more as needed

2 cloves garlic, minced

1 tablespoon minced fresh ginger

3 stalks yellow chives (see Note), cut into 1-inch (2.5-cm) pieces

3 cups (200 g) thickly sliced napa cabbage

1 tablespoon dark soy sauce

1 teaspoon granulated sugar

1 teaspoon ground white pepper

sesame oil

1. In a medium bowl, combine the cornstarch, 2 teaspoons of the wine, and 1½ teaspoons of the light soy sauce. Trim any excess fat or skin from the pork and slice the meat against the grain into short, thin pieces, 1 to 2 inches (2.5 to 5 cm) by ¼ inch (6 mm). Toss the pork with the marinade and let sit for at least 10 minutes but no more than 1 hour.

2. Drain the rice cakes thoroughly. Drain the mushrooms through a fine-mesh sieve to remove any grit, reserve 3 tablespoons of the stock, discard the stems, and slice the mushrooms.

3. Heat a well-seasoned wok over high until smoking. Add the oil and swirl to coat. Add the garlic and ginger and stir-fry quickly until fragrant. Add the pork and stir-fry until just cooked, 2 to 3 minutes. Remove the pork from the wok and set aside.

4. Return the wok to high heat. Add more oil if necessary. Add the mushrooms and stir-fry for 2 minutes. Add the yellow chives and stir-fry briefly.

5. Add the cabbage and stir-fry for another minute, then return the pork to the wok. Stream in the remaining 2 tablespoons of wine.

6. Gently slide in the rice cakes and mix to combine. Add the reserved mushroom stock. Cover and simmer for 3 to 5 minutes.

7. Remove the lid, add the dark soy sauce, remaining 2 tablespoons of light soy sauce, sugar, and white pepper. Continue to stir-fry, until the ingredients are well combined and the rice cakes are soft but chewy. Just before serving, finish with a few drops of sesame oil.

STICKY RICE BALLS THREE WAYS

汤圆: 鲜肉, 芝麻, 菜猪油 | tāng yuán: xiān ròu, zhī ma, cài zhū yóu | *Makes 12 big rice balls*

Part of the fun of the New Year's celebration is the preparation for and anticipation of the festivities. My mom's tradition as a child was to lay out brand-new clothes for the New Year and make sticky rice balls. She told me that she was the rice-ball maker in her family. She would stay up late the night before New Year's Eve to make black sesame sticky rice balls. She was the second youngest of six siblings and the best at shaping them. While I typically buy glutinous rice flour at a nearby Chinese grocery store, when my mom and dad were children, they made their own flour. Every year, they'd rent a special mortar and pestle and manually grind glutinous rice and water into a fine, powdery flour. The water, my dad said, is critical to making the flour super-fine. So, when I buy my own flour, I make sure to purchase one that is ground in a water mill.

Shanghainese enjoy rice balls in both sweet and savory preparations. I love both, so I included them here. All Shanghainese buns and pastries have simple identifiers for telling the difference between sweet and savory. Sweet versions are always round and smooth, while savory ones will have a tail hinting at the filling inside.

NOTE: If you can find it, use fatty ground pork, with about a 4:6 fat-to-lean-meat ratio. The ground meat will be more pale, and you should be able to see specks of fat throughout. Not all stores will sell ground pork with enough fat in it, so a mix of pork belly and ground pork can also be used. Each filling will make 12 rice balls; if you want to make all three at once, triple the amount of glutinous rice flour and water.

MEAT FILLING

4 tablespoons (75 g) ground pork
½ teaspoon dark soy sauce
½ teaspoon light soy sauce
¼ teaspoon salt
1 tablespoon Shaoxing wine
1 teaspoon granulated sugar
2 drops sesame oil
pinch of ground white pepper
2 tablespoons Ginger-Scallion Water water (page 257)
2 tablespoons Jellied Stock (Pi Dong) (page 257), diced

SESAME FILLING

⅓ cup (45 g) black sesame seeds
1 tablespoon (10 g) white sesame seeds
¼ cup (50 g) sugar
1½ teaspoons dried osmanthus petals, 桂花 *gui hua*
(continued)

1. **MAKE THE MEAT FILLING:** Combine the pork, soy sauces, salt, wine, and sugar and, using chopsticks, stir in one direction (see page 133, step 1) until well combined. Add the sesame oil, white pepper, and ginger-scallion water and stir until the liquid is completely incorporated and the mixture resembles a paste. Add the *pi dong* and gently mix. Refrigerate until ready to assemble.

2. **MAKE THE SESAME FILLING:** Toast the black and white sesame seeds in a pan over low for 3 to 5 minutes, keeping an eye on them, as they can burn suddenly. Once toasted, the sesame seeds will be slightly darker in color, very fragrant, and easily crushable between your fingers.

3. Grind the sesame seeds with a mortar and pestle while still warm. When the seeds start to release their oils, add the sugar. Continue to grind for 1 minute. Add the dried osmanthus and the salt. Grind for another 2 to 3 minutes, until mostly homogenous. Add 1 tablespoon of water and the lard, using a fork to combine thoroughly. Alternatively, this process can be done easily in a food processor: first grind the sesame seeds, then add the sugar, osmanthus, and salt. Add the water and pork lard with a fork as above. Refrigerate to harden for 30 minutes—this will facilitate the assembly process. *(continued)*

salt

3 tablespoons pork lard
(store-bought or homemade,
page 271), duck fat, or butter

GREENS FILLING

½ teaspoon salt, plus more
for the cooking water

½ pound (225 g) Chinese spinach,
油菜 *yu choy*, or other greens,
like baby bok choy

2 tablespoons granulated sugar

½ teaspoon minced ginger

2 tablespoons pork lard
(store-bought or homemade,
page 271)

1 tablespoon sesame oil

RICE BALL DOUGH

2 cups (250 g) water-based
glutinous rice flour,
plus more for dusting

1 cup (240 ml) warm water

4. **MAKE THE GREENS FILLING:** In a pot of boiling water with a pinch of salt, blanch the *yu choy* until the greens are vibrant green, 1 to 2 minutes. Transfer immediately to an ice-water bath. Drain and wring to remove the excess water, then chop as finely as you can. Combine the greens with the sugar, ginger, salt, lard, and sesame oil until well combined. Refrigerate for 2 hours.

5. **MAKE THE RICE BALL DOUGH:** Make a well in the center of the rice flour in a bowl. Stream in ½ cup (120 ml) of the warm water, mixing with chopsticks continuously until a loose mixture starts to come together. Turn the dough out onto a lightly floured surface. Knead until a tacky (but not sticky) dough comes together. If the dough sticks to your hand, add more glutinous rice flour. If it's too dry, add water, 1 teaspoon at a time. It should have a texture much like Play-Doh. Knead until smooth, about 3 minutes.

6. Bring a pot of water to a boil over high. Pinch and roll 1 teaspoon of dough into a ball, then gently flatten it into a disc. Boil it until the disc rises, 3 to 5 minutes. Remove the disc with a slotted spoon and let it cool slightly. Incorporate the cooked disc into the dough, kneading until completely incorporated and smooth. This extra step will make the dough super malleable and elastic, creating a silky soft and chewy texture when cooked. Set the dough aside and cover with plastic or a damp towel. Let rest for 20 minutes.

7. **ASSEMBLE THE RICE BALLS:** Divide the dough in half, and keep one half covered while you work. On a lightly floured surface, with your hands roll the dough into a log 1 inch (2.5 cm) in diameter. Divide it into 6 equal pieces (about 35 g each) and roll the pieces into balls. Cover with a damp towel or plastic wrap.

8. Working with one dough ball at a time, use your thumb to press down the center while your fingers press the edges up into a bowl shape. Take 1 teaspoon of filling and place it in the middle of the wrapper. Close the edges. Wrap your right hand around and squeeze gently while drawing up the sides of the bowl and slowly pinching the opening closed. If making meat balls, the traditional shape is a teardrop: Simply close the edges and pinch the dough off to make a teardrop shape. If making sesame balls, gently place the ball pinched side down, then roll quickly but lightly to smooth out. If making greens balls, shape into a rounded cylinder.

9. Repeat with the rest of the dough. At this point, you can freeze the rice balls until just before you're ready to serve or up to 3 months. They'll also last in the refrigerator, tightly covered, for up to 1 day.

10. Fill a large pot with water to 1 inch (2.5 cm) below the rim and bring to a boil over high. Gently slide in up to 4 rice balls at a time, stirring gently to prevent sticking.

11. **TO COOK THE MEAT AND GREENS RICE BALLS:** Bring the water back to a gentle simmer, then keep the heat on medium-high to stay just below boiling—if you reach boiling the rice balls will overcook. Once the balls float, after about 5 minutes, simmer for another 5 to 6 minutes. If cooking from frozen, cook for an additional 2 minutes.

Serve hot with some of the cooking water—this water isn't meant to be slurped up, but is a way to keep the rice balls hot for consumption. Be careful when eating: The *pi dong* will become soupy, and we are often scalded when we eat these!

12. **TO COOK THE SESAME RICE BALLS:** Bring the water back to a gentle simmer, then keep the heat on medium-high to stay just below boiling—if you reach boiling the rice balls will overcook. Cook for 5 minutes, until the balls float to the top. Add the remaining 1 teaspoon of osmanthus and cook for another 30 seconds. Serve hot with sweet fermented glutinous rice wine, or with candied osmanthus, dried osmanthus, or both, or none—the variations are endless.

SWEET RICE WINE AND RICE BALL SOUP

酒酿圆子 | jiǔ niàng yuán zi | *Makes 4 servings*

This dish is often eaten on the first day of the Lunar New Year. You'll find this fermented glutinous rice dessert soup, usually with sticky rice balls, as a final offering to round off a meal in most restaurants and households. My mom made this at home frequently during my childhood. It's simple to make: a quick fermentation makes the glutinous rice looser in texture and sweet, with just a hint of aromatic wine. My mom once over-fermented the glutinous rice and proceeded to have it for breakfast, and then (she tells me with an embarrassed chuckle) went to school tipsy. Needless to say, she was sent home.

There are many ways to dress this scrumptious dessert, but the addition of sticky rice balls is a must, whether they're plain or of the black sesame variety (see Sticky Rice Balls Three Ways, page 113). I like to add a little dimension to mine with a few petals of dried osmanthus, goji berries, or a light wisp of beaten egg. In Suzhou, tangerine segments are added for a particularly bright variation.

1 cup (125 g) water-based
    glutinous rice flour,
    plus more for dusting
    and the baking sheet
5 tablespoons rock sugar,
    plus more if needed
1 large egg
1 teaspoon cornstarch
½ cup (120 ml) fermented
    rice wine (recipe follows)

1. Make a well in the center of the flour in a bowl. Stream in ½ cup (120 ml) of water, mixing with chopsticks continuously, until a loose mix starts to come together.

2. Turn the dough onto a lightly floured surface. Knead until a tacky (but not sticky) dough comes together. If the dough sticks to your hand, add more glutinous rice flour. If it's too dry, add water, 1 teaspoon at a time. It should have a texture much like Play-Doh. Knead until smooth, about 3 minutes.

3. Bring a pot of water to a boil over high. Pinch and roll 1 teaspoon of dough into a ball, then gently flatten it into a disc. Boil it until the disc rises, 3 to 5 minutes. Remove the disc with a slotted spoon and let it cool slightly. Incorporate the cooked disc into the dough, kneading until completely incorporated and smooth. This extra step will make the dough super malleable and elastic, creating a silky soft and chewy texture when cooked. Set the dough aside and cover with plastic or a damp towel. Let rest for 20 minutes.

4. On a lightly floured surface, with your hands, roll the dough into a log. Divide it into 4 equal pieces. Cover the remaining dough while working on one quarter. Roll into a log, about ½ inch (12 mm) in

diameter. Use a knife or pinch off ½-inch (12-mm) segments. Gently roll each segment between your palms into a ball. Set aside on a flour-dusted baking sheet. Repeat with the remaining dough. At this point, you can either freeze the balls for a few months or serve them immediately.

5. Bring 4 cups (960 ml) of water to a boil over high in a saucepan. Add the rice balls, stirring to prevent them from sticking together. Reduce the heat to low and simmer until the rice balls float, about 3 minutes. Add the sugar and stir to dissolve.

6. Meanwhile, beat the egg vigorously and set it aside. In another small bowl, dissolve the cornstarch in 1 teaspoon of water. Stream the slurry into the soup while stirring to thicken to your preference.

7. Reduce the heat to as low as possible. Drizzle the egg over the surface of the soup, count to five, then stir in the fermented rice wine. Adjust the sugar to taste, adding more if desired, and serve warm.

FERMENTED RICE WINE 酒酿 | jiǔ niàng | *Makes about 2 cups*

NOTE: All equipment used must be sterilized. Any hint of oil or grease will ruin the ferment.

1 ¼ cups (250 g) glutinous (sweet) rice
1 Chinese wine yeast ball, 酒曲 *jiu qu* (available at Asian markets)
¾ cup (180 ml) boiled water, cooled to warm, plus more as needed

1. Rinse the rice thoroughly, then soak in water overnight.

2. Drain the rice and spread it across a heatproof plate. Poke throughout with chopsticks to create a few holes to allow steam to reach all the rice. Place the plate in a steamer over 2 inches (5 cm) of simmering water and steam on medium-high for 20 minutes, until tender and cooked. Check periodically to make sure the water hasn't all cooked off. Set aside.

3. Meanwhile, crush the wine yeast ball with a mortar and pestle until coarse. Mix all but 1 teaspoon of the crushed yeast with ½ cup of the warm water. While the rice is still warm to the touch but not hot, pour the yeast-water mixture over it, then mix thoroughly to incorporate.

4. Pour the rice mixture into a sterilized fermenting vessel. Make a small well in the center. Sprinkle the remaining teaspoon of crushed yeast over the surface. Cover loosely with plastic wrap, then a tea towel over that, and let ferment in a warm place, between 75°F and 85°F (25°C and 30°C).

5. Check after 2 days: The rice should be soft and pulpy but still recognizable as grains of rice. The characteristic sweet, fermented aroma should be present. The well you created should have filled with liquid, and the liquid level should have now reached the level of the rice. Give it a taste—you don't want it to be too sour. It should taste sweet with a hint of wine, and the rice should be porridge-like in texture. If the rice does not yet have these characteristics, let it ferment for another day.

6. Transfer the rice wine to a vessel with a tight lid and keep in the fridge (which basically slows fermentation) for up to 3 months.

ROCK SUGAR PORK HOCK

冰糖蹄膀 | bīng táng tí bǎng | *Makes 4 servings*

Venture from the hustle and bustle of the main streets to the neighborhoods of Old Shanghai and the numerous water towns surrounding the city, and you'll find heaps of luminous, mahogany rounds of pork hock, ready for purchase. Rock Sugar Pork Hock is 农家菜 *nong jia cai*, "farmer's home-style food," and it epitomizes how rustic, simple, and full of flavor these dishes are. It's similar to the famous red braise, but with a lot more rock sugar and a few more spices. It's meant to be richer, more luscious, and "warmer." My mom said that her mother made this often in winter, and that it is a particularly suitable dish for fixing the body, especially for women. The skin and fat are rendered into a melty, tender covering that flavors the meat tucked below. All you need is a pair of chopsticks to gently pull off pieces of meat—a knife is not necessary. In fact, people will often buy whole pieces of hock from street vendors to nibble on as they continue their walk.

NOTE: If using a clay pot, remember to heat the pot up slowly to prevent any sudden temperature changes, which could crack the pot.

1 pork hock, bone in and skin on

2 scallions, cut into 2-inch (5-cm) segments

2 thin slices fresh ginger

2 tablespoons neutral cooking oil, such as canola or grapeseed oil

2 whole star anise

7 whole cloves

1 (3-inch/7.6-cm) piece cassia bark or cinnamon stick

¼ cup (60 g) rock sugar, crushed slightly with a mortar and pestle

¼ cup (60 ml) Shaoxing wine

2 tablespoons light soy sauce

3 tablespoons dark soy sauce

1. Fill a pot with 3 inches (7.5 cm) of water and bring to a boil over high. Add the pork hock and boil for 5 minutes. Remove any remaining hairs with tweezers after boiling the hock.

2. Smack the scallions and ginger with the flat side of a cleaver to loosen the fibers.

3. In a clay pot or Dutch oven, heat the oil over medium. Add the star anise, cloves, and cassia bark and fry until aromatic. Add the scallions and ginger and briefly stir-fry. Add the rock sugar and let the sugar melt. Add the wine and the light and dark soy sauces. Pour in 3 cups (720 ml) of water and bring to a boil.

4. When the liquid is boiling, gently place the pork hock in the pot. The water should just cover the pork without completely submerging it. Add more water if necessary. Return to a boil over high, then reduce the heat to low. Cover and simmer for 2 hours.

5. Use tongs to gently turn the pork hock over and simmer, partially covered, for another 1½ hours. Carefully remove the pork from the broth.

6. Increase the heat to medium-high and reduce the sauce until thick and gleaming. Return the hock to the clay pot and spoon the sauce over it. Serve hot in the clay pot or on a serving dish.

SNOW VEGETABLE AND BAMBOO SIMMERED FISH

雪菜笋丝煮鱼 | xuě cài sǔn sī zhǔ yú | *Servings will vary*

This is a stunningly aromatic dish. Its punch of flavor is threefold: snow vegetable contributes tang (the characteristic earthy tartness from its brief fermentation), which also takes away any overly "fishy" odors; the fish contributes a meaty, yet delicate, flavor, its fat rendering into a milky broth; and the fresh winter bamboo, a crisp delicacy that is available only for a short period, soaks up all of the other flavors while imparting a gorgeous fragrance to the soup. Preparing this fish starts in much the same way as Steamed Fish (page 106), with a quick marinade of wine and aromatics. My grandmother used to make this for my mom with any fish she could get her hands on—if the fish was too big, she'd just chop it into segments. The meatier the fish, the better it will be for this dish, as the flesh is more likely to stay intact through a long simmer. Yellow croaker is a classic Shanghai fish, well-known for its tender, sweet flesh, with enough body to withstand some cooking.

Add a handful of cooked noodles to create one of the most famous noodle soup dishes in Shanghai: yellow croaker noodles.

NOTE: I used yellow croaker, but you can also use sea bass. I like to prepare a whole fish, but you can also fillet the fish (use the bones to make stock), or just use precut fillets for simplicity (purchase about 1 pound/455 g).

1 (1-pound/455-g) yellow croaker or sea bass (see Note)

coarse sea salt

2 tablespoons Shaoxing wine

2 slices plus one small peeled nub fresh ginger

2 scallions, white and pale green parts only, cut into 1-inch (2.5-cm) segments

3 tablespoons neutral cooking oil, such as canola or grapeseed oil

2 cups (480 ml) just-boiled water

½ cup (150 g) snow vegetable, rinsed a few times with cold water to remove excess saltiness, wrung dry, and finely chopped

1 fresh bamboo shoot (2¾ ounces/75 g), woody parts removed, blanched, and cut into thin slivers

¼ teaspoon ground white pepper

1. Rinse the fish and pat dry thoroughly with a paper towel. Use a sharp knife to cut three or four diagonal slits in the thickest part of the fish on both sides, reaching the bone.

2. Rub a thin layer of salt all over the fish, including in the slits and inside the belly. Brush 1 tablespoon of the wine over both sides, making sure to reach inside the diagonal slits and the belly. Place 2 slices of the ginger and two-thirds of the scallions into the belly of the fish. Let sit for 20 to 30 minutes.

3. Rub the inside of a well-seasoned wok with the small peeled nub of ginger. Heat the oil over medium-high. When the oil is shimmering, gently slide in the fish. Fry undisturbed until golden brown, 3 to 4 minutes. As you fry, tilt the wok and swish the oil so that every part of the fish touches the hot oil. Wiggle the wok a little bit, and if the fish moves, it is ready to flip. If it's stuck to the wok, let it cook a bit more. Carefully flip the fish and cook the other side for another 3 to 4 minutes.

4. Add the remaining 1 tablespoon of wine and let it cook off. Gently pour the just-boiled water down the sides of the wok (not directly on the fish), then add the finely chopped snow vegetable and bamboo. Cover and cook for 10 minutes over high, until the fish is cooked through and the broth has become milky. Test this by using chopsticks to poke at one of the diagonal slits—if the flesh is opaque and easily flakes, the fish is cooked.

5. Season with salt and ground white pepper. Carefully transfer to a large serving bowl.

PORK-STUFFED FRIED DOUGH

油面筋塞肉 | yóu miàn jīn sāi ròu | *Makes 30 fried-dough meatballs*

When I told my father-in-law that I was writing a book, this was the first dish he told me to include. It's a bit hard to translate and describe, but it's essentially an oil-fried dough stuffed with meat, which is then cooked in a tasty broth. The fried dough soaks up all the broth and becomes wrinkly, like a soaked cloth.

This recipe makes about thirty meatballs, but you can stretch it further by stuffing each one with less meat than I recommend to create doughier, wrinklier meatballs—it's all up to you.

NOTE: After stuffing all the balls, you may also have filling left over. At this point, the moisture from the filling will actually have softened and broken down the fried dough interiors, so that there is more give inside, providing you more room to stuff in a bit more filling.

NOTE: Adjust the cooking time depending on how large the meatballs are and how much meat is in each one. You can always cut one open to check doneness.

FRIED-DOUGH MEATBALLS

30 oil-fried dough puffs (available at Asian markets)
1 pound (455 g) ground pork
2 tablespoons light soy sauce
2 tablespoons dark soy sauce
1 tablespoon granulated sugar
¼ teaspoon ground white pepper
2 tablespoons Shaoxing wine
1 teaspoon cornstarch
1 large egg, beaten
3 tablespoons Ginger-Scallion Water (page 257)

COOKING BROTH (for 8 meatballs)
makes 2 to 4 servings

1 tablespoon neutral cooking oil, such as canola or grapeseed oil
1 slice fresh ginger
1 scallion, cut into 1-inch (2.5-cm) segments
2 whole star anise
2 tablespoons Shaoxing wine
¼ cup (60 ml) just-boiled water
1 tablespoon light soy sauce
1 tablespoon dark soy sauce
2 teaspoons rock sugar
sesame oil

1. **MAKE THE FRIED-DOUGH MEATBALLS:** Prepare the fried dough puffs by sticking a chopstick into each puff to create a hole without going through to the other side. Use your fingers to gently break up the fibers in each puff, hollowing it out to become a sphere. Set aside.

2. In a medium bowl, combine the pork, light and dark soy sauces, sugar, white pepper, wine, cornstarch, and egg, and mix with chopsticks or a small spatula in one direction (see page 133, step 1). Add the ginger-scallion water. Use chopsticks to mix in one direction until the mixture resembles a sticky paste.

3. Stuff 1 tablespoon of the meat into each fried dough puff with a small spatula or spoon. At this point, you can freeze the meatballs for later (thaw them before using), or cook some of them in the broth.

4. **MAKE THE BROTH:** Heat the oil in a pan over medium. Fry the ginger, scallion, and star anise until fragrant.

5. Place the meatballs, opening side down, in the pan in a single layer and cook undisturbed for 30 seconds to seal the meat in. Gently add the wine and cover the pan immediately for 30 seconds. When the alcohol has evaporated, add the just-boiled water, light and dark soy sauces, and sugar.

6. Bring to a boil over high, then reduce the heat to medium-low. Braise the meatballs, partially covered, for 15 to 20 minutes. The sauce will be absorbed deliciously into the now wrinkly dough. Finish with a few drops of sesame oil.

BRAISED SHIITAKE AND TOFU

冬菇豆腐煲 | dōng gū dòu fu bāo | *Makes 4 servings*

Dried shiitakes are a staple in every Chinese household. You can buy them at any Asian grocery store, though Japanese varieties are the best. There are different "grades" of shiitake available, and 冬菇 *dong gu,* "winter mushroom," is the highest. It's what I use when shiitakes are the main ingredient, as in this dish. The intense flavor from the shiitakes and the umami of dried shrimp elevate this simple dish to another level.

NOTE: You can skip using a clay pot and use a Dutch oven or saucepan instead, but if you are using a clay pot, be sure to heat the pot slowly to prevent sudden temperature changes. Soft tofu can be harder to find, but it's the perfect texture between firm and silken tofu, with enough integrity to stay intact during cooking but soft enough to avoid becoming rubbery. If you can't find soft tofu, use silken or firm tofu.

10 high-quality dried shiitake mushrooms
1 teaspoon dried shrimp, 虾米 *xiā mǐ*
1 (1-pound/455-g) brick soft tofu (see Note)
¼ cup (60 ml) neutral cooking oil, such as canola or grapeseed oil, for frying
4 cloves garlic, smashed with the flat side of a cleaver
3 (1-inch/2.5-cm) pieces peeled fresh ginger
1 red Thai chili pepper, deseeded and roughly chopped
3 tablespoons light soy sauce
1 tablespoon Shaoxing wine
2 teaspoons granulated sugar
1 tablespoon cornstarch, if needed
kosher salt
ground white pepper
1 young garlic shoot or scallion, green parts only, chopped into ½-inch (12-mm) pieces
sesame oil

1. Boil water in a kettle. Pour it over the dried shiitake and shrimp in a heatproof bowl to cover and soak them for 1 hour, until the mushroom caps are soft. Drain, retaining the stock. If the stock contains any dirt or grit, strain through a fine-mesh sieve. Stem and halve the mushrooms. Set them and the shrimp aside.

2. Gently cut the tofu into 12 pieces by halving the block, then cutting 6 smaller rectangles from each half. Let them sit on a shallow plate for 1 hour to allow excess water to seep out. Pour off the excess water.

3. In a wok or a tall pot for deep-frying, heat ¼ cup of oil over medium-high to between 375°F and 400°F (190°C and 205°C). This temperature is essential to quickly create the brown crust that will keep the soft tofu intact. Working in batches of 3 or 4 pieces at a time, use a metal spatula to gently ease the tofu into the hot oil. When the tofu is browned on all sides and a light crust has formed, 2 to 3 minutes per side, remove with a slotted spoon to paper towels.

4. To the same pot of oil, add the garlic, ginger, and chili pepper. Stir-fry briefly, until fragrant. Add the mushrooms and shrimp and stir-fry for 1 to 2 minutes. Remove from the heat.

5. Heat a tablespoon of oil in a clay pot (see Note) over low. Add the tofu, and mushroom-shrimp mixture. Add enough stock retained from soaking the shrimp and mushrooms to cover the tofu. Add the soy sauce, wine, and sugar and stir to combine. Slowly bring to a boil over medium heat, then reduce the heat to low and simmer for 10 to 15 minutes.

6. Increase the heat to medium-high and reduce the liquid until saucy, 10 to 15 minutes. It should be thick enough to coat the back of a spoon. If still too thin, mix the cornstarch with 1 tablespoon of water and gently stir the slurry into the sauce.

7. Season with salt and white pepper. Finish with the garlic greens and a few drops of sesame oil.

THE INVIGORATING FIRST BOWL OF NOODLES

头汤面 | tóu tāng miàn

I will never forget the bowls of breakfast noodles my father would make me before tests. When I was growing up, my mom was always the one who prepared us for school, heating up our daily cup of milk and cooking breakfast. Except on test days. On those stressful pre-exam mornings, my dad let my mom sleep in and prepared a special treat for us: a piping-hot bowl of noodles.

The dish wasn't traditional—no pork lard or long-simmered high stock. It was simply a bowl of noodles swimming in steaming-hot chicken soup, flavored with soy sauce, vinegar, chili oil, garlic, scallions, and a fried egg. It was delicious. It was perfect. It filled us up and left us more awake and energized than a cup of coffee would. What I realized later, as I spent more time in China and took more of an interest in Chinese food, was that this ritual is rooted in tradition: the breakfast bowl of noodles is an institution that extends back centuries.

When I first heard breakfast noodles described as 头汤面 *tou tang mian*, "head soup noodles," I was confused. A soup for the head? Further conversations and research revealed that it refers to the first bowl of noodles of the day. The saying 面要头汤, 浴要浑汤 *mian yao tou tang, yu yao hun tang* means: "Eat noodles as early as possible, as the soup from that first batch will be the lightest in color and the taste the freshest and cleanest." Nowhere is it more important than in Suzhou, a water city crisscrossed with canals that is famous for its noodle bowls. People from all over the region travel to Suzhou to try the noodles. Their flavor embodies what Suzhou cuisine is about: food that is refined, seasonal, and seemingly simple, yet complex in flavor. Days in Suzhou start with noodles, particularly in the chillier seasons of autumn and winter. It's a time-honored ritual that I have gladly adopted.

On the surface, a bowl of Suzhou noodles is simple, especially compared with their better-known counterparts in other Asian countries, like ramen. There are several important components to Suzhou soup noodles, and the Suzhounese are notoriously picky about their noodles: the soup must be fresh, aromatic with the addition of lard; the noodles should be chewy, yet thin, cooked to exactly the right texture; and there must be toppings. I'm less picky, but when all the boxes are checked, what results is an irresistible bowl of noodles.

There are two important parts to a perfect noodle soup: the making and the serving.

In making, you need to consider:

汤 *tāng*, "stock": The soup base is a major part of the dish—usually 高汤 *gao tang*, "High Stock" (page 277), which is made by simmering chicken and pork for a long time, often with an additional hit of umami, such as dried scallops. An authentic Suzhou stock is clear, not too greasy, and without impurities. It's fragrant, fresh, and moderately salty. Some families keep the recipe for their stock a carefully guarded secret, because without a good base there cannot be a superb bowl of noodles.

汁 *zhī*, "juice": Additional flavoring comes from the "juice," which is really the braising liquid released when meats are cooked. Classic examples are the juice from Mom's Shanghai Red-Braised Pork Belly (page 93) and braised fish. The juice is a concentrated collection of rendered fat and stock from the meat. The Suzhounese are very particular about this. One time, Alex's uncle took us to a noodle shop and opted for dry sauced noodles instead of soup. However, he really wanted a thick slice of pork belly as a topping. The 阿姨 *ayi*, "matron," of the shop tersely told him no, this is a topping that is specifically for soup noodles, not for dry sauced noodles.

油 *yóu*, "lard": The finishing touch. Lard is a tiny dollop of magic that increases the fragrance of any stock. However, lard's contribution isn't just fragrance: it will melt and disperse, floating on the surface of the stock and keeping the warmth in. When the noodles are added, they pass through that layer of melted lard, which coats the strands.

面 *miàn*, "noodles": Noodles must be cooked in clear water. When serving, ensure that only noodles are transferred over, without excess cooking water that will dilute the soup. You can do this by holding the noodles with a long pair of cooking chopsticks and gently shaking them to release excess liquid, then gently sliding them off the chopsticks into the bowl, so that not only do the noodles retain their lovely round shape but also no soup splashes out.

青 *qīng*, "greens": There will always be some form of greens in the soup, for color, flavor, and fragrance. In the winter and early spring, young garlic leaves are the aromatic of choice, and when they're not available, scallions are abundant. I try to add both if I can—the more the better.

浇头 *jiāo tóu*, "toppings": What the bowl of noodles is called, as well as the price, is dictated by the toppings, a luxurious menu of pork, offal, mushrooms, bamboo, greens, and more. Classics include 焖肉 *men rou*, "pork belly"; 炒肉 *chao rou*, "fried meat"; 卤鸭 *lu ya*, "soy duck"; 香菇 *xiang gu*, "shiitake mushrooms"; and 清炒虾仁 *qing chao xia ren*, "fried shrimp." Anything that can contribute both protein and juice is a fair contender. See Sauced Noodles (page 204) for additional topping ideas.

For serving, the 碗烫 *wan tang*, "bowl," needs to be hot, otherwise it will bring down the temperature of the whole dish. And old noodles sitting in hot soup will soak up too much water and cook further, becoming soggy and unappetizing. Therefore, noodles should be freshly cooked and added just before serving, so that the temperature and texture are perfect.

There used to be giant noodle halls in Shanghai, and they were busiest in the morning as their main business was breakfast noodles. They were lively, informal establishments, crowded with workers who shuffled in before the start of their day. People arrived hungry and bleary-eyed and left satiated and energized. These days, giant noodle halls have been replaced by smaller, family-run shops, but the concept and intentions are the same. It's not a giant leap to incorporate these intentions into your own home, as my dad did with his loving gesture of sending us off to take our exams invigorated and clear-minded.

I will always associate noodle soup with love and well-wishes from my parents, with good luck and precious memories. With utter certainty, I know that I will make pre-test noodles for my future children.

SUZHOU PORK BELLY NOODLE SOUP

苏式焖肉面 | *sū shì mèn ròu miàn* | *Makes 1¾ pounds of pork belly*

Alex's 外公 *wai gong*, "maternal grandfather," in Suzhou is a known fatty meat lover. This is one of his favorite dishes—melt-in-your-mouth pork belly that is lightly complemented with aromatics, so that the natural taste of the pork is undisguised. It is the most tender pork belly I've ever had—it practically falls apart when you take a bite, and it is simply fabulous when paired with soup noodles or rice. People in Suzhou will wake up early and line up for this meat, sometimes for hours. Due to hip and back pain, *wai gong* cannot easily line up, so Alex's 外婆 *wai po*, "maternal grandmother," will line up for him, because he loves this dish that much. The meat sits in a fragrant broth and can be cut up into chunks or sliced thinly. Much of the grease from the fat and skin will render out from this cooking process, leaving clean, flavorful, tender, but not too greasy, pork belly.

NOTE: The amount of water will depend on the size of your pot. Make sure the water just covers the pork belly. Too little water will yield a dry pork belly. Too much will become a soup.

1¾ pounds (800 g) skin-on pork belly
4 tablespoons kosher salt, plus more as needed
1 bunch scallions
4 slices fresh ginger
3 whole star anise
4 dried bay leaves
2 tablespoons Shaoxing wine
1 tablespoon soy sauce
1 tablespoon rock sugar
1 teaspoon salt

NOODLE SOUP
makes 2 servings
chicken stock or High Stock (page 277), as needed
½ cup (120 ml) reserved broth from cooking the pork belly
10½ ounces (300 g) fresh Shanghai thin noodles, cooked to al dente (or similar amount in dried noodles)
2 or 3 slices cooked pork belly
scallion or young garlic greens, finely chopped
kosher salt
ground white pepper

1. **PREPARE THE PORK BELLY:** Place the pork belly in a shallow bowl and massage salt onto every surface. Lay a piece of parchment paper over the pork belly and place a heavy object on top to press it down. Refrigerate for 6 hours or overnight.

2. Rinse the pork belly with water and pat dry with a paper towel. Slice into three pieces.

3. Bring a pot of water to a boil over high. Boil the pork belly for 5 minutes. Drain and discard the water.

4. Rinse the pot and fill with enough water to cover the meat. Add the scallions, ginger, star anise, and bay leaves. Bring to a boil, then add the wine. Add the pork belly and make sure the water level just covers it (see Note). Add the soy sauce, sugar, and salt.

5. Return to a boil over high, then reduce the heat to medium-low and keep the water at the gentlest boil for 30 minutes. Then reduce the heat to as low as possible, so that the liquid barely bubbles. Cover and simmer for 5 hours.

6. Remove from the heat. Let the pork belly cool completely in the broth, about 1 hour. Using a sharp knife, cut the pork into chunks or lengthwise into ½-inch (12-mm) slices. If you try to cut the pork before it's completely cool, it can fall apart (that's how tender it is!). To store, place the pork in a container with some of the remaining broth and refrigerate for up to 4 days; discard any remaining broth. You can also freeze for up to 3 months.

7. **MAKE THE NOODLE SOUP:** Bring the stock and reserved broth from cooking the pork belly to a boil. Add the cooked, drained noodles. Top with the pork belly and scallion and season with salt and white pepper. Pork belly from the fridge or freezer will heat through upon contact with the hot soup.

LION'S HEAD MEATBALLS

狮子头 | shī zi tóu | *Makes 8 medium or 4 large meatballs*

As a child, I always revered this dish. A refined dish that is reserved for special occasions, in part because of its regal name, it is truly special. During the Cultural Revolution, when my mom grew up, meat was rationed, often reserved for the working men in the family. A treat like this was something to be treasured and eaten on special occasions, such as the New Year.

This meatball resembles a stone statue of a lion, hence the name. The characteristically giant, lumpy meatball is often served one at a time, nestled in a clear, enchantingly aromatic broth. Traditionally, pork belly or shoulder is minced by hand for this dish, and I recommend doing so because it gives you full control over the size of the mince. Unlike when stuffed in buns, the meat should be minced coarsely, a little bit smaller than kernels of corn. The larger pieces allow for gaps within the meatball that retain both the fat rendered from the meat and the broth it's simmered in to make an astonishingly tender meatball. There are many variations of this dish. I particularly love the Suzhou version, where the sweet flesh of hairy crab is added. Winter bamboo or water chestnuts can also be incorporated for some extra crunch.

There are two main ways to cook this: 清炖狮子头 *qing dun shi zi tou,* "clear broth–simmered lion's head meatball," is my favorite, as the flavor of the giant meatball is given the chance to truly shine in a light wine broth. 红烧狮子头 *hong shao shi zi tou,* "red-braised lion's head meatballs," is a Shanghai classic, where smaller meatballs are simmered in the beloved red braise.

1 pound (455 g) pork belly, minced by hand (page 270) into corn-sized chunks

1 tablespoon kosher salt

3 teaspoons granulated sugar

3 tablespoons Shaoxing wine

1 teaspoon ground white pepper

1 large egg, beaten

2 tablespoons cornstarch

⅓ cup (45 g) winter bamboo or water chestnuts, finely diced (optional; fresh, frozen, or canned all work)

¼ cup (60 ml) Ginger-Scallion Water (page 257)

CLEAR BROTH METHOD

napa cabbage leaves, for lining the pot

2 cups (480 ml) High Stock (page 277) or chicken stock

3 slices fresh ginger

1 scallion

(continued)

MAKE THE MEATBALLS USING THE CLEAR BROTH METHOD:

1. In a large bowl, combine the minced pork belly with the salt, sugar, wine, white pepper, egg, and cornstarch. Mix in the winter bamboo, if using. Add the ginger-scallion water and mix to combine. Traditionally, these meatballs are made by stirring the mixture with chopsticks in one direction. Supposedly, the fibers of the pork will line up when you persist in just one direction, creating a meltingly tender meat. (Alternatively, use your hands to mix gently and thoroughly, which is my preferred method.) The mixture should be soft but not wet.

2. Pour some hot water in a clay pot, Dutch oven, or other heavy-bottomed pot to warm it. Discard the water. Gently line the bottom of the pot with napa cabbage leaves.

3. Shape the meatballs with your hands: Take a quarter of the mixture (or one-eighth for smaller meatballs) in one palm and slap the meat from one hand to the other. This slapping motion will remove any excess air, letting the meatball come together into a ball without losing its texture. Repeat with the remaining mixture. Gently place the meatballs on top of the cabbage leaves and cover them with additional cabbage leaves so there is a final layer of cabbage leaves on top.

4. In a separate pot, heat the stock and slowly pour it into the clay pot beside the meatballs, making sure not to pour it directly *(continued)*

1 tablespoon Shaoxing wine

1 teaspoon kosher salt, plus more
as needed

2 dried bay leaves

ground white pepper

4 stalks Chinese spinach, 油菜
you cai (yu choy), trimmed

RED-BRAISED METHOD

2 tablespoons neutral cooking oil,
such as canola or grapeseed oil

2 tablespoons light soy sauce

1 tablespoon dark soy sauce

¼ cup (60 ml) Shaoxing wine

1 cup (240 ml) just-boiled water

3 whole star anise

2 whole cloves

2 tablespoons rock sugar

onto the balls. The stock should come three-quarters of the way up the meatballs. Add the ginger, scallion, wine, 1 teaspoon of salt, and bay leaves.

5. Bring to a boil over high, then reduce the heat to low, cover, and simmer gently for 2 to 2½ hours.

6. Remove the top layer of napa cabbage leaves. Adjust the seasoning with salt and ground white pepper. Add the *yu choy,* cover, and simmer until tender, about 10 minutes. The soup is ready to serve.

MAKE THE MEATBALLS USING THE RED-BRAISED METHOD:

1. Shape 8 meatballs as described in step 1 and step 3, without layering the meatballs on napa cabbage in the clay pot. Warm a clay pot, Dutch oven, or other heavy-bottomed pot as in step 2.

2. Heat the oil in a pan. Gently add the meatballs in a single layer and pan-fry until all surfaces are golden yellow. Place the browned meatballs in the warmed clay pot or other braising pot. Add all the remaining red-braised method ingredients to the pot—the stock should come three-quarters of the way up the meatballs. Bring to a boil over high, then reduce the heat to low and simmer for 40 minutes. Increase the heat to high and reduce the broth until a glistening, dark sauce develops, about 10 minutes. Serve.

TATSOI WITH WINTER BAMBOO

塌棵菜炒冬笋 | tā kē cài chǎo dōng sǔn | *Makes 2 servings*

One winter, my husband and I were wandering down a street in Old Shanghai that was lined with bags full of greens, bamboo, and fermented goods. I was immediately drawn to the tatsoi, its gleaming rosettes of dark green leaves like a luscious bouquet. The kind *ayi* selling them informed me that they had been freshly plucked from the snow in the mountains outside of Shanghai, and thus would be as fresh and rich in flavor as I could find. Tatsoi, also known as tat soy, spoon mustard, or rosette bok choy, is a low-growing cabbage in the Brassica family with a rich, intense flavor, available only for a short season in the winter months. Tatsoi pairs well with winter bamboo shoots or pork. Baby tatsoi leaves are often included in ready-to-go salad mixes, but finding whole rounds can be difficult. I've found them in the United States at farmers' markets in early winter, but if you can't find tatsoi, bok choy makes a good substitution.

NOTE: To break the tatsoi apart, cut off the base to free up the individual leaves. Rinse and drain. Cut the stems to make approximately 2-inch (5-cm) pieces. To process winter bamboo, use a cleaver to make a cut lengthwise along the bamboo shoot, cutting it down to approximately half the thickness. Then use your hands along each side of the cut to peel off the woody layers, revealing a pale yellow, tender shoot. If you are using frozen bamboo, blanch 1 to 2 shoots in boiling water for 1 minute, then drain and rinse with cold water.

½ pound (225 g) fresh winter bamboo shoots (1 to 2 shoots)

kosher salt

2 tablespoons neutral cooking oil, such as canola or grapeseed oil

1 tablespoon pork lard (optional; store-bought or homemade, page 271)

2 slices fresh ginger, smacked with back of a cleaver to loosen its fibers

10½ ounces (300 g) tatsoi, 塌棵菜 *ta ke cai* (see Note)

5 tablespoons (75 ml) chicken stock or High Stock (page 277)

½ teaspoon granulated sugar

cooked white rice, for serving

1. Slice the bamboo into very thin slices (about 1/16 inch/2 mm).

2. Bring a pot of water with a pinch of salt to a boil over high, add the bamboo, and cook for 2 minutes. Drain and rinse with cold water.

3. Heat a well-seasoned wok over high. Add the oil and lard, if using, and swirl to coat. Add the ginger and stir-fry until fragrant. Add the bamboo shoots and stir-fry for another 1 to 2 minutes. Add the tatsoi and stir-fry until the greens just begin to wilt.

4. Stir in the stock and sugar. Bring to a boil over high, then cover, reduce the heat to low, and simmer for 2 to 3 minutes. The tatsoi stems should retain some crispness. Serve with freshly steamed white rice.

chūn

SPRING

Spring is an enchanting season of growth, birth, and new things. During this time, the heavier, warming dishes of winter are replaced with more delicate dishes that showcase natural flavors and fresh ingredients. Spring ingredients are given a warming treatment, such as with Oil-Braised Spring Bamboo (page 144), to ease the transition into the new season.

Traditionally, winter is a more stationary season, but spring is full of energy. We stretch our arms and begin to move. We're motivated again. It's time to reestablish balance. In Shanghai, the transition is subtle, but palpable. It's like the whole city comes alive, shaking off the frost.

In the spring, tender, leafy greens and young shoots are abundant. River shrimp—succulent, with thin, delicate shells—are the delicacy of choice. Freshwater shrimp are at their most plentiful in this season, and the Shanghainese never fail to take advantage of in-season seafood.

FORAGING SPRING BAMBOO

As we drove up a mountain to a bamboo forest somewhere outside of Hangzhou, we saw a tiny woman with beautiful long braids framing her face walking down. Her face was ruddy and lined, almost as if in a perpetual smile. She was dressed head to toe in blue, the pouch of her apron-like garment spilling over with thin bamboo shoots. When we said hello, she assured us there was still plenty of bamboo left to forage. There had just been a thunderstorm, after all.

We proceeded on foot and entered the bamboo forest. These bamboo were delicate and slim, mellow green in color, and swaying with the wind. On the ground, we saw that the *ayi* was right—it was studded with sharp ends pointing up to the sky, from just a peek to a foot in height. We carefully navigated our way around the shoots. Picking them is simple: just grab the base and break it off. Soon we, too, had armfuls of young bamboo shoots.

There are hundreds of varieties of bamboo in China, varying with the temperature and climate in different regions. In the wet markets, bamboo shoots are always labeled with where they're from: Hangzhou, Anji, Lin'an, usually from the mountainous Zhejiang province. Bamboo is a type of grass and incredibly functional, used as a building material and to make furniture, tools, musical instruments, clothing, paper, and more. It's also a staple ingredient in Chinese cooking, and one I love to introduce to friends who aren't familiar with Chinese cuisine.

There are two broad categories of bamboo shoots: 冬笋 *dong sun*, "winter bamboo shoots," and 春笋 *chun sun*, "spring bamboo shoots." Their names refer to the season in which they are foraged. In winter, the shoots are larger and often called 毛笋 *mao sun*, "hairy bamboo," because of the fibers coating the shoots. They're almost three inches in diameter and more stout, ending in a slightly curved point. Winter bamboo shoots are buried and dug up from the earth, usually in late winter and early spring. Always choose shoots that are solidly golden, which indicates they were snugly protected by the earth until being dug up.

Spring bamboo, on the other hand, is longer, slimmer, straighter, and more delicate, with a short season of availability, usually from the beginning of March to the end of April. There are many varieties. The ones we foraged were wild mountain bamboo—green, slim, and delightfully tender. I haven't been able to find them in North America. The bamboo shoots that are available frozen in the United States are slightly thicker, about 1 1/2 inches in diameter, and have a brown exterior. I love using these in stir-fries or braises. They're more tender and fragrant in flavor than their winter counterparts. There's a saying, 雨后春笋 *yu hou chun sun*, "after rain comes spring bamboo." Bamboo's growth accelerates after rain, exposing green shoots that were previously buried underground.

After we finished foraging, our host showed us how to peel off the woody layer to reveal the pale green and white shoots. She did it with a flourish, nicking the shoot with her bamboo knife and then whirling the shoot with her other hand, as she peeled the woody layer off. As I slowly unpeeled one, she prepped five more shoots. At home, I still prep bamboo shoots the "slow" way, using a knife to make a cut lengthwise and then peeling the layers off.

My parents planted a variety of slim bamboo in their yard in California. With a big grin on his face, my dad told me that they forage young shoots in their little bamboo patch, catching them before they shoot up toward the sky, and make Oil-Braised Spring Bamboo (page 144). For now, I'm left with scouring Chinese markets for fresh bamboo and often have to make do with frozen.

OIL-BRAISED SPRING BAMBOO

油焖笋 | *yóu mèn sǔn* | *Makes 4 servings*

Chinese people look forward to spring bamboo every year because its season is ephemeral. Spring bamboo is more delicate, sweet, and tender than winter bamboo. I love using it in soups, but my absolute favorite way to make spring bamboo is in this dish. It's called "oil-braised," but it's not greasy. It's a simple, flavor-packed dish and goes fabulously with white rice. If I have any leftovers, I chop it up and use it as a topping for noodles.

The way to cut bamboo, or any cylindrical food, is using the 滚刀 *gun dao*, "rolling knife," method (see page 20).

NOTE: If you find fresh wild rice stem *(jiao bai)*, do not hesitate to pick up a few stems and use them instead of spring bamboo shoots. They're hard to find in the United States, but they're one of my favorite water vegetables, just as fragrant and even more tender than bamboo shoots. Their preparation is similar to that of bamboo shoots; you peel and blanch them before using.

17½ ounces (500 g) fresh or frozen spring bamboo shoots (see Note)

3 tablespoons neutral cooking oil, such as canola or grapeseed oil

2 thin slices fresh ginger, crushed lightly with the side of a cleaver to loosen the fibers

2 whole star anise

2 tablespoons rock sugar, crushed coarsely with a mortar and pestle

2 tablespoons Shaoxing wine

2 tablespoons light soy sauce

1 tablespoon dark soy sauce

sesame oil

1 scallion, chopped

1. Bring a pot of water to a boil over high. Slide in the bamboo shoots and boil for 1 minute. Remove with a slotted spoon and set aside. When cool enough to handle, cut the bamboo into wedges and set aside.

2. Heat the oil in a well-seasoned wok over medium. Add the ginger and star anise and fry until fragrant. Reduce the heat to low, then dissolve 1 tablespoon of the sugar in the hot oil. Add the reserved bamboo, increase the heat to medium-high, and stir-fry until slightly browned, about 3 minutes.

3. Add the remaining 1 tablespoon of sugar, the wine, the light and dark soy sauces, and 1 cup (240 ml) of water. Cover and boil over high for 2 minutes. Reduce the heat to medium-low and simmer for 10 to 15 minutes.

4. Remove the lid, increase the heat to high, and reduce the sauce until thick. Right before serving, add a few drops of sesame oil for extra fragrance. Top with the scallion.

WUXI SPARERIBS

无锡小排 | wú xī xiǎo pái | *Makes 4 servings*

Wuxi, a city adjacent to Suzhou, is the sweetest city in Jiangsu. Jiangsu cuisine often gets described as "sweet," but, as I mentioned earlier, that description oversimplifies the cuisine. Yes, locals love sweet dishes, and these ribs may be on the sweeter side, but with that sweetness is a whole symphony of flavors working together to make a complexly spiced sweet-and-savory dish. It is seductive, with chunky pieces of rib braised until they're so tender the meat literally slides off the bones. You will be licking the braising juice off your fingers and spooning the sauce over rice.

Traditionally, red yeast rice is used in the braise to give it that glowing red color, but I find it doesn't contribute much to the taste, so I omit it. If you want to use it, simply steep it in hot water and use that liquid for the braise.

NOTE: You can ask your butcher to cut the ribs in half lengthwise, leaving you with long strips of spareribs, about 2 inches (5 cm) wide.

2 pounds (910 g) pork spareribs (about 1 side of ribs), cut in half lengthwise

1 tablespoon kosher salt

4 tablespoons (60 ml) light soy sauce

5 tablespoons (75 ml) Shaoxing wine

neutral cooking oil, such as canola or grapeseed oil

6 scallions, roughly cut into 2-inch (5-cm) segments

4 slices fresh ginger

2 tablespoons dark soy sauce, plus more as needed

1 tablespoon black vinegar

2 pieces star anise

1/3 teaspoon fennel seeds

1/2 teaspoon whole cloves

1 (3-inch/7.5-cm) piece cassia bark or cinnamon stick

3 tablespoons rock sugar, plus more as needed

about 3 cups (720 ml) chicken, pork, or vegetable stock, or High Stock (page 277), or water

1 teaspoon cornstarch (optional)

1. Carefully cut the spareribs between every other bone, so you end up with square two-bone pieces. Rub the salt over the ribs and refrigerate overnight or for up to 12 hours. This tenderizes the meat and helps it keep its flavor during a long braise.

2. Rinse and pat the ribs dry.

3. In a large bowl, mix together 2 tablespoons of the light soy sauce and 1 tablespoon of the wine. Add the ribs, toss to coat, and let marinate for 15 minutes—reserve this marinade when you fry the ribs.

4. Heat a wok with enough oil to deep-fry, 2 to 3 inches (5 to 7.5 cm), being sure to use a splatter shield to protect yourself from burns. Working in batches as necessary, slide the ribs into the hot oil and fry until golden brown, about 3 minutes. Remove the ribs with a slotted spoon. (If you don't wish to deep-fry, just sauté the ribs in a large skillet in 3 tablespoons of oil until brown.)

5. With the flat side of a cleaver, smash the scallions and ginger. Heat 2 tablespoons of oil in a heavy-bottomed pot over high heat. Add the ginger and scallions and stir-fry briefly until fragrant. Pour in the reserved marinade from step 3. Add the remaining 4 tablespoons (60 ml) of wine, the remaining 2 tablespoons of the light soy sauce and the dark soy sauce, vinegar, star anise, fennel seeds, cloves, cassia bark, sugar, and stock. The stock will barely cover the ribs; they do not need to be completely submerged.

6. Bring to a boil over high, then reduce the heat to low and simmer, covered, for 1 1/2 hours, until the meat is easily pierced with a chopstick. Check occasionally to see if you need to add more stock or water so the bottom of the pot isn't dry.

7. Remove the lid. Taste and add more sugar and dark soy sauce to your preference. Increase the heat to high and reduce the liquid until thick and glistening, coating the ribs in a glossy sauce, 10 to 15 minutes. If you want an even thicker sauce, combine the cornstarch with 1 teaspoon of water, and gently stream the slurry in. Remove the ribs to a plate and strain the sauce, then return the ribs to the pot, toss to coat with the sauce, and serve hot.

CHIVE BOXES

韭菜盒子 | *jiŭ cài hé zi* | *Makes 12 dumplings*

You'll often find these freshly cooked on the streets, encased in a thin skin folded much like an envelope. To me, this was *the* after-school treat. My mom makes a home-style variation that I associate with the short break between arriving home from school and beginning after-school activities or homework. Instead of the street-style thin, crispy version, my mom uses slightly leavened dough, and the resulting skin is a fluffy, pillow-like *mantou*. It's not too puffed and not too thin. My mom also pleats the dough, rather than wrapping it like an envelope, to create something akin to a giant palm-sized dumpling. She then pan-fries it to get a crunchy finish that's stuffed with a piping-hot, fragrant filling.

NOTE: Wrapping these may be harder than wrapping the other dumplings, because the filling is loose and more difficult to compress. To make it easier, I don't close them by pleating; instead I fold over and seal the wrappers, then pleat them along the sealed edge.

DUMPLING WRAPPERS

2 cups plus 2 tablespoons (300 g) all-purpose flour, plus more for dusting

3 teaspoons baking powder

¾ cup (180 ml) lukewarm water, plus more if needed

½ teaspoon pork lard (store-bought or homemade, page 271), or vegetable oil

FILLING

3 tablespoons neutral cooking oil, such as canola or grapeseed oil

3 large eggs, beaten

¼ cup tiny dried shrimp, 虾皮 *xia pi* (see page 30)

1⅓ cups (150 g) finely chopped chives

1¾ ounces (50 g) vermicelli, cooked, cooled, and cut into ½-inch (12-mm) pieces

¼ teaspoon ground white pepper

1 teaspoon sesame oil

1½ teaspoons kosher salt

neutral cooking oil, such as canola or grapeseed oil, for frying

1. **MAKE THE WRAPPERS:** Mix the flour and baking powder together in a bowl and make a well in the center. Use one hand to stream in the lukewarm water while using the other hand to mix with chopsticks until a workable dough is formed. Once the dough is a loose mix, add in the lard or oil and knead to combine. The dough will be on the dry side, but if it is too dry to come together, add more water, 1 tablespoon at a time.

2. Knead the dough on a lightly floured surface until soft and elastic, 7 to 10 minutes. At this point, the dough should not stick to your hands or your kneading surface—it should bounce back at the press of a fingertip. Cover with plastic wrap and let rest at room temperature for 30 minutes.

3. **MEANWHILE, PREPARE THE FILLING:** Heat 2 tablespoons of oil in a nonstick pan. Swirl one-half of the beaten eggs across the pan so that a thin layer cooks. Gently remove and set aside. Repeat with the remaining beaten eggs. When the cooked eggs are cool enough to handle, cut into thin strips.

4. Heat another tablespoon of oil in your pan and add the dried shrimp. Cook until the shrimp turn golden brown and aromatic. Let cool.

5. Mix the egg and shrimp with the remaining filling ingredients in a medium bowl, adding the salt just before forming the dumplings.

6. **SHAPE THE DUMPLINGS:** Divide the dough in half. Work with one half while keeping the other half covered with plastic wrap.

7. Divide the dough into 6 equal pieces. Dust the work surface lightly with flour. Use your palm to press down the cut side of each piece to form a flat disc. Use a rolling pin to flatten the disc further. Use one hand to hold the edge of the circle so that it is half lifted off the surface. Use your other hand with the rolling pin to flatten the portion on the surface. Rotate the dough as you go so that you flatten the entire circumference. This creates a wrapper that is thinner on the edges and thicker in the center. The wrapper should be 4 to 5 inches (10 to 12 cm) in diameter. Repeat with the remaining discs. *(continued)*

STIR-FRIED PEA SHOOTS

清炒豆苗 | qīng chǎo dòu miáo | *Makes 4 servings*

If you've never had 豆苗 *dou miao,* "pea shoots," then you should immediately head to your local Asian supermarket and pick up a bag of these bright green vegetables.

Preparing pea shoots is simple: The bottoms of the stems can be tough, so I rip them off at the base of the first leaves and discard the tough ends, and then tear the leaves in half if they're still too long. I then rinse them in cold water and drain them. The key to this dish is high heat, a quick stir-fry, and exploding garlic for seasoning. This is a very quick preparation: it won't take long for the pea shoots to begin to wilt and turn bright green, so that they are juicy and tender but still crunchy. If you can hold a conversation with someone while making this dish, your wok isn't hot enough.

NOTE: If the pea shoots are silty, rinse thoroughly and soak in cold water for 1 hour to remove any additional sediment. Be sure to lift the pea shoots out of the water (rather than pouring the silty water back over the clean shoots!).

3 tablespoons vegetable oil
5 cloves garlic, sliced finely
1 pound (455 g) fresh pea shoots, cleaned and dried
kosher salt

1. Heat a well-seasoned wok over high. Add the oil and swirl to coat. Immediately add the garlic, stir-frying until it explodes into fragrance, 爆香 *bao xiang.*

2. When the garlic is golden—be careful, as this goes quickly—add the pea shoots in one batch. Stir-fry for a few seconds until coated with oil and slightly wilted.

3. Add a big pinch of salt while stirring and tossing the vegetables to evenly distribute the salt.

4. Keeping the heat on high, cover the wok for 30 seconds to 1 minute, until the shoots are bright green and shiny. Uncover and serve immediately.

SHEPHERD'S PURSE AND TOFU SOUP

荠菜豆腐羹 | jì cài dòu fu gēng | *Makes 4 servings*

My parents emigrated from China to Oregon for graduate school. There, with their more experienced foraging friends, they'd often go for hikes and forage shepherd's purse, a distinctively fragrant, grassy weed, for a taste of home. It pairs well with pork (a classic Shanghai wonton mix is shepherd's purse with pork, see Shanghai Big Wontons, page 89). Slivers of pork add depth and flavor to this soup, but it could easily be made vegetarian by omitting the pork—shepherd's purse is the true star. To elevate the presentation, chefs with excellent knife skills slice tender tofu into impossibly thin slivers, which then float on the surface of the soup, a beautiful mosaic of green and white. My rudimentary knife skills limit me to cubes of tofu, but I love the texture of tofu in this soup regardless of presentation. Shepherd's purse is hard to find fresh (unless you're an expert and knowledgeable forager), but it's easily found frozen in Chinese supermarkets.

¼ cup plus 1 teaspoon (40 g) cornstarch

1 teaspoon Shaoxing wine

1 teaspoon light soy sauce

pinch of granulated sugar

3½ ounces (100 g) pork loin or shoulder

½ pound (225 g) fresh or frozen shepherd's purse (about half a frozen package)

½ pound (225 g) silken tofu, drained of excess water

2 tablespoons neutral cooking oil, such as canola or grapeseed oil

4 cups (960 ml) stock or water, plus more as needed

2 teaspoons kosher salt

1 teaspoon ground white pepper

1 teaspoon sesame oil

1. Mix 1 teaspoon of the cornstarch with the wine, soy sauce, and sugar in a medium bowl. Trim any excess fat or skin from the pork and slice the meat against the grain into short, thin pieces, about 1 x ¼ inch (2.5 cm x 6 mm). Toss the pork with the marinade and let sit for at least 10 minutes but no more than 1 hour.

2. Meanwhile, wash the shepherd's purse thoroughly. If you're using frozen shepherd's purse, defrost completely and rinse thoroughly.

3. Bring a pot of water to a boil over high. Blanch the shepherd's purse for 15 seconds, until wilted. Transfer immediately to an ice-water bath. Rinse and wring out the excess water. Remove the tough stem at the end of each bunch, then finely chop the shepherd's purse.

4. Slice the tofu into ½-inch (12-mm) cubes.

5. Heat the oil in a well-seasoned wok or heavy-bottomed pot over high. Add the pork and quickly stir-fry until the meat turns white. Remove the pork to a plate.

6. Add the stock, cover, and bring to a boil, then reduce the heat to medium and keep at a simmer. Gently add the shepherd's purse, and add back the pork, stirring to disperse. Gently slide in the tofu cubes. To mix without disintegrating the tofu, place the back of your ladle on the surface of the soup and make gentle circular motions. Season with the salt and white pepper.

7. In a small bowl, combine the remaining ¼ cup of cornstarch with ¼ cup (60 ml) of water and mix until no lumps remain. Turn the heat to low. With one hand gently stirring the soup, slowly drizzle in half of the slurry. The soup should thicken nicely. Add more of the slurry if you want the soup to be thicker. Slowly turn the heat back up to get a gentle simmer. Taste and adjust the seasoning. Drizzle in the sesame oil.

8. Ladle the soup into individual bowls, and serve.

FLOWERING CHIVES AND PORK SLIVERS

韭菜花炒肉丝 | *jiǔ cài huā chǎo ròu sī* | *Makes 2 to 4 servings*

This dish is in regular rotation in my kitchen in spring. When chive flowers are at their finest, I make this at least twice a week. The crunchiness and juiciness of the flowering chives combined with tender, lightly seasoned pork are irresistible—and the dish is quick to make. You'll be able to find flowering chives at most Asian grocery stores.

1 teaspoon cornstarch

3 teaspoons Shaoxing wine

1 teaspoon light soy sauce

1½ teaspoons plus 1 pinch of granulated sugar

¼ pound (115 g) pork loin, belly, or shoulder

7 ounces (200 g) flowering garlic chives (about 1 large bunch)

2 tablespoons neutral cooking oil, such as canola or grapeseed oil

1-inch (2.5-cm) piece fresh ginger, julienned

3 cloves garlic, sliced

1 teaspoon kosher salt

1. Mix together the cornstarch, 1 teaspoon of the wine, soy sauce, and pinch of sugar in a medium bowl. Trim any excess fat or skin from the pork and slice it against the grain into short, thin pieces, 1 to 2 inches (2.5 to 5 cm) by ¼ inch (6 mm). Toss the pork with the marinade and let sit for at least 10 minutes but no more than 1 hour.

2. Cut the chives into 1- to 2-inch (2.5- to 5-cm) segments. You should have about 4 cups. Set aside.

3. Heat a well-seasoned wok over high until smoking. Reduce the heat to medium-high, then add the oil. Once the oil is shimmering, add the ginger and garlic and stir-fry until fragrant. Add the pork and stir-fry until just cooked, 2 to 3 minutes.

4. Add the flowering chives, the remaining 2 teaspoons of wine, the remaining 1½ teaspoons of sugar, and the salt and fry until aromatic, 1 to 2 minutes. Don't cook the chives for too long, or they lose their crispness!

QING TUAN

青团 | qīng tuán | *Makes 12*

If there were any dish to truly mark and celebrate spring, it would be this emerald treat served during 清明节 Qing Ming Jie. This festival, also known as the Tomb Sweeping Festival, usually occurs in early April and is a time when families gather together and travel to their loved ones' final resting places to sweep their graves, light joss sticks (incense), burn paper money and clothes, and offer fruits and flowers, with the goal of communicating with their ancestors. It's a poignant day of sentiment, emotion, and conversation.

The jewel green color comes from 艾草 *ai cao*, "mugwort." Mugwort is grown outside of China, too, and I'm lucky enough to know some folks in New England who have mugwort growing wild in their yards. It's delightfully fragrant and earthy, and it's popularly used to brew in teas. My mom often remarks that the *qing tuan* of her childhood was far superior to what's available now. True *qing tuan* needs that earthy, grassy mugwort fragrance.

There are many different filling options, including 马兰头 *ma lan tou*, "Indian aster," tofu mix (similar to Indian Aster with Tofu, page 181), and younger generations enjoy the more recently popular filling made from salted duck yolk and pork floss. However, my favorite filling will always be sweet red bean paste.

NOTE: You can make the red bean paste ahead of time and store it in the fridge for up to 1 week.

RED BEAN PASTE

7 ounces (200 g) dried adzuki beans, soaked in cold water overnight

2 tablespoons vegetable oil or pork lard (store-bought or homemade, page 271)

½ cup (100 g) granulated sugar

¼ cup (60 ml) hot water

STICKY RICE DOUGH

⅓ cup plus 1 tablespoon (50 g) water-based white rice flour

1¾ cups (200 g) water-based glutinous rice flour

2 tablespoons granulated sugar

1½ teaspoons vegetable oil or pork lard (store-bought or homemade, page 271), plus more for brushing

3 tablespoons (40 ml) boiling water

(continued)

1. **MAKE THE RED BEAN PASTE:** Drain the adzuki beans and place them in a medium saucepan with enough water to submerge the beans by ½ inch (12 mm). Bring the water to a boil, uncovered, then simmer on low for 30 to 45 minutes, until the beans are tender and easily crushable. Be careful: as the water cooks off it will be easy to burn the beans—but don't add too much water either. If the water looks like it is going below the level of the beans, add ½ cup more at a time.

2. Remove the beans with a slotted spoon and press them through a fine-mesh sieve. This step will both mash the beans and remove the skins, creating a super-smooth paste (alternatively, puree the beans in a food processor).

3. In a separate sauce pan, combine the mashed beans with the vegetable oil and half of the sugar. Add the hot water. Bring the bean mixture to a boil over medium, then reduce the heat to low.

4. Simmer the bean puree, cooking off the liquid. The red bean puree should simmer with a few bubbles. Stir in the remaining sugar. Be patient and stir frequently with a wooden spoon to prevent burning or sticking. It will soon begin to thicken. Let cook for 25 to 30 minutes, until the paste is so thick that the wooden spoon shifts the paste in one block across the surface of the pan. Let cool.

5. **MAKE THE STICKY RICE DOUGH:** Mix together the rice flour, glutinous rice flour, sugar, and vegetable oil in a bowl. Set aside.

6. In a small bowl, add the boiling water to the wheat starch while stirring with chopsticks with your other hand. Moving quickly at this stage will prevent the mixture from becoming clumpy. *(continued)*

¼ cup (30 g) wheat starch

7½ ounces (220 g) Mugwort Puree (recipe follows)

It should be a very thick paste. This wheat starch paste will serve the dough in two ways: by making it incredibly soft and sticky, and by stabilizing it. Set aside.

7. **ASSEMBLE THE QING TUAN:** Stream the hot mugwort puree into the flour mixture, using the other hand to stir until a workable dough is formed. Stir in the wheat starch paste.

8. When the dough is cool enough to handle, knead by hand until smooth. It will become uniformly green, soft, and almost Play-Doh-like in texture. Chunks of dough should be easy to tear, but the dough should not be dry. Cover with plastic wrap and let rest at room temperature for 10 to 15 minutes.

9. Divide the red bean paste into 12 1-inch (2.5-cm) balls. Store any remaining red bean paste in an airtight container in the fridge for up to a week.

10. Divide the sticky rice dough into 12 equal portions. Work with one portion at a time, covering the remaining dough with a damp towel or plastic wrap.

11. Take one portion of the dough and roll it between your palms to form a ball. Press your thumb into the ball, forming a hole. With your thumb in the dough ball and your other fingers outside the ball, pinch and rotate to press the edges up into a bowl shape.

12. Take a ball of red bean paste and place it in the middle of the bowl. Close the edges and gently press to seal. Place the folded side down on a board, place your palm on top, and quickly but lightly roll to smooth out. Repeat with the remaining dough and red bean paste balls. At this point, you can freeze the balls on a parchment paper–lined baking sheet, then transfer to a freezer-safe container. They keep in the freezer for a month.

13. Line a steamer with parchment paper with holes cut in it. Place the balls in a single layer on top, with about 1 inch (2.5 cm) of space between them. Steam for 10 minutes over 1½ inches (3.8 cm) of simmering water over medium.

14. While hot, brush the rice balls with vegetable oil to make them glisten and to prevent them from sticking together. Let cool slightly, then serve warm. These can be made ahead: wrapped tightly with plastic, they can be kept in the fridge for a few days and in the freezer for up to a month in a freezer bag. To reheat, remove the plastic, place the balls in a lined steamer, and steam for 3 to 5 minutes before serving warm.

MUGWORT PUREE

3½ ounces (100 g) fresh mugwort
1½ cups (360 ml) cold water

1. Bring a pot of water to a boil over high. Blanch the mugwort for 10 to 15 seconds, or until it changes to a dark green color. Drain.

2. Place the blanched mugwort and cold water in a medium pan. Bring to a boil over high, then reduce the heat to medium-low and simmer for 2 minutes, until the mugwort is very soft and tender.

3. Puree the mugwort with the water in a blender until smooth.

SCALLION-BRAISED FAVA BEANS

葱油蚕豆 | cōng yóu cán dòu | *Makes 4 servings*

Cooking in spring in Shanghai revolves around three classic, seasonal types of produce: spring bamboo, celtuce, and fava beans. Other herbs and weeds are used, but these three are the cardinal greens of spring. One spring, I went with my grandmother-in-law to one of Suzhou's largest wet markets. We passed rows and rows of thin, woodsy spring bamboo (freshly dug from the mountains, a sign informed us); gorgeous stems of celtuce, with leaves already stripped and bagged separately; and heaping piles of fresh, plump fava beans. Fava beans are on regular rotation in spring because there are so many ways to cook them. This preparation, with just a touch of scallion aromatics, is my favorite. In the West, it is customary to remove the thin skin encasing each bean, but in China, it's fried along with the bean, taking on flavor as well as trapping in moisture, making the beans incredibly tender. Young fava beans are best for this.

Other ways to make fava beans include braised in dark soy sauce with five-spice powder; stir-fried with snow vegetable and chili pepper; stir-fried with chives; and cooked with rice to make fava bean rice (similar in technique to Celtuce-Leaf Rice, page 168).

2 tablespoons neutral cooking oil, such as canola or grapeseed oil
3 scallions, finely chopped
1½ cups (200 g) shelled fava beans, skins on
¾ teaspoon granulated sugar
kosher salt
¼ teaspoon

1. Heat a well-seasoned wok over high. Add the oil and swirl to coat. Add one-third of the scallions and stir-fry until fragrant. Add the fava beans and stir-fry for a few seconds. Add ¾ cup (180 ml) of water, the sugar, and salt and bring to a boil.

2. Cover the wok and reduce the heat to medium-low. Simmer until the beans are tender, about 10 minutes. If too much water is reduced and the mixture is becoming dry, add a little more water a tablespoon at a time.

3. Remove the lid and increase the heat to high to reduce any remaining liquid. Sprinkle the beans with the remaining scallions and stir-fry until fragrant. Serve immediately.

OIL-EXPLODED SHRIMP

油爆虾 | yóu bào xiā | *Makes 4 servings*

The Shanghainese eat freshwater shrimp in droves in springtime. They are particularly plentiful in April and May. During a recent trip, Alex and I visited a few shrimp farmers in Jiangsu. A lovely couple showed us their small-batch shrimp setup. They place shrimp baskets—basically long, cylindrical nets that stretch a few yards—in a small pond next to their home, and the shrimp swim into the net on their own. When the nets are full, the farmers wade into the pond and drag them out, scooping up all the shrimp in the process.

Oil-Exploded Shrimp sounds more aggressive than it is. It's cooked using a technique very familiar to the Shanghainese: deep-fried in a flash, then stir-fried more deliberately with a sauce. The quick deep-fry "shocks" the shrimp, separating the flesh from its shell, yielding a super-crisp exterior with succulent, tender meat. The deep-fried shrimp absorb the sauce in the subsequent stir-fry, so that every bite is ripe with flavorful sauce. That stir-fry is done in the residual oil from the deep-fry, letting the sauce take on all the umami shrimp flavor.

NOTE: This whole dish comes together very quickly—have all the ingredients ready before you begin.

1 pound (455 g) whole, unpeeled shrimp (about 15 to 20 heads, depending on size)

1 scallion, cut into 2-inch (5-cm) segments

3 slices fresh ginger

1 cup (240 ml) neutral cooking oil, such as canola or grapeseed oil

2 tablespoons Shaoxing wine

2 tablespoons rock sugar, crushed coarsely with a mortar and pestle, or granulated sugar

2 tablespoons light soy sauce

2½ teaspoons black vinegar

1. Using kitchen shears, trim the pointy spikes from the head of each shrimp and snip off the legs. Remove the black vein along the back with a toothpick (although, in true home-style fashion, it's okay to leave it in). Alternatively, use sharp kitchen shears to snip along the back to both remove the vein and make an opening in the shell for ease of eating later. Rinse thoroughly and pat dry with paper towels.

2. With the flat side of a cleaver, smash the scallion and ginger.

3. Heat the oil in a wok over high until it reaches 375°F to 400°F (190°C to 205°C) on a deep-frying thermometer. Place the shrimp into a long-handled metal sieve or spider and gently slide them into the hot oil. Use the sieve to gently stir and flip the shrimp. After 10 seconds, use the sieve to remove the shrimp to paper towels. After this first fry, the shrimp should be orange and starting to curl up. Work in batches as necessary.

4. Let the oil heat up again. Slide the shrimp in again and fry for another 15 to 20 seconds, until they crisp up and turn golden yellow. Remove with the sieve. Pour the oil into a heatproof container. (This shrimp-infused oil is actually fabulous in other dishes, and a little goes a long way!) Wipe the outside of the wok to make sure there are no oil drips and return the wok to the heat.

5. When the residual oil in the wok begins to shimmer, add the scallion and ginger and stir-fry until aromatic.

6. Add the shrimp, stir-fry once or twice, and add the wine. Stir-fry once or twice, and then add the sugar and soy sauce. Stir-fry to mix—it will bubble, and caramelization is the goal.

7. Keep stir-frying as the sauce becomes thick, coating the shrimp. Splash with the vinegar, stir-fry for another 5 seconds, then remove to a plate with the sauce. Serve hot.

SCALLION OIL NOODLES

葱油拌面 | cōng yóu bàn miàn | *Makes 2 servings*

You haven't experienced Shanghai until you've had a bowl of scallion oil noodles. It's a quintessential old Shanghai dish, a humble, yet extremely satisfying, bowl of noodles. This dish highlights the secret of that complex umami flavor used in many of Shanghai's signature dishes: scallion oil. Scallions are slowly fried in oil so that their flavor infuses it. This flavored oil serves as the base of this dish. Dried shrimp is an excellent addition that supplies an extra bit of umami. If you're craving something with more protein, fry some ground pork in your scallion oil until browned and crisp, then turn off the heat and proceed with the recipe.

NOTE: You can also make scallion oil ahead of time. Quadruple the recipe (everything but the noodles) below and follow the steps. Let it cool and pour it into a sterile jar; it will keep in the fridge for up to 1 month. Use it anytime to elevate any dish you're making.

1½ teaspoons dried shrimp
6 to 8 scallions, cut into 1-inch (2.5-cm) segments
3 tablespoons neutral cooking oil, such as canola or grapeseed oil
1 tablespoon dark soy sauce
2 tablespoons light soy sauce
½ teaspoon black vinegar
1 tablespoon crushed rock sugar or granulated sugar
pinch of ground white pepper
½ pound (225 g) fresh Shanghai-style thin noodles, cooked to al dente (or 2 servings of any dried noodles—I've used soba and ramen noodles to great effect.

1. Place the dried shrimp in a small bowl with hot water to cover and soak for 30 minutes. Drain and pat dry with a paper towel.

2. Smash the scallions with the side of a meat cleaver. Pat dry with a paper towel to avoid water droplets causing the oil to splatter during stir-frying.

3. Heat the oil in a well-seasoned wok over medium-low. Add the scallion segments and let them fry slowly, so they turn yellow without burning. Stir occasionally so the segments brown evenly. This slowly rendered-out flavor is essential to this recipe—be patient and let the toasty flavor infuse the oil. I usually let the scallions cook for 20 to 30 minutes, but for a deeper flavor cook them at a lower heat for longer, even up to 1 hour. Reduce the heat to low, add the shrimp, and cook for another 5 minutes.

4. Meanwhile, mix together the dark and light soy sauces, vinegar, and sugar.

5. Increase the heat to medium and immediately pour the soy sauce mixture into the wok. Fine bubbles and foam will form in the sauce (if it bubbles too much, your heat is too high) and begin to caramelize. Stir to dissolve the sugar and let simmer for 2 to 3 minutes to thicken. Turn off the heat. Add the white pepper. Add the cooked noodles to the wok and toss to combine. Divide the noodles between two bowls, making sure to scoop up the scallion segments.

CELTUCE-LEAF RICE

莴笋叶菜饭 | wō sǔn yè cài fàn | *Makes 4 to 6 servings*

Celtuce leaves are often bundled up and sold separately from the stem. In the market, you may find a pile of beautiful pale green stems, with a small stump of cut-off leaves at the tail, and in the leafy greens section, a bag of lush celtuce leaves. The leaves are often called *cai*. They are delicate, fragrant, and can be used just as you would bok choy: stir-fried, added in soups, et cetera. A delightful way to use these leaves is in celtuce-leaf rice. This is a version of 菜飯 *cai fan*, "greens rice," a quintessential Shanghai home-style dish that is in the back pocket of every Shanghai cook. It hits all the marks: luxurious 口感 *kou gan*, "mouthfeel," and fragrance from the rice and greens, and umami from the salt pork.

Classic *cai fan* includes salt pork, bok choy, and rice, cooked in a clay pot so that the bottom layer becomes crisp and crunchy. Since the development and ubiquity of rice cookers, a lot of home cooks just toss everything in a rice cooker. I use my trusty cast-iron rice pot, which holds heat well and cooks rice beautifully, to get that crisp layer on the bottom. Using celtuce leaf instead of bok choy adds an especially lovely fragrance to the dish. You can also replace the salt pork with Chinese sausage, pancetta, or bacon or omit it completely. I like a lot of vegetables in this dish, but you can adjust the amount to your preference.

NOTE: You can add diced fresh spring bamboo if it's available and cook it with the greens. If using a clay pot, first warm it up with hot (not boiling) water, then discard the water; this will prevent the pot from cracking over the heat.

7 ounces (200 g) celtuce leaves or bok choy, leaves separated and rinsed thoroughly

3 teaspoons kosher salt

2½ ounces (75 g) salt pork (optional; use salt pork belly if you can)

1½ cups (275 g) large-grain rice, soaked for 30 minutes in cold water

1 teaspoon pork lard (store-bought or homemade, page 271), or neutral cooking oil

1 (1-inch/2.5-cm) peeled nub plus ½ teaspoon minced ginger

1 cup (240 ml) hot water or High Stock (page 277)

1 teaspoon granulated sugar

ground white pepper

1. Slice the celtuce leaves into ribbons, then sprinkle with 1 teaspoon of the salt. Let stand for 2 hours. This softens the leaves and removes their bitterness. Rinse and drain. If using bok choy, trim the tough stems, rinse the leaves thoroughly, and slice into ribbons.

2. Cut the salt pork into thin slices. Rinse and drain the rice.

3. In a medium-sized heavy pot with a lid, heat the pork lard or oil over medium-high. Brown the salt pork, rendering out the fat. Using chopsticks, use the nub of ginger like a paintbrush to spread the fat halfway up the sides of the pot. Add the minced ginger and toast until fragrant. Add the celtuce leaves and cook for a few minutes, until the color begins to change to a bright green.

4. Add the drained rice and toast until translucent.

5. Add the hot water or stock, sugar, remaining 2 teaspoons of salt, and white pepper.

6. Increase the heat to high and bring to a boil; cook the rice for about 5 minutes, or until most of the liquid has been absorbed. Poke a few holes halfway in the rice to allow steam to escape. Cover and reduce the heat to medium; cook for 5 minutes. Keeping the lid on, reduce the heat to as low as possible and cook for 20 minutes more (the rice can simmer on the lowest heat for up to 10 minutes more if you want a more golden crust).

7. Turn off the heat and let sit, covered, for 5 minutes, then serve hot. Be sure to scrape the bottom and sides of the pot to get that golden crust.

SCALLION OIL CELTUCE

葱油莴笋 | cōng yóu wō sǔn | *Makes 2 servings*

The first time I had celtuce, I thought, *Why is this vegetable so underutilized in the West?* Celtuce has very quickly become one of my most coveted spring vegetables—it's versatile, fragrant, and refreshing. After a quick salt marinade to coax out the water, the stem is ready to eat raw. Hot oil briefly sizzles and cooks the scallion, and then it's tossed with the celtuce to make a truly refreshing, light dish. You can reserve the leaves to make Celtuce-Leaf Rice (page 168).

2 large or 3 small celtuce stems

1 teaspoon salt

1 scallion, white and pale green parts cut into 1-inch (2.5-cm) segments, green parts finely chopped

2 tablespoons neutral cooking oil, such as canola or grapeseed oil

1 teaspoon granulated sugar

1. Remove the outer fibrous layer of the celtuce stems with a vegetable peeler or a paring knife; otherwise you may get some tough, stringy slivers. Cut the stems into 3-inch (7.5-cm) segments, then carefully cut the segments into thin planks. You should have about 3 cups (300 g) of prepared celtuce.

2. Sprinkle the salt over the slivers and mix to combine. Let sit for 30 minutes to 1 hour.

3. Drain any excess water. Rinse the celtuce and squeeze out as much liquid as possible. The celtuce slivers should be soft and flexible.

4. Place the darker green parts of the scallion on top of the celtuce, in one pile.

5. Heat the oil in a well-seasoned wok over medium-high until shimmering. Add the white and pale green parts of the scallion and cook until they begin to yellow, then remove and discard.

6. Pour the hot flavored oil over the pile of dark green scallions and celtuce. Add the sugar and toss the celtuce to distribute the seasoning evenly. Serve at room temperature or chilled. The salad will keep in the fridge for up to 1 week.

WATER EGG

蒸水蛋 | zhēng shuǐ dàn | *Makes 2 to 3 servings*

I once found my husband trying to re-create one of his favorite childhood egg dishes. He had beaten an egg with some water and stuck it in the microwave. It was not a success. Rubbery bits of egg clung to the bowl. "It's supposed to be silky," he told me, "like pudding, and you eat it with generous drizzles of soy sauce and sesame oil." His description immediately evoked one of my own childhood memories, and I instantly knew what he was talking about. The steamed water egg—a delicious, savory custard.

Perhaps due to its simplicity and amazing flavor and texture, some variation of this dish makes an appearance across multiple cuisines in Asia, such as the *chawanmushi* in Japan. I love it with just a few garnishes, but another favorite way to eat it is with clams. To make the clam version, steam cleaned clams until they open, collect the clam juice and reserve the clams, and then add the juice to the water with the egg. Then scatter the clams into the egg mixture before steaming. It yields a strong, fragrant clam custard. As a delicate variation, you can also scatter the egg mixture with raw, peeled, deveined freshwater shrimp and extend the cooking time by 10 minutes.

I add in a touch of soy sauce and a tiny dollop of lard for extra flavoring, but that is entirely optional. You can eat it on its own or spoon it over a bowl of white rice.

3 large eggs
1 ¼ cups (300 ml) High Stock (page 277) or water, kept warm
½ teaspoon pork lard (optional; store-bought or homemade, page 271)
½ teaspoon salt
1 tablespoon plus 1 teaspoon light soy sauce
1 ½ teaspoons dark soy sauce
1 teaspoon rock sugar, crushed coarsely with a mortar and pestle
½ teaspoon sesame oil
red chili oil (optional; page 273)
1 scallion, thinly sliced

1. Beat the eggs thoroughly in a large bowl. Slowly stream in the warm stock or water, whisking constantly to incorporate. Add the lard (if using), salt, and 1 teaspoon of the light soy sauce and whisk vigorously until well combined.

2. Strain the egg mixture through a fine-mesh sieve and divide into two or three small serving bowls, such as ramekins.

3. If there are still frothy bubbles remaining, use a sieve to scoop them out—you want the surface to be as still as possible.

4. Prepare a steamer or steaming rack. Bring the water to a boil over high. Cover the egg bowls with aluminum foil or heatproof plastic wrap. Carefully (wear gloves to prevent steam burns) place the bowls in the steamer. Cover the steamer, reduce the heat to medium, and steam for 10 minutes.

5. Meanwhile, mix together the remaining 1 tablespoon of light soy sauce, the dark soy sauce, and sugar in a small saucepan. Heat over medium-high until boiling, then turn down to low and simmer for 2 to 3 minutes, until the sugar is dissolved. Remove from the heat and add the sesame oil and a drizzle of chili oil (if using).

6. Take one of the egg bowls out of the steamer to assess doneness. If the center has only a slight wobble when jiggled, the steamed egg is ready. If the center wobbles a lot and is obviously not set, let the bowls steam for another 2 minutes.

7. Divide the soy sauce mixture among the bowls, top with scallions, and serve immediately.

SCALLION-ROASTED FISH

葱烤鲫鱼 | cōng kǎo jì yú | *Servings will vary*

Scallions may be the most commonly used aromatic in Shanghainese cooking. When cooked slowly over a small flame, scallions take on a toasty, almost smoky flavor that is undeniably umami. This dish takes full advantage of that flavor. Long segments of scallions are toasted to become the base for this fish. The fish is drenched in a rich, thick sauce and then blanketed in a layer of scallions.

1 (1 to 1½ pounds/455 to 680 g) river carp, bass, branzino, barramundi, or any meaty fish, scaled and gutted

3 tablespoons coarse sea salt

5 tablespoons (75 ml) Shaoxing wine

4 slices plus one small peeled nub fresh ginger

10 to 15 scallions—2 cut into 2-inch (5-cm) segments, 1 finely chopped, and the remaining cut into approximately 4-inch (10-cm) segments

¼ cup (60 ml) neutral cooking oil, such as canola or grapeseed oil

⅓ cup (80 ml) light soy sauce

2 tablespoons dark soy sauce

1 tablespoon black vinegar

1 cup (240 ml) High Stock (page 277)

2 tablespoons rock sugar

1 teaspoon cornstarch

1. Rinse the fish and pat dry thoroughly with a paper towel. Use a sharp knife to cut three or four diagonal slits in the thickest part of the fish on both sides, reaching the bone. Rub a thin layer of the salt all over, including in the cuts and inside the belly of the fish.

2. Brush 2 tablespoons of the wine over both sides, making sure to reach inside the diagonal slits and the belly. Place 2 slices of the fresh ginger and the 2-inch (5-cm) scallion segments into the belly of the fish. Let sit for 20 to 30 minutes, then rinse and pat the fish dry.

3. Rub the inside of a well-seasoned wok with the small peeled nub of ginger. Heat the oil in the wok over medium-high. When the oil is shimmering, gently slide in the fish. Fry slowly until golden brown, 3 to 5 minutes. Tilt the wok and swish the oil so that every part of the fish touches the hot oil. When the fish is properly fried it will easily come off the wok, so if it is immobile and stuck, keep frying. Carefully flip and cook the other side for another 3 to 5 minutes. Turn off the heat and place the fish on a plate.

4. Discard all but 2 tablespoons of the oil. Reheat the oil in the wok over high. Add the remaining 2 pieces of ginger and let them explode into fragrance, 爆香 *bao xiang*. When aromatic, add the 4-inch (10-cm) scallion pieces, reduce the heat to medium, and cook until the scallions yellow and become aromatic, 15 to 20 minutes.

5. Return the fish to the wok on top of the scallions, then add the remaining 3 tablespoons of wine and let it cook off, 2 to 3 minutes. Add the light and dark soy sauces, vinegar, stock, and sugar. The broth should reach about halfway up the fish. Reduce the heat to low, cover, and simmer for 5 to 8 minutes. Periodically raise the lid and spoon the braising liquid from the bottom of the wok over the fish.

6. When the fish is cooked through—if you poke it with chopsticks the meat should easily flake off the bones—carefully lift it onto a plate.

7. Increase the heat to high and reduce the sauce in the wok until thick. Mix the cornstarch with 1 teaspoon of water and slowly stream in the slurry while stirring the sauce. You may not need all of the cornstarch mixture—add it in gradually, until the sauce reaches the thickness you desire.

8. Turn off the heat and spoon the sauce over the fish. Sprinkle with the finely chopped scallions and serve.

SHANGHAI FRIED THICK NOODLES

上海粗炒面 | shàng hǎi cū chǎo miàn | *Makes 4 servings*

The origins of this dish are a mystery to me—my parents aren't sure, and so far my research hasn't yielded an answer. All I know is, it's somehow become woven in with Shanghai cuisine. Many Chinese restaurants in America boast this dish with Shanghai in its name. It's very simply flavored, and its real charm comes from the thick, chewy noodles. It's incredibly quick to make using the classic Chinese stir-fry technique of high heat to meld the ingredients together.

In Shanghai, the green of choice is 鸡毛菜 *ji mao cai*, which literally translates to "chicken feather greens," basically very young bok choy—delicate and utterly fragrant. The first time I truly appreciated this green was at a restaurant in Shanghai. I really wanted vegetables with my meal, and this was recommended to me. A bowl of delicately boiled young bok choy leaves in a pale broth was set before me and my husband. It was quite possibly the simplest yet most delicious bowl of greens I had on that trip. Unfortunately, *ji mao cai* is hard to find in America. So, I use baby bok choy, which I blanch first to make sure it will cook quickly.

NOTE: If you can't find fresh Shanghai thick noodles, substitute Japanese udon noodles. They're rounder and thicker but work well.

1 teaspoon cornstarch
1 teaspoon Shaoxing wine
1 teaspoon plus a pinch of granulated sugar
2 tablespoons plus 1 teaspoon light soy sauce
4 ounces (100 g) pork loin or shoulder
1 pound (455 g) fresh Shanghai noodles (see Note)
2 tablespoons neutral cooking oil, such as canola or grapeseed oil, plus more for drizzling
7 ounces (200 g) 鸡毛菜 *ji mao cai* or baby bok choy, rinsed thoroughly and leaves separated
1 clove garlic, minced
1 teaspoon minced fresh ginger
2 scallions, cut into 1-inch (2.5-cm) segments
1½ teaspoons dark soy sauce
pinch of ground white pepper
½ teaspoon black vinegar

1. Combine the cornstarch, wine, pinch of sugar, and 1 teaspoon of the light soy sauce in a medium bowl. Trim any excess fat or skin from the pork and slice the meat against the grain into short, thin pieces, 1 to 2 inches (2.5 to 5 cm) by ¼ inch (6 mm). Toss the pork in the marinade and let sit for at least 10 minutes but no more than 1 hour.

2. Meanwhile, bring a pot of water to a boil. Add the noodles and cook for 2 minutes, stirring to break up the strands. Drain the noodles, then drizzle with a touch of oil to prevent them from sticking together.

3. Blanch the bok choy in a pot of boiling water for 1 minute, then transfer it to an ice-water bath and set aside.

4. Heat 2 tablespoons of the oil in a well-seasoned wok over medium-high. Add the garlic and ginger and stir-fry until aromatic. Add the pork slivers and fry until pale and just cooked, 2 to 3 minutes. Remove the pork mixture to a plate and set aside.

5. Return the wok to medium-high heat. Add the scallions and stir-fry until fragrant. Add the noodles and stir-fry until hot. Add the dark soy sauce, the remaining 2 tablespoons of light soy sauce, and the remaining 1 teaspoon of sugar and stir to combine.

6. Return the pork to the wok, then add the drained, blanched bok choy. Stir-fry until well combined and hot, then add the ground white pepper. Right before serving, stir in the vinegar.

SCALLION OIL–POACHED CHICKEN

葱油鸡 | cōng yóu jī | *Makes 4 servings*

This poached chicken is refreshing, clean, and fragrant. It's also incredibly tender. This poaching method is one of my favorite ways to cook chicken. When the chicken is served cold, it's a forgiving recipe that's hard to overcook. The chicken is gently boiled in water with aromatics, then the heat is turned off and the chicken slowly poaches, lid snugly in place, for half an hour. This is a crucial resting period. The still-hot stock slowly cooks the chicken just right, so that while the flesh is fully cooked, the bone marrow may still be pink. If you're nervous, you can check the doneness with a meat thermometer—the thickest part of the chicken should reach 165°F (74°C). After removing the chicken from the pot, you plunge it into an ice bath that shocks it, rendering it superbly succulent and pure in flavor.

There are many recipes in this book that highlight scallions as the main flavor, but instead of the toasty scallion flavor that Scallion Oil Noodles (page 167) relies on, this dish capitalizes on fresh scallions.

The flavoring is subtle and meant to complement the chicken, so the quality of the chicken is paramount. I like to use a free-range, young whole chicken. In China, people use only one species of chicken for this dish, 三黄鸡 *san huang ji*, "three-yellow chicken," called such because of its yellow feet, skin, and beak. This small chicken is known to have flavorful, tender flesh.

You can make this into 白斩鸡 *bai zhan ji*, "white cut chicken." It's one of the simplest Shanghainese dishes and brilliantly pure in flavor. To make this variation, follow all the steps below, but instead of making a scallion oil sauce to pour over it, serve as is, chilled, with a side of high-quality soy sauce for dipping.

This dish does wonderfully after a day in the fridge, giving it time to absorb all the flavors.

(See recipe on next page.)

NOTE: Don't break down the whole chicken while warm, otherwise the meat will fall apart. Wait until it is completely cooled, then chop the chicken into slices. For a small chicken, about 2½ pounds, the poaching time of 30 minutes is perfect. If the thermometer hasn't reached 165°F (74°C), return the pot to a boil, then immediately remove the chicken from the heat, cover it, and let it poach for another 15 minutes. If you don't feel like making a whole chicken, use chicken legs instead. Simply decrease the boiling time to 3 minutes, and then poach for 25 minutes.

4 scallions

1 (2-pound/910-g) young chicken

3 slices fresh ginger

2 tablespoons Shaoxing wine

½ teaspoon sesame oil, for brushing

1 recipe Scallion Oil Sauce (recipe follows)

1. Separate the white and pale green parts of 2 scallions. Set the dark green parts aside. Julienne the white and pale green parts, then soak them in cold water until ready to use.

2. In a large stockpot, bring enough water to cover the chicken to a boil over high. Gently dunk the chicken in the boiling water, then lift it out, then dunk it back in again, two or three times. This step evens out the temperature throughout the whole chicken, allowing for more uniform cooking.

3. Place the chicken completely in the water and return the water to a boil. Add the remaining 2 scallions and the green parts of the others, the ginger, and wine. Cover, reduce the heat to medium, and gently boil the chicken for 7 minutes (a larger chicken may need 10 to 12 minutes). Remove from the heat and let sit with the lid on, undisturbed, for 30 minutes.

4. Meanwhile, prepare a large pot of ice water. Gently remove the chicken from its cooking liquid and place it in the ice water, reserving 1 cup (240 ml) of the chicken stock for the scallion oil sauce. Let the chicken sit in the cold water for 15 minutes, turning it periodically to ensure complete cooling. If the ice melts, add more to keep it cold. If you poke the chicken with chopsticks, it should release a transparent, colorless liquid, not a red one.

5. Drain the chilled chicken and pat dry. Brush the skin with sesame oil for extra fragrance. Cut the chicken into thick slices, then pour scallion oil sauce over it and garnish with the julienned scallions. Serve chilled.

SCALLION OIL SAUCE

6 scallions

2 teaspoons minced fresh ginger

2 teaspoons kosher salt

3 tablespoons neutral cooking oil, such as canola or grapeseed oil

1 teaspoon Sichuan peppercorns

1 cup (240 ml) chicken stock (reserved in the recipe above)

1. Slice the white parts of the scallions into 1-inch (2.5-cm) segments on a diagonal and set aside. Finely chop the green parts and toss them with the ginger and salt; place the mixture in a small saucepan and set aside.

2. Heat the cooking oil in a small saucepan over low, then add the white parts of the scallions and cook until they become golden yellow and fragrant, 10 to 15 minutes.

3. Add the Sichuan peppercorns and stir for 30 seconds, then pour the mixture through a fine-mesh sieve into the saucepan with the green parts of the scallions. Pour the reserved stock into the saucepan and bring to a boil over high. Remove from the heat and let cool slightly before pouring over the chilled slices of chicken.

INDIAN ASTER WITH TOFU

香干马兰头 | xiāng gān mǎ lán tóu | *Makes 4 servings*

Every spring, my mom used to forage in the meadows for Indian aster, or *Kalimeris*, a fragrant, herby weed. The Chinese characters for this weed include the one for horse, because apparently horses love eating it. This dish is unassuming on first sight, but its textures and unique tastes will captivate: delicate and aromatic, with just a touch of sugar and fragrant sesame oil to bring out its natural, earthy flavor. Served cool, it is refreshing and can easily be spooned over rice or noodles. Unfortunately, it's almost impossible to find fresh Indian aster outside of China, but you can find high-quality frozen aster in most Chinese supermarkets, sometimes labeled "Chinese cress." Or you can substitute 茼蒿 *tong hao*, "chrysanthemum leaves," another earthy, herblike green.

10½ ounces (300 g) fresh or frozen Indian aster, 马兰头 *ma lan tou*

¼ pound (115 g) smoked tofu, 豆腐干 *dou fu gan*

3 teaspoons kosher salt

2 teaspoons granulated sugar

3 teaspoons sesame oil

1. Wash the Indian aster thoroughly, discarding any yellowing leaves. If you're using frozen Indian aster, defrost completely and rinse thoroughly.

2. Bring a pot of water to a boil over high. Blanch the aster for 15 seconds, until just wilted. Transfer to an ice-water bath, then strain and wring out any excess liquid. Finely mince the aster.

3. Finely dice the tofu.

4. In a large bowl, combine the aster, tofu, salt, sugar, and sesame oil. Let sit for 10 minutes in the fridge. Adjust the seasoning to taste and serve chilled.

SHANGHAI-STYLE PORK ZONGZI

鲜肉粽子 | xiān ròu zòng zi | *Makes 12 dumplings*

During the Dragon Boat Festival, which falls on the fifth day of the fifth lunar month, usually at the end of May or in early June, dragon boat races fly by on rivers and everyone eats zongzi, glutinous rice dumplings enclosed snugly in lotus or water bamboo leaves. There are innumerable varieties of zongzi, usually passed down through the generations. Shanghai's savory pork belly zongzi is my favorite—glutinous rice is marinated in soy sauce with fatty pork belly, then it is wrapped in a pyramidal shape in the leaves of a particular type of bamboo, 箬叶竹 *ruo ye zhu, Indocalamus longi-auritus.* (These leaves are available dried in most Chinese markets and need only be rehydrated.) The zongzi are then tied with kitchen twine and simmered for hours, until the meat and glutinous rice are tender and melty and suffused with the fragrance of bamboo, which lends a subtle flavor that complements the pork filling.

Other variations of this sticky rice dumpling include white zongzi, dipped in sugar after cooking, and red bean zongzi, containing pockets of red bean paste. My mom used to make large batches, not just for our family to eat, but to give away to our neighbors and family friends.

It turns out that my mom's sentiment is grounded in tradition. She grew up in poverty in Shanghai. Her apartment building had communal kitchens shared by four to five families. This fostered a strong sense of community. During the Dragon Boat Festival, each family would make their own zongzi and gift a few to their neighbors. My mom's family is Shanghainese through and through, so they made the traditional pork zongzi of the region. But other families hailed from different parts of the country, and they would make their own versions. Even if another family was from Shanghai and made pork zongzi, my mom reminisced, the flavor would still be different. Zongzi is totally familial, and only more special as a result. My mom said that her mom never really taught her how to make them. Instead, she learned by observation and proximity (or, as I say, osmosis). When she moved to America, she re-created it, finding comfort in the familiar taste of home.

NOTE: Plan ahead: The bamboo leaves and glutinous rice need to be soaked separately for at least 8 hours or overnight. You will need kitchen twine to tie up the dumplings to help them hold their shape.

30 dried bamboo leaves (two per zongzi and a few backups in case of rips)
3 cups (600 g) glutinous (sweet) rice
(continued)

1. Two nights before you plan to serve the dish, soak the bamboo leaves in water on a rimmed baking sheet. In a bowl, completely cover the glutinous sticky rice in water. Let both sit for at least 8 hours or overnight.

2. **MARINATE THE PORK:** Mix all of the pork marinade ingredients in a bowl. Cut the pork belly into ½-inch (12-mm) slices and place them in the pork marinade for at least 2 hours at room temperature or overnight in the fridge.

3. **MARINATE THE RICE:** Mix all of the rice marinade ingredients in a bowl. Drain the sticky rice and place it in the rice marinade for at least 1 hour.

4. To wrap the dumplings, place 2 bamboo leaves on top of each other (trimming sharp points so they don't puncture the leaves), offset slightly for more surface area. Bring the bottom edge up and around to form a cone. Scoop marinated sticky rice into the cone— it should fill the cone up to 1 to 1½ inches (2.5 to 3 cm) below the edge. *(continued)*

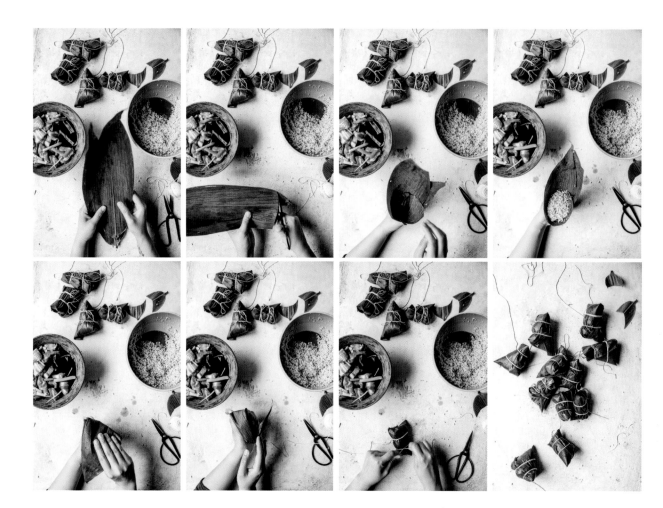

PORK MARINADE

½ cup (120 ml) light soy sauce
3 heaping teaspoons granulated
  sugar
3 slices fresh ginger
4 scallions, roughly chopped
3 tablespoons Shaoxing wine

1 pound (455 g) boneless
  pork belly or pork butt

RICE MARINADE

½ cup (120 ml) light soy sauce
1 tablespoon dark soy sauce
1 tablespoon salt
1 tablespoon granulated sugar

5. Place two pieces of pork belly on top, and then top with another handful of sticky rice to cover the pork. At this point the filling should be about ³/₈ inch (1 cm) below the edge of the cone. Fold the two leaves over the top of the cone and use kitchen twine to secure the leaves (see photographs). Repeat until you have 12 zongzi in all.

6. Place the wrapped zongzi in a large stockpot, then pour water over to cover. Bring to a boil over high, then reduce the heat to low and simmer, covered, for 8 hours. If the water dips below the level of the zongzi, add boiled water and bring back to a simmer. Turn off the heat and leave the zongzi, covered, in the cooking water overnight.

7. The next day, rinse the zongzi and let drain for an hour. Store in the fridge for up to 1 week, or freeze them for up to 2 months. To reheat from the fridge, reboil the zongzi for 5 minutes. To reheat from frozen, let them thaw in the fridge for a few hours, then reboil for 12 to 15 minutes. They are best reboiled, as microwaving them can dry them out, but sometimes I do microwave if I'm short on time: from the fridge, microwave for 1 minute, then remove the leaves and microwave for another 30 seconds. From the freezer, microwave for 1 minute, then remove the leaves and microwave for another 2 minutes, until the interior is thoroughly heated.

夏

xià

SUMMER

When I was young, I suffered from eczema. One summer, my mom took me to a doctor in Shanghai. The prescription did not include any topical ointments or creams, but rather, lifestyle modifications, particularly in relation to food. "Avoid any warming foods," I was told. "Avoid overheating the body and disrupting your energy—no spicy foods, no oily foods, nothing too sweet, especially in the summer. Eat sour things and drink plenty of fluids." We left unsatisfied. These lifestyle modifications weren't particularly new to us—my mom's cooking had already shifted to the summer dishes that were mentioned, such as chilled noodles and mung bean soup.

Chinese cuisine pairs foods with the seasons based on whether they are "hot" or "cold" in terms of their effects on the body. Summer calls for cooling foods to prevent inflammation, hence my mom's belief that her chilled mung bean soup prevents skin flares.

Food is a tool to balance the hot climate. Mung beans, bitter melon, watermelon, cucumber, lotus root, and bean sprouts are believed to keep the body cool. Chilled dishes, like cold noodles, mung bean soup, and drunken chicken, are prepped. The effect of eating something as juicy and cold as drunken chicken after walking around in the heat and humidity is immediate and almost as good as a cold shower.

FOUR HAPPINESS WHEAT GLUTEN

四喜烤麸 | sì xǐ kǎo fū | *Makes 4 servings*

烤麸 *kao fu* is a wheat gluten. How you use it and its texture are sort of like tofu, but it is made with wheat rather than soy. Sold dried or frozen, it rehydrates beautifully, a bit like a sponge, absorbing all the sauce in whatever dish it is used in.

Chinese names for dishes are often poetic instead of descriptive, elevating the dish to something extraordinary. I love the name of this dish, which draws on the four additions to *kao fu*: yellow lily flowers, two types of mushrooms, and peanuts. I've had this dish served with a bit of extra sauce on top of noodles or on the side, a chilled dish packed with flavor. The texture of *kao fu* is soft and elastic, and it is believed to neutralize heat and quench thirst. As it's served chilled, it soaks up all the sauce, so that every bite releases flavor and a punch of juice.

2 (3½-ounce/100-g) pieces dried or fresh wheat gluten, 烤麸 *kao fu*

4 dried shiitake mushrooms

7 or 8 dried wood-ear mushrooms

¼ cup (9 g) dried yellow lily flowers

1 teaspoon kosher salt

¼ cup (30 g) raw peanuts, skin on

2 tablespoons neutral cooking oil, such as canola or grapeseed oil

2 thin slices fresh ginger

1 scallion, roughly chopped into 2- to 3-inch (5- to 7-cm) segments

2 tablespoons Shaoxing wine

2 tablespoons light soy sauce

1 tablespoon dark soy sauce

2 tablespoons rock sugar

1 whole star anise

sesame oil

1. If using dried wheat gluten, soak it in cold water for at least 2 hours or overnight.

2. In a separate heatproof bowl, soak the dried mushrooms and lily flowers in just-boiled water to cover until soft, about 1 hour. Reserve the mushroom soaking liquid when draining. Run it through a fine sieve to remove any grit.

3. Tear the wheat gluten into 1-inch (2.5-cm) cubes rather than cutting it (tearing gives the *kao fu* natural edges that will soak up the cooking juices more effectively). Discard the shiitake stems and cut the caps into quarters. Tear the wood-ear mushrooms into bite-sized pieces. Strain the lily bulbs from the soaking liquid and cut them into 2-inch (5-cm) segments.

4. Bring a pot of water to a boil over high and add the salt. Boil the peanuts and lilies for 10 minutes. Remove with a slotted spoon.

5. Bring the water back to a boil. Blanch the wheat gluten for 1 to 2 minutes, then place it in an ice-water bath and let cool. Drain the wheat gluten and squeeze out the excess water. Pat dry with paper towels.

6. Heat a well-seasoned wok over high. Add the oil and swirl to coat. Add the ginger and scallion and cook until they explode into fragrance, 爆香 *bao xiang*. Discard the aromatics. Working in batches if necessary, add the wheat gluten to the wok and cook until the outsides of the pieces are brown and crispy, about 2 minutes. Add the shiitake and wood-ear mushrooms, lilies, and peanuts and stir-fry for 1 minute. Add the wine, light and dark soy sauces, sugar, star anise, and 2½ cups (600 ml) of reserved mushroom liquid with water. Stir to combine and bring to a boil. Reduce the heat to low, cover the wok, and simmer for 30 minutes, stirring occasionally to prevent the contents from sticking to the bottom of the wok.

7. When the *kao fu* is soft and soaked with flavor, increase the heat to high and reduce the sauce until it is thick. Finish with a few drops of sesame oil, then serve at room temperature or chill in the fridge before serving cold.

SCALLION-GINGER CLAMS

葱姜蛤蜊 | cōng jiāng gé lí | *Makes 4 servings*

Ginger, scallion, and garlic make up the aromatic trio in Shanghai cooking. They add fragrance and depth and neutralize the "meatiness" or "fishiness" of pork and seafood. This dish utilizes all three to lusciously season clams. The clams typically used in Shanghai are dime-sized, paper-thin-shelled clams called 海瓜子 *hai gua zi*, "seeds from the sea." I admit, they're a pain to eat because the morsel of flesh extracted from one clam is about the size of a pumpkin seed, but that flesh is so sweet and tender, it's worth it. I can't find these clams where I live, so I use littleneck or razor clams, when they're available. There are three simple steps: steam the clams open, quickly stir-fry with sauce, and then finish with sizzling-hot oil over ginger and scallions. Every step includes aromatics and another layer of flavor. I imagine this would be a marvelous way to prepare mussels, too.

FOR STEAMING THE CLAMS

1 pound (455 g) littleneck or razor clams

2 scallions, roughly chopped into 2-inch (5-cm) segments

3 or 4 slices fresh ginger

2 tablespoons Shaoxing wine

FOR FRYING THE CLAMS

1 tablespoon neutral cooking oil, such as canola or grapeseed oil

2 cloves garlic, minced

1 teaspoon minced fresh ginger

2 scallions, white and pale green parts minced and dark green parts reserved

2 tablespoons light soy sauce

1 tablespoon granulated sugar

FOR FINISHING

1 teaspoon minced fresh ginger

2 tablespoons neutral cooking oil, such as canola or grapeseed oil

1. **PREP THE CLAMS:** Rinse the clams thoroughly under cold water. Discard any cracked or open shells. Soak in cold water for 10 to 20 minutes if they are sandy.

2. Smack the scallions and ginger with the flat side of a cleaver

3. Fill a large saucepan with enough water to come ½ inch (12 mm) up the sides of the pan. Add the scallions, ginger, and wine. Bring to a boil over high, add the clams, then cover and cook for 3 minutes, until all the clams open. Remove the steamed clams with a slotted spoon and set aside. Discard any clams that are not open.

4. **FRY THE CLAMS:** Heat a well-seasoned wok over medium-high. Add the oil and swirl the wok to distribute it. Add the minced garlic, ginger, and the white and pale green parts of the scallions. Stir-fry until fragrant.

5. In a small bowl, whisk the soy sauce with the sugar. Add the clams to the wok, and then immediately pour in the soy sauce mixture. Turn off the heat. The soy sauce mixture will bubble and caramelize, becoming thick and aromatic. Toss with the clams to coat.

6. Transfer the clams to a plate, making sure to pour any remaining sauce over them.

7. **FINISH THE DISH:** Pile the minced ginger and the reserved dark green parts of the scallions on top of the clams. In a small saucepan, heat the oil until it bubbles when a chopstick is inserted, 2 to 3 minutes. Pour it over the ginger-scallion garnish (you'll hear the sizzling!) and serve.

SHANGHAI COLD SESAME NOODLES WITH CLASSIC WOK-FRIED EGG

上海冷面加荷包蛋 | shàng hǎi lěng miàn jiā hé bāo dàn | *Makes 4 servings*

Mom always pulled this dish out on the hottest, busiest days. The sauce is nutty from the sesame paste and tangy from the black vinegar. Sometimes my mom added shredded cooked chicken.

The soy sauce wok-fried egg is classic Shanghai, and it is my absolute favorite addition to any noodle dish, soup or otherwise. For much of my childhood, I thought the whole world made fried eggs this way. It's cooked lightning-fast in a sizzling-hot wok, then touched with soy sauce, so that the outside is crispy and savory, encasing that molten golden yolk. A Chinese-style wok is important, as the rounded bottom allows the oil to pool around the egg, so that it almost deep-fries.

COLD NOODLES

17½ ounces (500 g) fresh Shanghai-style thin noodles, or any kind you prefer

1 tablespoon plus 1 teaspoon sesame oil

2 tablespoons light soy sauce

2 tablespoons black vinegar

2 tablespoons rock sugar, crushed coarsely with a mortar and pestle

1 to 2 tablespoons red chili oil (optional; store-bought or homemade, page 273)

3 cloves garlic, grated (optional)

1 tablespoon creamy peanut butter

2 tablespoons sesame paste (if using tahini, add an extra tablespoon sesame oil)

WOK-FRIED EGGS

2 tablespoons neutral cooking oil, such as canola or grapeseed oil

4 large eggs

1 teaspoon dark soy sauce

2 teaspoons light soy sauce

1 teaspoon granulated sugar

TOPPINGS: minced scallions, julienned cucumber, shredded cooked chicken, fresh bean sprouts, 1 teaspoon minced fresh ginger (optional), toasted white sesame seeds

1. **MAKE THE COLD NOODLES:** Cook the noodles until al dente, then drain and rinse them under cold water. Toss with 1 tablespoon of the sesame oil to prevent them from sticking.

2. Combine the soy sauce, vinegar, and sugar in a small saucepan. Heat over medium-high until the mixture boils, then turn the heat to low and simmer for 2 minutes until the sugar dissolves. Remove from the heat and stir in the remaining 1 teaspoon of sesame oil. Add the chili oil and garlic, if using. In a separate bowl, combine the peanut butter and sesame paste with 1 tablespoon of cold water and slowly whisk to form a thin paste. Add the soy sauce mixture to the peanut butter mixture and whisk to combine. Adjust the seasoning to taste.

3. Add 3 tablespoons of the sesame sauce to the noodles. Toss to combine, then add more sesame sauce if necessary.

4. **FRY THE EGGS:** Heat a well-seasoned wok over medium-high. Once smoke starts curling up from the wok, add the oil and swirl to coat, then reduce the heat to medium. Add the eggs to the wok and cook for 90 seconds. The oil and heat will work their magic, and the egg whites will cook immediately and curl up, adopting what's called a tiger pattern, 虎皮状 *hu pi zhuang*, which allows for maximum absorption of the sauce.

5. Flip the eggs gently but quickly. If the wok and oil are properly heated, the eggs should not stick to the wok at all. Cook for another 30 seconds. Whisk together the dark and light soy sauces, sugar, and 1 teaspoon of water. Reduce the heat to low and drizzle in the sauce. The soy sauce should bubble satisfactorily. Simmer for 2 to 3 minutes.

6. Remove the fried eggs from the pan and place them on top of the noodles. Finish with your choice of toppings and sprinkle with the toasted sesame seeds.

MUNG BEAN SOUP WITH LILY BULB

百合绿豆汤 | bǎi hé lǜ dòu tāng | *Makes 4 servings*

Mung bean soup is a classic Shanghai summer dish used to keep the body from overheating, and you'll often see this in both soup and popsicle form. My mom always throws in a handful of dried lotus bulbs, giving the soup a floral fragrance and extra texture.

I was told that this soup would not only keep me cool but also "cure" acne and rashes, or so my mom believed. Cold, creamy, and thick, it is something I still make and eat every summer, not so much in the hopes of clear skin but because it's cooling and delicious—and can be made ahead. An ice-cold bowl of this after running around on a hot summer day is as thirst quenching as a glass of water.

1 cup (195 g) dried mung beans
½ cup (18 g) dried lily bulbs
2 tablespoons rock sugar, crushed coarsely with a mortar and pestle, plus more as needed

1. Soak the mung beans in water to cover for at least 2 hours or overnight.

2. Drain the mung beans and place them in a medium heavy-bottomed pot with the dried lily bulbs. Fill the pot with water to 1 inch (2.5 cm) from the rim. Bring to a boil, then reduce the heat to a simmer. Simmer for 30 minutes.

3. Add the rock sugar and stir to dissolve. Taste and adjust the sweetness to your preference. Simmer for another hour, until the mung beans are soft and have "bloomed" and burst open.

4. Adjust the thickness of the soup to your preference—simmer more if you desire a thicker soup or add water if you want a thinner soup. Let cool, then chill in the fridge for at least 2 hours before serving.

SEASONED STEAMED EGGPLANT

凉拌茄子 | líang bàn qié zi | *Makes 4 servings*

Everyone needs at least one reliable and reproducible recipe for entertaining. This is mine, because it's easy, unique, and universally pleasing. This dish can be prepared ahead of time, with ample time in the fridge to cool down. I find that eggplant can be a polarizing vegetable—some people dislike the texture, but others have no problem with it. I used to dislike eggplant until I discovered the steaming method. Eggplant is often fried with a lot of oil and ends up being too heavy for my tastes, but steamed eggplant is light and a wonderful vessel to soak up sauce. It's a fast way to cook eggplant, and even more important, the texture transforms and becomes silky soft, tender, and creamy.

NOTE: The first step is a trick to keep that gorgeous purple on the eggplant, otherwise it will turn brown. You can omit this step, though; it has no effect on the taste. When layering eggplant in the steamer, I've found that piling the pieces yields the best result. Place the bottom layer skin down to prevent oversteaming, then pile the other eggplant segments on, crisscrossing them to create air pockets so steam can reach every piece.

2 eggplants (about 12 ounces/350 g total), such as Japanese or Chinese varieties

2 teaspoons white vinegar

2 tablespoons light soy sauce

1½ teaspoons dark soy sauce

1 teaspoon black vinegar

1 tablespoon granulated sugar

1 teaspoon sesame oil

½ teaspoon ground white pepper

1 teaspoon minced fresh ginger

2 scallions, thinly sliced crosswise

3 cloves garlic, minced

2 tablespoons neutral cooking oil, such as canola or grapeseed oil

2 teaspoons red chili oil (optional; store-bought or homemade, page 273)

1½ teaspoons toasted white sesame seeds, store-bought or self-toasted (see page 113, step 2)

cilantro leaves

1. Cut off the base of each eggplant, then cut each eggplant into 3 segments. Halve each segment lengthwise so that you have 6 pieces total per eggplant.

2. Add the white vinegar to a large bowl of water. Add the eggplant pieces and let them sit in the vinegar water for 10 to 15 minutes.

3. Set a bamboo steamer over 2 inches (5 cm) of water in a wok, and bring the water to a boil over high. Place a layer of eggplant skin side down in the steamer, then pile the remaining pieces on top (see Note), working in batches if necessary.

4. Cover and steam the eggplant over high for 5 to 7 minutes, until soft and easily pierced with a chopstick. The texture should be silky soft and creamy but still firm enough to hold its shape. Set the steamed eggplant aside in a colander to cool slightly.

5. Meanwhile, mix together the light and dark soy sauces, black vinegar, sugar, sesame oil, and white pepper. Set the sauce aside.

6. When the eggplant is cool enough to handle, tear each piece lengthwise into strips about ³/₈ inch (1 cm) wide. Arrange the eggplant strips on a plate. Pile the ginger, half of the scallions, and the garlic in the center of the eggplant.

7. In a small saucepan, heat the oil until it bubbles when a chopstick is inserted, 2 to 3 minutes. Pour the hot oil over the aromatics. They should sizzle and release a gorgeous fragrance.

8. Drizzle the soy sauce mixture and chili oil, if using, over the eggplant. Top with the remaining scallions, the toasted sesame seeds, and cilantro leaves. Serve immediately at room temperature.

SUN-DRIED AND PRESERVED GREENS WITH STEAMED PORK BELLY

梅菜扣肉 | méi cài kòu ròu | *Makes 4 servings*

In the city of 绍兴 Shaoxing, an old water town southeast of Shanghai, 臭美 *chou mei*, "fermented funk," is prized and savored. Shaoxing is renowned for its cooking wine, which is used in most Chinese cooking, but this is also the city where 梅干菜 *mei gan cai*, "sun-dried fermented greens," are made. These greens (which can be mustard greens, amaranth, or even napa cabbage) are salted, dried, and then fermented, creating a funky, tangy dish that pairs well with pork. This is a quick and inexpensive way to add a punch of flavor to any dish.

The pork belly goes through a series of steps meant to cook out the grease, crisp up the skin, and prep it for steaming. The preparation is long but worth it. The result is a very clean and light pork belly, perfect for summer, or so my dad says. He calls it "like paper," with a distinctive texture that is neither rubbery nor meltingly tender like braised pork belly. Instead, it's pure and dry, full of a bewitching fragrance that comes from steaming it under a generous cap of fermented greens, exchanging aromas and flavors.

When buying dried *mei gan cai*, try to find a package that specifically states "Shaoxing." The darker the *mei gan cai*, the longer and headier the ferment, and the better the flavor. The amount of soy sauce used can vary depending on the potency of the fermented greens.

NOTES: Rinse the *mei gan cai* very thoroughly to remove dirt—an overnight soak followed by 5 to 6 rinses will do it. Rinse until there is no debris left in the water. You can make this dish ahead of time—letting it sit overnight in the fridge will only improve the flavor. Simply steam it again to reheat before serving.

3½ ounces (100 g) dried fermented mustard greens, 梅干菜 *mei gan cai*, rinsed and soaked (see Notes)

about 1 pound (455 g) boneless skin-on square or rectangle of pork belly

2 thin slices plus ½ teaspoon minced fresh ginger

3 scallions, cut into 2-inch (5-cm) segments, plus 1 tablespoon chopped scallion

2 whole star anise

2 dried bay leaves

1 tablespoon dark soy sauce, plus more for the marinade

2 tablespoons light soy sauce

1 tablespoon rock sugar, coarsely crushed with a mortar and pestle

2 tablespoons Shaoxing wine

neutral cooking oil, such as canola or grapeseed oil, for the wok

1 tablespoon cornstarch dissolved in 1 tablespoon water

cooked white rice, for serving

1. Finely chop the *mei gan cai*. You should have about 3 cups of fermented mustard greens. Set aside.

2. Place the pork belly in a large pot and add enough water to cover. Crush the slices of ginger and the scallion segments with the flat slide of a cleaver to release the aromatics. Add the sliced ginger, scallions, star anise, and bay leaves to the pot and bring the water to a boil. Boil for 5 minutes, flip the pork belly over, then boil for another 5 minutes. Remove the pork to a shallow plate with tongs and let cool, reserving the water in the pot.

3. Pour a pool of dark soy sauce in the shallow plate. Dip all sides of the pork belly into the soy sauce to darken it. Use a chopstick or toothpick to poke holes into the skin. Dip all sides of the pork belly in the soy sauce again. Place the pork, skin side down, in the soy sauce and let sit for 10 minutes.

4. Remove the pork belly from the soy sauce and place it skin side down on a wire rack over a baking sheet; let it air-dry for 10 minutes. Flip the pork belly and place it skin side up on the rack; let it air-dry for another 10 minutes.

5. Meanwhile, mix together the remaining 1 tablespoon of dark soy sauce, the light soy sauce, rock sugar, and wine in a mixing cup.

6. Heat a well-seasoned wok over low, then add enough oil to cover the skin of the pork (about 3 tablespoons). Place the pork belly skin side down in the hot oil and immediately cover the wok with a lid to contain the oil splatter. Cook for 6 to 8 minutes, until the skin is crackled. Briefly fry the other sides of the pork belly until golden. Transfer to the pot with the reserved warm water and let soak for about 20 minutes, until the rind is soft and plump. Reserve the oil in the wok.

7. When cool enough to handle, slice the pork into ¼-inch (6-mm) slices. Place the slices in a heatproof bowl, skin down, and fan the slices out slightly. Pour in half of the soy sauce mix.

8. Set the wok with reserved oil over medium-high, stir-fry the minced ginger in the reserved oil until aromatic. Add the *mei gan cai* and stir-fry. Pour in the other half of the soy sauce mix, then stir-fry to incorporate the sauce. Turn off the heat.

9. Spread the *mei gan cai* mixture in a generous layer over the pork belly, making sure the pork is covered completely, and place in a bamboo steamer or steamer basket. Steam, covered, over 2 inches (5 cm) of water on high for 20 minutes, then reduce the heat to medium-low and steam for another 60 minutes.

10. Gently pour out the excess liquid in the bowl by tipping it into a small saucepan. Place a plate or a large shallow bowl on top of the bowl in the steamer, then carefully flip the bowl so the pork belly sits on the plate, skin side up, on a bed of fermented greens. Sprinkle with the remaining chopped scallion.

11. Bring the reserved liquid to a boil and reduce into a thick sauce. Slowly stream in the cornstarch slurry as needed to thicken the sauce. Spoon the sauce over the pork belly and serve with rice.

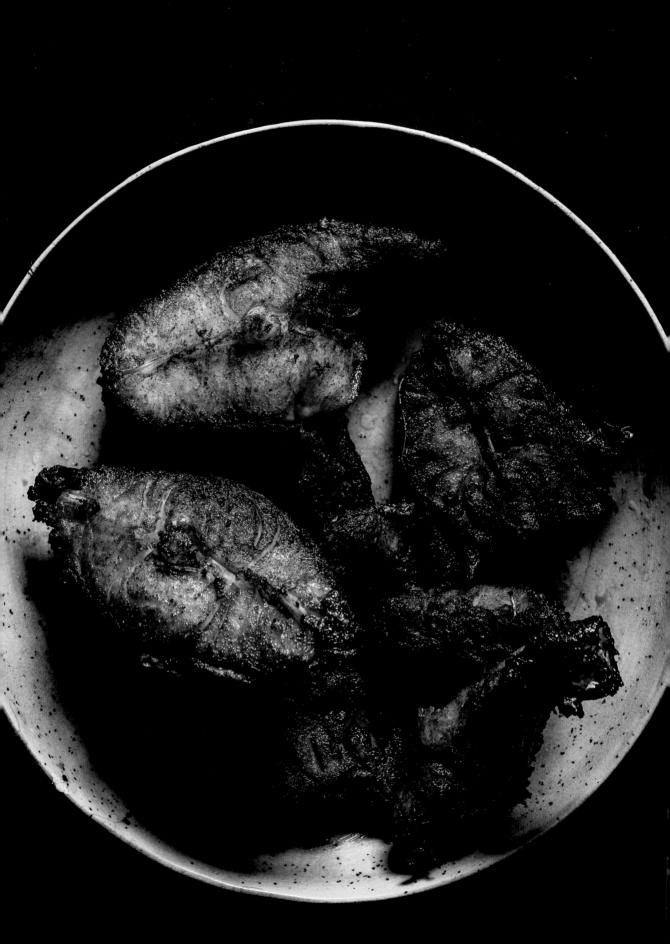

SHANGHAI "SMOKED" FISH

上海熏鱼 | shàng hǎi xūn yú | *Makes 4 servings*

There are a few "must-eats" when touring Shanghai cuisine, including red-braised pork belly (Mom's Shanghai Red-Braised Pork Belly, page 93), Celtuce-Leaf Rice (page 168), Shanghai Big Wontons (page 89), and this dish. It's served as a cold or room-temperature appetizer, and has a sweet, tangy flavor. It's not really smoked, but the sauce has a lovely smoky taste, hence the name. Done right, each piece of fish will have a fragrant, smoke-infused crust, with a delicate, tender interior. It's important to use rock sugar in this dish, as it adds to the caramelized taste and thick texture of the sauce. Make this one day in advance—this dish will mature with the sauce, soaking up that smokiness.

NOTE: Have your fishmonger cut and prepare the fish. The slices can't be too thin, otherwise they will fall apart during cooking. If the slices are too thick, the sauce won't permeate throughout the flesh: between ½ inch and ¾ inch (6 mm and 2 cm) is just right.

2 whole star anise

1 (3-inch/7.5-cm) piece cassia bark or cinnamon stick

3 dried bay leaves

3 slices fresh ginger

1 whole carp, grass carp, pomfret, mackerel, or sea bass (about 1½ pounds/680 g), cut into ¾-inch (2-cm) slices (see Note)

3 tablespoons plus ½ teaspoon dark soy sauce

¼ cup (60 g) rock sugar, crushed coarsely with a mortar and pestle

¼ cup (60 ml) Shaoxing wine

⅓ cup (80 ml) light soy sauce

2 tablespoons black vinegar

neutral cooking oil, such as canola or grapeseed oil, for frying

1. In a medium saucepan, combine 2 cups (480 ml) of water with the star anise, cassia bark, bay leaves, and ginger. Bring to a boil over high, then reduce the heat to medium and simmer for 15 minutes.

2. Meanwhile, toss the fish with ½ teaspoon of the dark soy sauce (use more as needed) until the fish slices are coated. Refrigerate until ready to cook.

3. Remove the aromatics from the saucepan with a slotted spoon. Add the rock sugar, wine, the remaining 3 tablespoons of dark soy sauce, the light soy sauce, and the black vinegar. Cover the pan and simmer the sauce over medium for 20 minutes. Fine bubbles should be present.

4. Remove the lid, then increase the heat to medium-high and reduce the sauce for 10 minutes, until thickened. Set aside in a large bowl.

5. Pat the fish slices dry with paper towels.

6. Add enough oil to your wok, or a deep pot, to cover a slice of fish. Heat the wok over medium-high and bring the oil to about 350°F (175°C) on a candy or deep-frying thermometer.

7. Working in batches, slide the fish slices into the wok in a single layer. Don't move them—let the fish fry and brown for 2 to 3 minutes, until a gentle push with a spatula shifts the slices easily. If the fish shows resistance when you push it, let it continue frying.

8. Remove the fish to a plate with a slotted spoon, bring the oil back to 350°F (175°C), then deep-fry the pieces again, this time flipped so the other side is down, until an even darker golden brown is achieved. At this point, if you lightly tap the fish with chopsticks, you will feel that it has acquired a hard surface.

9. Place the fried fish directly into the prepared sauce one at a time. This step "smokes" the sauce and caramelizes the sauce even further.

10. Repeat with the remaining fish slices, then let all the pieces sit in the sauce in the fridge for a few hours before serving. The dish is even better after overnight marination in the fridge. Serve chilled.

SAUCED NOODLES

拌面 | bàn miàn

We pulled up by Tai Hu on a beautiful sunny day in the spring. Alex's uncle drove us there with one goal in mind: to eat noodles. A heavy plastic curtain sealed up the shop, and we pushed it aside and stepped in. We were met by a cacophony of chopsticks hitting bowls, slurps, and the hum of conversation. Several servers pointed us toward an open kitchen in the back, full of gleaming chrome and large, circular wooden chopping boards and bathed in a fluorescent light.

"Tang mian? Ban mian?" (Soup or dry sauced?) a matronly server asked me, then immediately followed up with, *"Xian zai ban di hao chi"* (Right now, dry sauced is better). Who was I to question her? I nodded my head in agreement, and she tossed a handful of floured noodles into a simmering vat of water. She pointed me toward the opposite side, where I was astounded to see a four-tier shelf full of toppings: 虾仁 *xia ren,* "river shrimp"; edamame with snow vegetable; snow vegetable fried with chili peppers; celery with minced meat; all kinds of fried offal; fried eggs; crispy tofu rolls; and a variety of meatballs covered in sticky rice or bathed in a gleaming sauce.

If sitting down to eat a piping-hot bowl of soup noodles is a foil to the cooler seasons, then eating *ban mian,* "dry sauced noodles," is the counterpart in warmer weather. There's no real recipe for it—the beauty of dry sauced noodles is that you can top them with anything, even a simple stir-fry of shiitake and minced pork (something I do frequently at home), because the flavoring from the toppings is often enough to coat the noodles and function as a sauce.

I chose a few of my favorite toppings, including shrimp, soy sauce fried egg, and lion's head meatballs, and watched as the bowl came together: hot noodles slipped into a bowl, then a few spoons of braising liquid, topped with heaping amounts of my selected toppings. I was handed the bowl and directed to another topping station, this time a do-it-yourself bar with fresh scallions, garlic, ginger, chili oil, and other condiments like soy sauce and vinegar.

I love the flexibility of *ban mian,* and the fact that there are so many paths you can take. It's really all about the thick braising liquid 卤汁 *lu zhi* (which is the best flavoring) from the topping. Dishes that will give you this are Mom's Shanghai Red-Braised Pork Belly (page 93), Wuxi Spareribs (page 147), Hairy Crab Tofu (page 45), Soy-Braised Duck Legs (page 219), Spiced Braised Beef Shank (page 212), and Shanghai "Smoked" Fish (page 203).

If you're lacking any topping with braising liquid, use this basic noodle recipe (makes 4 servings):

3 tablespoons light soy sauce
2 tablespoons dark soy sauce
2 tablespoons black vinegar
½ teaspoon fennel seeds
1 whole star anise
½ teaspoon Sichuan peppercorns
1 tablespoon rock sugar, crushed
    coarsely with a mortar and pestle
¼ teaspoon sesame oil
dash of ground white pepper
1 pound (500 g) cooked noodles

TOPPINGS: minced garlic,
    red chili oil, scallions (optional)

1. Combine the soy sauces, vinegar, aromatics, and sugar with 3 tablespoons of water in a small saucepan. Heat over medium-high until boiling. Turn the heat to low and simmer for 5 minutes, until the sugar is completely dissolved. The sauce should thicken slightly.

2. Strain the sauce, stir in the sesame oil, and a add dash of white pepper. Use immediately with noodles. When cooled, the sauce can be stored in a sterilized container in the fridge for up to 3 days.

TOMATO AND EGG STIR-FRY

西红柿炒鸡蛋 | xī hóng shì chǎo jī dàn | *Makes 4 servings*

This dish brings back memories of childhood meals and early college days with Alex (this dish, along with steak, is his favorite food). I grew up eating this dish, but it wasn't until college that I realized how ubiquitous it was—although, like many dishes in this book, each family adds their own special twist. Some families use ketchup to boost the flavor. Others add *dou ban jiang*, "fermented broad bean paste."

The combination of jammy, sweet tomatoes with soft, wok-scrambled eggs is irresistible over rice with the juice spooned over the top, savory and sweet flavors in perfect balance (like so much of Shanghai cuisine!). There is a great texture contrast, and best of all, it's entirely dictated by the cook.

The tomatoes you use are paramount: fresh, in-season tomatoes will ensure the best flavor and juice content. However, this is such a staple dish, I cannot resist making it in the winter, too (with a bit of added sugar to offset the tang of the off-season produce).

I also love using this dish as a topping for Sauced Noodles (page 204), reducing the sauce a bit more and sometimes adding miso or rehydrated shiitake mushrooms for extra flavor.

6 large eggs

1½ teaspoons kosher salt

2 tablespoons neutral cooking oil, such as canola or grapeseed oil

3 medium tomatoes, cut into wedges

1 teaspoon Shaoxing wine

2 teaspoons rock sugar, finely crushed with a mortar and pestle, or granulated sugar, plus more as needed (depending on the sweetness of the tomatoes)

1 scallion, sliced finely into discs

cooked white rice, for serving

1. Combine the eggs with the salt. Beat with chopsticks or a fork until the egg yolks and whites just come together.

2. Heat a well-seasoned wok over high. Add the oil and heat until smoking—if you add a drop of egg, it should instantly bloom and puff up.

3. Immediately slide in the beaten eggs (you'll hear a sizzle) and stir-fry until large dollops of fluffy scrambled egg begin to form. Use your spatula to fold the uncooked parts into the cooked parts to ensure even cooking.

4. After 40 to 45 seconds, when large curds of golden-yellow scramble form, add the tomatoes and gently press them with your spatula to release their juices, which will temper the eggs and prevent them from cooking too fast. Add the wine and sugar and continue to stir.

5. Reduce the heat to medium-low, cover, and cook the eggs for 3 to 4 minutes, until the tomatoes are soft and the eggs have absorbed their flavor.

6. Increase the heat to high and reduce the cooking liquid to your preferred consistency. If your tomatoes aren't very juicy, add a few tablespoons of water; with the right in-season tomatoes, this is unnecessary.

7. Sprinkle with the scallions and serve with white rice.

SWEET-AND-SOUR RIBS

糖醋小排 | táng cù xiǎo pái | *Makes 2 large or 4 small servings*

This dish is an homage to the sweet flavor often attributed to Southern Chinese cuisine. It's a signature Shanghai cold dish, with a truly harmonious balance of sweet, savory, and tart. During the cooling process, the flavors meld together, transforming these simple ingredients into something more potent. These are nothing like the sweet-and-sour dishes you see on takeout menus in North America.

These sweet-and-sour spareribs have a crispy exterior and tender interior; are coated with a thick, sweet, tart sauce; and are served chilled or at room temperature. We deep-fry them, then use the 炒糖色 *chao tang se* method (see page 20), sautéing them in oil with melted sugar, which not only tenderizes the spareribs but also gives them that caramelized brown color.

NOTE: You can ask your butcher to cut the ribs in half lengthwise for you, leaving you with two long strips of spareribs, each roughly 2 inches (5 cm) wide.

2 pounds (910 g) pork spareribs (about one side of ribs), cut in half lengthwise (see Note)

3 tablespoons plus 2 teaspoons light soy sauce

5 tablespoons (75 ml) Shaoxing wine

1 tablespoon vegetable oil, plus more for frying

4 tablespoons (60 g) rock sugar, finely crushed with a mortar and pestle

2 (1-inch/2.5-cm) pieces fresh ginger

3 tablespoons black vinegar

1 tablespoon rice vinegar

2 cups (480 ml) just-boiled water or stock

toasted white sesame seeds

cooked white rice, for serving

1. Cut the spareribs between every other bone, so you end up with 1½- to 2-inch (4- to 5-cm) square two-bone pieces.

2. Place the ribs in a pot of cold water to cover and bring to a boil over high. Boil for 1 minute, then drain and pat dry.

3. In a medium bowl, stir together 2 tablespoons of the light soy sauce and 1 tablespoon of the wine. Add the ribs, toss to coat, and let rest for 15 minutes.

4. Meanwhile, heat about 1 inch (2.5 cm) of vegetable oil in a well-seasoned wok over medium-high (be sure to use a splatter shield to protect yourself from the hot oil). When a chopstick dipped in the oil causes bubbles (or a candy or deep-frying thermometer reads 360°F/180°C), the oil is ready. Working in batches, very carefully slide the ribs into the oil and fry them for 2 to 3 minutes, until golden brown. Reserve the rib marinade.

5. Using a slotted spoon, remove the ribs to paper towels. Allow the oil to return to temperature between batches. (If you prefer, sauté the ribs in a pan with 3 tablespoons of oil until brown.)

6. Discard the cooking oil and, in the clean wok, combine 1 tablespoon of vegetable oil with 2 tablespoons of the rock sugar. Over low heat, and stirring often, slowly melt the sugar into the oil. Add the ribs and stir to coat them in the melted sugar. Add the ginger.

7. Return the heat to medium-high, then add the reserved marinade, the remaining 4 tablespoons (60 ml) of wine, the remaining soy sauce, 2 tablespoons of the black vinegar, the rice vinegar, 2 tablespoons of rock sugar, and enough just-boiled water to barely cover the ribs. Bring to a boil over high, then reduce the heat to medium-low and simmer the ribs gently, covered, until the meat is easily pierced with chopsticks, 1 to 1½ hours.

8. Remove the lid. Increase the heat to high and reduce the liquid, stirring occasionally, until it is thick and syrupy, coating the ribs in a glossy sauce, 10 to 15 minutes. Remove the wok from the heat and stir in the remaining 1 tablespoon of black vinegar. Let cool; serve at room temperature.

FATHER-IN-LAW'S NANJING SALTWATER DUCK

南京盐水鸭 | *nán jīng yán shuǐ yā* | *Makes 4 servings*

After we'd been living in Boston for two years, Alex's mom, dad, and sisters—who were in New York visiting family friends—decided to take the four-hour bus ride to be with us for Thanksgiving. I was very excited, and nervous, to host a classic American Thanksgiving with turkey, sweet potatoes, stuffing, and pies—the works. They arrived with a stockpot and two large packages wrapped in a lot of plastic. Alex and I knew what that meant: his father was making his famous saltwater duck. Alex's dad, Nu Xu, grew up in Nanjing, a city renowned for its love of duck, particularly when cooked this way. For as long as I have been with Alex, his dad has made saltwater duck for every get-together, even vacuum-sealing them for us to take with us on the plane home.

It turned out they had bought two fresh ducks in New York, began the salting process there, and then wrapped them up in bags and brought them on the bus as if they were luggage. That Thanksgiving, we had a lovely classic menu, plus succulent saltwater ducks (which beats roast turkey any day).

Traditionally, the duck is 风干 *feng gan*, "wind-dried," similar to the way Soy-Braised Duck Legs are prepared (see page 219), but Nu Xu prepares his duck a bit differently. When it comes to saltwater duck, there is no one I trust more than my father-in-law, whose saltwater duck I have been eating for more than a decade. This is the method he taught me (in great secrecy), and the one I always use.

The duck is seasoned with salt and toasted Sichuan peppercorns, which add fragrance and take away some of the duck's gaminess. It sits, curing, for over twenty-four hours so that the salt has a chance to really seep in, preserving and contributing to the duck's flavor.

NOTE: Try to get a fresh whole duck, one that's not too fatty and has not been previously frozen. It's difficult to source, but try a local poultry farm—the quality of the duck truly makes a difference in this recipe. And plan ahead— the duck must salt-cure for 1½ to 2 days before cooking.

4 to 5 tablespoons sea salt
2 tablespoons Sichuan pepper-
    corns
1 fresh whole duck (about
    5 pounds/2.3 kg)
7 slices fresh ginger
5 scallions, roughly chopped
3 tablespoons Shaoxing wine

1. In a well-seasoned wok over medium heat, toast the salt with the Sichuan peppercorns until fragrant. Let cool to room temperature.

2. Rinse and clean the duck. Pat it dry thoroughly with paper towels. Massage the salt-and-peppercorn mixture inside and outside the duck, especially behind the wings and over the breasts and legs. Let sit at room temperature, uncovered, for 36 to 48 hours. The longer the salt-cure, the saltier it is.

3. Stuff the duck with 3 slices of the ginger and 2 of the scallions.

4. In a large, deep stockpot, combine the wine, the remaining ginger and scallions, and enough water to cover the duck. Bring to a boil over high and gently set the duck in the water. Reduce the heat to medium and cook, covered, at a gentle boil for 20 minutes, adjusting the heat as necessary. Remove from the heat and let sit, covered, for another 5 minutes.

5. Return the liquid to a boil over high and boil gently for another 10 to 15 minutes. Pierce a thick part of the duck (the breast or thigh). If blood bubbles up, cook the duck for another 5 minutes and check again. There should be only clear liquid when the flesh is pierced. Remove the duck and let cool to room temperature.

6. When cool, break down the duck and cut it into slices (this is even easier if you chill it in the fridge). Eat immediately or let the duck sit overnight in the fridge—the meat will taste even better the next day.

SPICED BRAISED BEEF SHANK

酱牛肉 | jiàng niú ròu | *Makes 4 to 6 servings*

My parents have made or bought this dish since I was a child. It's essentially Chinese roast beef, and it is wonderful as a cold appetizer with a splash of braising liquid and dipped in chili oil, but it also transforms into a magically tender topping for noodle soup, cooked in the leftover braising liquid. Also known as 卤牛肉 *lu niu rou,* "five-spice stewed beef," it goes through rounds of cooking and steeping in a spiced braising liquid, resulting in tender slices of beef with jellied tendons.

2 pounds (910 g) beef shank, 牛腱 *niu jian*

2 tablespoons neutral cooking oil, such as canola or grapeseed oil

3 cloves garlic, crushed

1 bunch scallions, chopped into 2-inch (5-cm) segments

1 tablespoon rock sugar, crushed coarsely with a mortar and pestle

1 teaspoon kosher salt

4 thin slices fresh ginger

2 dried bay leaves

2 (3-inch/7.5-cm) pieces cassia bark or cinnamon stick

1 black cardamom pod

2 pieces dried orange or tangerine peel

1 teaspoon black peppercorns

1 tablespoon fennel seeds

5 whole cloves

1 tablespoon Sichuan peppercorns

3 whole star anise

¼ cup (60 ml) Shaoxing wine

¼ cup (60 ml) light soy sauce

2 tablespoons dark soy sauce

sesame oil

red chili oil (store-bought or homemade, page 273), for serving

1. Trim any excess fat from the beef shank. Place the beef shank in a large pot and add enough water to cover. Bring to a boil over high, then reduce the heat to medium and simmer for 2 to 3 minutes. Discard the cooking water and rinse the shank clean. Cut the shank into 3 pieces.

2. In a fresh or cleaned pot, heat the cooking oil over medium-high. Add the garlic and three-quarters of the scallions and cook until they explode into fragrance, 爆香 *bao xiang.* Reduce the heat to medium-low. Add the rock sugar and cook until melted and the scallions are golden. Add the beef shank pieces and brown them on all sides, 6 to 8 minutes total.

3. Add the remaining ingredients, except the sesame and chili oils, and enough water to just cover the beef shank. Bring to a boil over high, then reduce the heat to low and simmer, covered, for 1 hour.

4. Remove from the heat and let steep for at least 3 hours or overnight, covered.

5. Bring back to a boil and adjust the heat to simmer an additional 30 minutes. The beef shank is done when a chopstick pierces the flesh with ease. Let the shank cool in its braising liquid, then refrigerate until completely cool.

6. Remove the shank pieces from the liquid and thinly slice them. Arrange the slices on a plate and drizzle with sesame oil and scatter with the remaining scallions.

7. Spoon some of the braising liquid over the plate and serve with chili oil for dipping. Use the leftover braising stock for soup.

CHILLED THOUSAND-YEAR EGG WITH TOFU

凉拌皮蛋豆腐 | liáng bàn pí dàn dòu fu | *Makes 4 servings*

My father has always said that soy in China is like dairy in America. I think soy is misunderstood here, often thought of only in relation to sickly sweet soy milk or the rubbery, firm tofu cubes commonly found in salads. Soy is as varied in form as dairy: there's the silky, soft tofu used in this dish; tofu skin that's used to wrap meat; and thickened soy custard, poetically called "tofu flower," that is simply delightful for breakfast. Walk into any wet market in China, and there will be vendors dedicated to everything tofu, showcasing beautiful blocks of fresh tofu in all its variations.

This dish is a beautiful way to use silken tofu. Delicately sliced tofu sits in a soy sauce–based marinade that permeates it. It's topped with thousand-year egg, a funky, fermented egg that is a delicacy in China (an acquired taste). The egg is then topped generously with fresh scallions, and the contrast of crisp, fresh scallions, creamy egg, and silky tofu is suitable for hot summer days.

NOTES: If you are not serving this dish immediately, keep the egg separate from the silken tofu so as to not cloud the tofu. Place the egg wedges on the tofu immediately before serving. If you want to truly get rid of all excess water, steam the tofu for 5 minutes, then chill it in the fridge.

1 (12-ounce/340-g) brick silken tofu (see Notes)
2 cloves garlic, minced
2 tablespoons light soy sauce
1½ teaspoons dark soy sauce
1 teaspoon sesame oil
1 tablespoon black vinegar
1 tablespoon granulated sugar
pinch of ground white pepper
3 scallions, thinly sliced crosswise
2 preserved thousand-year eggs, 皮蛋 *pidan*, peeled and cut into 8 wedges each
fresh cilantro, roughly chopped
red chili oil (optional; store-bought or homemade, page 273)

1. Slice the tofu vertically and horizontally for a ½-inch crosshatch while still in the container, then drain off any excess water. Place the tofu in a serving bowl.

2. In a separate bowl, whisk together the garlic, light and dark soy sauces, sesame oil, vinegar, sugar, and white pepper. Add half of the scallions and mix to combine.

3. Just before serving, drizzle half of the sauce over the tofu. Place the wedges of thousand-year eggs on top.

4. Drizzle the remaining sauce over the eggs and garnish with the remaining scallions and fresh cilantro. Drizzle with chili oil, if using.

SWEET-AND-SOUR LOTUS ROOT

糖醋莲藕 | táng cù lián ǒu | *Makes 4 servings*

Lotus root is the stem of the lotus flower, a powerful symbol of femininity, beauty, innocence, and purity. This flower floats on the water, anchored into the muddy bottom of ponds and lakes by these stems, which can grow up to four feet long. The woody stem is comprises segments that look a bit like sausage links. When sliced, they reveal a beautiful interior with numerous circular rivets that give the slices a pleasing pattern.

Look for lotus roots that are firm without any visible soft spots or bruising. Once peeled and sliced, place them in a bowl of cold water with a few drops of white vinegar to preserve their pristine, pale flesh. They can then be boiled into soups, baked into chips, or stir-fried, like they are in this dish. Cooked lotus roots will be tender and crisp, and they absorb sauces and flavors readily.

NOTE: If the lotus root doesn't produce enough starch, mix together 1 teaspoon cornstarch and 2 teaspoons water, then add the slurry to the dish at the end to thicken the sauce.

1 (½-pound/250-g) lotus root segment
white vinegar
2 teaspoons neutral cooking oil, such as canola or grapeseed oil
1 tablespoon goji berries, soaked in warm water for 1 hour
1 scallion, sliced on the diagonal

SWEET-AND-SOUR SAUCE

1 tablespoon black vinegar
1 tablespoon rice vinegar
2 tablespoons rock sugar, crushed coarsely with a mortar and pestle, or granulated sugar
2 tablespoons light soy sauce
salt
ground white pepper, to taste

1. Peel the lotus root with a vegetable peeler, then carefully slice it into ¼-inch (6-mm) slices. Place the slices in a bowl of cold water with a few drops of white vinegar to help prevent discoloring and let soak for 10 minutes.

2. Drain the lotus root and pat dry with paper towels.

3. In a well-seasoned wok, heat the cooking oil over medium-high until shimmering. Add the lotus root and stir-fry for 2 to 3 minutes. Add 3 tablespoons of water, cover, and simmer for 5 minutes. Remove the lid and let the water evaporate completely.

4. Drain the goji berries and pat them dry with paper towels.

5. Whisk together the sauce ingredients. Add the sauce, goji berries, and scallions to the lotus root in the wok and stir to combine. Add salt or ground white pepper to taste. Serve hot.

SOY-BRAISED DUCK LEGS

酱鸭腿 | jiàng yā tuǐ | *Makes 4 servings*

When I asked my mom about this dish, she told me, "I remember watching 外婆 *wai po,* your grand-mother, make this." We walked through the dish together, and I was amazed that she was able to re-create it from her long-ago memories.

In most Shanghainese sauces, light soy sauce is the main ingredient, contributing a savory umami flavor, and a touch of dark soy sauce is added for extra color. In this dish, dark soy sauce is high-lighted, utilizing its molasses-like consistency and color to intensely flavor the duck, coating it like lacquer. The other important ingredient is rock sugar. It may seem like this recipe calls for a large quantity, but that amount is needed to balance the dark soy sauce and create that lacquer-like glaze. Crushed rock sugar is sprinkled not in the sauce but directly onto the duck skin, bringing out the color and crisping it up. It's decadent.

Similar to Father-in-Law's Nanjing Saltwater Duck (page 211), the duck is first salted and briefly cured before cooking (风干 *feng gan,* "wind-dried," page 20), creating tender, flavorful duck. Try to choose not-too-fatty legs from a smaller duck to make this dish.

Soy duck is a wonderful accompaniment to rice or noodles. The sauce is pure liquid gold, packing a punch of flavor when combined with stock. Scoop it over the duck or white rice or use it as a sauce for dry sauced noodles or noodle soup—just don't discard it.

NOTE: Be sure to rub the duck with kosher salt or coarse sea salt with large granules; fine salt will too easily dissolve and absorb into the meat.

4 (2.2-pound/960-g) duck legs
about 2 teaspoons kosher salt (see Note)
3 slices fresh ginger
2 scallions, cut into 2-inch (5-cm) segments
2 tablespoons dark soy sauce, plus more for brushing the duck legs
1 tablespoon neutral cooking oil, such as canola or grapeseed oil
2 whole star anise
1 (3-inch/7.5-cm) piece cassia bark or cinnamon stick
1 dried bay leaf
¼ cup (60 ml) Shaoxing wine
2 tablespoons light soy sauce
1 teaspoon red yeasted rice, ground into a powder with a mortar and pestle (optional, for color)
(continued)

1. Rinse and clean the duck legs, trim away any excess fat, and dry thoroughly with paper towels.

2. Rub the salt over the duck legs in a thin layer. Let sit for 2 hours, ideally in an area with good air circulation (I place them next to an open window).

3. Rinse the salt off the duck legs with cold water. Bring a pot of water with 1 slice of the ginger and half the scallions to a boil, then add the duck legs and simmer for 5 minutes. Remove the duck legs to an ice-water bath to stop the cooking.

4. Pat the duck legs dry thoroughly with paper towels. Brush the legs with dark soy sauce and let sit for 30 minutes, skin side up, in the fridge.

5. In a well-seasoned wok or heavy-bottomed pan, heat the oil over medium-high, then add the duck legs, skin side down, and fry until yellowed and some fat has rendered out, 5 to 7 minutes. Render more if you want crisper duck. Set aside.

6. In the hot rendered duck fat, combine the remaining scallion, 2 slices of the ginger, and the star anise, cassia bark, and bay leaf and stir-fry until fragrant. Add the duck legs, skin side up this time. Pour in the wine and light soy sauce with 2 tablespoons of dark soy sauce. Stir in the red yeasted rice, if using, then add enough stock to come halfway up the duck legs. Increase the heat to high and bring back to a boil, uncovered. Meanwhile, sprinkle the crushed rock sugar over the skin of the duck legs—this will crisp up and flavor the skin and give it a bright color. *(continued)*

High Stock (page 277) or water
¼ cup (50 g) rock sugar, crushed coarsely with a mortar and pestle
cooked rice or noodles, for serving

7. When the liquid comes to a boil, reduce the heat to medium-low and begin ladling the stock over the duck, dissolving the rock sugar. Once all the sugar has dissolved, simmer, partially covered, over medium-low for about 1½ hours. Chopsticks should easily pierce the flesh at this point.

8. Remove the lid, increase the heat to medium-high, and reduce the sauce. As it reduces, ladle the braising liquid over the duck legs to ensure they are the same bright red everywhere. This process could take as long as 30 minutes, during which the duck will darken visibly. The sauce will start to bubble very finely, almost like a foam. Let it bubble for an additional 5 minutes. At this point, the sauce should be thick and flavorful, coating the duck as you spoon it over the legs.

9. Remove the duck legs from the wok and let them cool completely before cutting into slices. Serve the duck chilled or just cooler than room temperature. I usually remove the chiled duck from the sauce and let the temperature come up a little as I reheat the sauce. Warm the sauce (skim off any excess fat first if you wish) and spoon it generously over the duck. Eat with rice or noodles.

GARLICKY CUCUMBERS

凉拌黄瓜 | liáng bàn huáng guā | *Makes 4 servings*

The perfect dish to combat summer heat: juicy cucumbers tossed in a tangy, garlicky sauce. I like to use small Taiwanese cucumbers for this dish—I find them juicier and fresher. This dish is best described as 清爽 *qing shuang*, "refreshing." Let the cucumbers crisp up by sitting for one hour in salt (not quite pickled), then toss generously with garlic, vinegar, and sugar. A few drops of sesame oil at the end will round the dish off. If you want some heat, you can drizzle some chili oil in to give it a kick! Serve at the start of any meal as a lovely chilled appetizer.

3 small cucumbers (English cucumbers preferred over American)

1 tablespoon kosher salt

5 cloves garlic—2 smashed and roughly chopped, 3 finely chopped

2 tablespoons black vinegar

2 teaspoons light soy sauce

2 teaspoons granulated sugar

sesame oil

2 teaspoons red chili oil (optional; store-bought or homemade, page 273)

1. Wash the cucumbers thoroughly, then cut them into wedges in the 滚刀 *gun dao* "rolling knife" style (see page 20) or in strips.

2. Combine the cucumber with the salt and smashed garlic and let sit for 1 hour.

3. Rinse the cucumbers, squeezing them slightly to wring out any excess water. Pat dry thoroughly with paper towels.

4. In a small bowl, stir together the vinegar, soy sauce, and sugar until the sugar is dissolved. Stir in the finely chopped garlic and a few drops of sesame oil.

5. Pour the garlicky marinade over the cucumbers and toss to combine. Drizzle with the chili oil, if using. Serve immediately. These will keep in the fridge for 3 to 5 days but are best eaten on the day they are made.

BLANCHED WATER SPINACH

白灼空心菜 | bái zhuó kōng xīn cài | *Makes 2 servings*

Traditionally, water spinach is stir-fried with garlic, but this 白灼 *bai zhuo*, "blanched," and seasoned method is my preferred way to eat this crisp, hollow vegetable, especially in the summer. This is a water plant that grows beautifully in higher temperatures and a lot of sunlight. Not only is the star ingredient cooling, it's literally a cool dish—blanched, then shocked in ice water, it's tossed with caramelized, still-hot soy-based seasoning and served at room temperature or cool. It's a quick, satisfying dish that I frequently make when entertaining. When I told my dad I was including this recipe, he immediately asked, "You included the fermented tofu, right? It has to be the white kind, not the red one." Yes, dear father, I've included it as an option. Fermented tofu is not for everyone, though, and this dish is delightful even without it.

Preparing the water spinach is the most time-consuming part, as you only use the stems. (Reserve the leaves for another use, such as stir-frying and serving over rice or to throw in soups.) Remove the tougher base of each stem by holding the bottom part with one hand and farther up the stem with the other while bending it. The stem will naturally break at a certain spot. If your leaves have long, nice stems, use those as well.

NOTE: Blanching, called 白灼 *bai zhuo*, is a technique that can be used with any tender, delicate greens. Tiny baby bok choy, 鸡毛菜 *ji mao cai,* is particularly delightful, and I've blanched napa cabbage, lettuce, and asparagus as well. If you wish to make a more chilled version of this dish, drain and place the water spinach in the fridge after chilling it in the ice-water bath.

10½ ounces (300 g)
    water spinach
1 tablespoon kosher salt
sesame oil
2 tablespoons Shaoxing wine
1½ teaspoons white fermented
    tofu, with brine (optional)
2 tablespoons light soy sauce
1 tablespoon granulated sugar
dash of ground white pepper
1 tablespoon neutral cooking oil,
    such as canola or grapeseed oil
3 cloves garlic, minced
1 teaspoon minced fresh ginger
1 dried chili pepper, chopped
    into ½-inch (12-mm) segments
    (optional)

1. Wash and drain the water spinach thoroughly. Prepare the spinach by removing its leaves, then holding the middle and base of each stem while bending it. The stem will naturally break where the stem is tough. Discard the tough base. Use your hands to tear the remaining stem into 2-inch (5-cm) segments. Prepare a bowl of ice water.

2. Bring a pot of water to a boil. Add the salt, a drizzle of sesame oil, and the wine. Gently slide in the water spinach stems and use chopsticks to turn them, allowing them full contact with the boiling water. The water spinach will turn brighter green rapidly. Once this happens, remove it with a large slotted spoon and place it in the ice water to stop the cooking. Remove the spinach from the ice-water bath and pat dry with paper towels (see Note).

3. Mix together the fermented tofu (if using), soy sauce, sugar, and white pepper.

4. Heat a well-seasoned wok over high until smoking. Add the oil and swirl to coat, then add the garlic, ginger, and dried chili pepper, if using, and cook until they explode into fragrance, 爆香 *bao xiang*. Add the soy sauce mixture to the hot wok and turn off the heat. The soy sauce will bubble and caramelize a bit, creating a thick, aromatic sauce.

5. Pour the sauce over the chilled water spinach. Toss to combine. Serve at room temperature or chilled.

DRUNKEN CHICKEN

醉鸡 | zuì jī | *Makes 4 servings*

Drunken chicken is a beloved summer dish in Southern China. This dish capitalizes on the potent fragrance of Shaoxing wine, which elevates the relatively simple ingredients to a new level.

It's satisfying when served cold on a hot, humid day. I like to make this with boneless legs (technically 醉鸡卷 *zui ji juan*, "drunken chicken roll"), as I usually can't eat that much drunken chicken, but if you want to do a whole chicken, increase the steaming time to twenty-five minutes.

2 chicken leg quarters
    (about 1½ pounds/630 g total)
1½ teaspoon salt
½ cup (120 ml) Shaoxing wine
6 thin slices fresh ginger
2 dried bay leaves
1 whole star anise
2 tablespoons light soy sauce

BRINE
1½ cups (360 ml) Shaoxing wine
2 tablespoons granulated sugar
2½ teaspoons sea salt
1 tablespoon dried goji berries

1. Debone the chicken legs with a sharp paring knife or scissors, reserving the bones for the stock (see step 2). Place skin side down on a cutting board and use the back of your knife to lightly tap across the chicken, especially in the meatier part, tenderizing each leg. Rub the legs on both sides with 1 teaspoon of the salt. In a large bowl, combine the legs with the wine. Let sit for 20 minutes.

2. In a small saucepan, combine the reserved bones, 2½ cups (600 ml) of water, the remaining ½ teaspoon of salt, the ginger, bay leaves, star anise, and soy sauce. Bring to a boil and simmer, partially covered, for 1 hour. Strain the stock and let cool, then place it in the fridge, as it must be completely cool before using to soak the chicken in step 5.

3. Meanwhile, rinse off the chicken and pat it dry with a paper towel.

4. On a sheet of aluminum foil or heat-safe plastic wrap, roll up the chicken legs tightly into a long log and seal by folding the ends under the log. Steam in a bamboo steamer or steamer basket over 2 inches (5 cm) of simmering water on medium-high for 20 minutes. Remove from the heat and prepare an ice-water bath while the chicken sits for 5 minutes with the steamer lid on tight. Transfer the leg roll to the prepared ice-water bath.

5. Whisk together the brine ingredients in a large nonreactive glass container. Remove the foil or plastic wrap from the chicken roll and add the chicken to the brine. Pour in enough of the now cold reserved broth to cover the chicken.

6. Cover the container and refrigerate the chicken for at least 24 hours—it will keep for up to 3 days. When you're ready to serve, remove the chicken from the brine, slice it, and serve cold or at room temperature.

风味小吃

fēng wèi xiǎo chī

STREET FOOD

At six in the morning, Shanghai is a different city. Instead of the usual cacophony of voices speaking musical Shanghainese, blaring announcements from buses, and cars honking in standstill traffic, intermingled with the bellow of traffic officers, I hear the quiet chirp of cicadas, the muffled footsteps of the early risers, and the quiet murmur of shop owners just beginning their day.

On a recent trip, fresh off a flight from America with jet lag fueling my early morning energy despite a restless night, I was in the mood for 包子 *bao zi*, "steamed stuffed buns." As I approached an intersection about three blocks from where I was staying that is known to be a hub for breakfast vendors, I saw other people walking away, clutching plastic bags of steaming *bao* and *shaomai*—I was close. I passed by a mundane wall and saw a small line of people forming ahead. I suddenly noticed a three-foot square opening, accompanied by a sign that said FABRICS, yet I could see that what was being sold was 煎饼 *jian bing*, "crispy breakfast egg crepe." In the dark background, I saw the promised bolts of fabric. I walked another block and reached the mother lode: an intersection where each corner boasted a breakfast shop, with more stands and vendors snaking along each street.

Wisps of steam from giant bamboo steamers obscured the menu, but no matter—I knew what I was going to get: pork *baozi*; 烧卖 *shaomai*; 豆浆 *dou jiang*, "warm soy milk"; and 油条 *you tiao*, "fried dough," all made fresh before my very eyes. Behind the main counter, where orders were filled, a small group of chefs was hard at work with face masks and arm covers in place. They worked quickly in assembly-line fashion, with one person rolling out dough, another shoving filling in, and a third rapidly pleating the buns. Yet another chef transferred the freshly pleated *bao* to a bottom ring in a stack of bamboo steamers, and then lifted the top layer to reveal cooked *bao*, ready for the customers.

The breakfast markets are where you'll find the classic, traditional foods of Shanghai, as well as the locals who cherish them. This is where you can immerse yourself in old Shanghai culture: sit down with a steaming bowl of soy milk elbow to elbow with a stranger; help yourself to toppings of tiny dried shrimp, scallions, chili oil, and fried dough; get a piping-hot bowl of noodles and slurp it up while standing; or order a ball of sticky rice and enjoy the hefty portion on your way to your next destination.

MORNING PORK BAO

鲜肉包 | xiān ròu bāo | *Makes 12 buns*

I call these morning pork buns because when I am in China, I get them almost every single day for breakfast. They are sold all over the city, usually from a cart or stand strategically placed on the way to a metro station or in a major center, to capture the attention of professionals making their way to work. I love starting the day off with fragrant, juicy pork hugged by a cloud-like bun, usually chased with some warm, sweet soy milk.

The secret to a perfectly moist filling is the fattiness of the ground pork and the flavored water. It's called 水陷 *shui xian*, "water filling," because the flavored water is incorporated into the meat filling, which mingles with the rendered pork fat while cooking, transforming it into an amazing juice that is the hallmark of breakfast buns.

The recipe is incredibly similar to *mantou* (see Scallion Flower Buns, page 236), but it has an important addition: baking powder. Baking powder gives the dough more height and tenderness. *Mantou* is like bread, dense yet tender, and is divine on its own, but it's not as fluffy and airy as *bao*, which is meant to hold some sort of filling.

NOTE: The ground pork must be fatty, about a 4:6 fat to lean pork ratio. The ground pork I find at the Chinese grocery store usually is perfect—it is a pale pink color with bits of white throughout. Otherwise, ask your butcher to mince some pork belly and combine it with ground pork. You can also use 3¾ cups (500 g) all-purpose flour in lieu of the cake flour combination.

DOUGH

1 teaspoon active dry yeast
1 tablespoon granulated sugar
1 cup (240 ml) warm water
2¾ cups plus 1 tablespoon (350 g) all-purpose flour, plus more for dusting
1¼ cups (150 g) cake flour
2 teaspoons baking powder
1 teaspoon pork lard (store-bought or homemade, page 271) or vegetable oil, plus more for greasing the bowl

(continued)

1. **MAKE THE DOUGH:** Combine the yeast, sugar, and warm water in a medium bowl. Let sit for 5 minutes to bloom to ensure that the yeast is indeed active. Foamy bubbles should appear on the surface.

2. **IF WORKING BY HAND:** Mix the flours in a bowl and make a well in the center. Sprinkle the baking powder around the outer edge of the flour so that it will be incorporated last. Gradually stream in the yeast mixture, mixing with chopsticks with your other hand. Once all the water is in and the dough is loosely mixed, add in the lard. Use your hands to knead the dough until it is soft, elastic, and so smooth it can be described as "three shines," 三光 *san guang*, about 10 minutes. Your hands, the dough, and the bowl should be "shiny," without anything sticking to them. If you try to stretch the dough, it should offer some resistance and pull back. If the dough is too tight, wet your hands with water and keep kneading. Be careful of how much extra water you add—the more hydrated the dough, the heavier it will be. Try to incorporate all the water and knead before adding extra water.

   IF USING A STAND MIXER WITH DOUGH HOOK: Combine the dry ingredients in the bowl, and mix on low until combined. Slowly stream in the yeast mixture. When the dough starts to come together, add the lard and increase the speed to medium. Mix until smooth and elastic and the dough pulls away from the sides of the bowl. The dough and bowl should be smooth and shiny—if not, add more flour gradually.

3. Place the dough in a large oiled bowl. Let rise in a warm place, covered, for 30 to 45 minutes, until about one and a half times its original size.

4. **MAKE THE FILLING:** Combine all the filling ingredients except the ginger-scallion water and salt in a large bowl. *(continued)*

17½ ounces (500 g) ground pork (see Note)

1 tablespoon plus 2 teaspoons light soy sauce

1 tablespoon dark soy sauce

1 tablespoon Shaoxing wine

1 tablespoon plus 2 teaspoons fine granulated sugar

pinch of ground white pepper

1 teaspoon sesame oil

1 cup (240 ml) Ginger-Scallion Water (page 257)

½ teaspoon salt

Use a spatula and mix in a circular motion, in one direction (see page 133, step 1). Add the ginger-scallion water in two batches, stirring to combine fully between additions. The motion is almost like whipping to incorporate air into the filling. Add the salt last. The texture should be thick, sticky, and paste-like, with no residual liquid.

5. **CHECK THE DOUGH:** If you pull the dough from the edge of the bowl and see a honeycomb of airy textures, the dough is ready. It should stretch easily without any elastic recoil. Punch down the dough and knead vigorously until smooth and shiny once more, 3 to 5 minutes. How vigorously you knead (which will get rid of the air bubbles from the rise) will dictate how smooth your resulting bun surface is.

6. On a lightly floured surface, roll the dough into a log with your hands. Divide the log into two portions. Cover one portion with plastic wrap while working with the other half.

7. Roll the log to about 8 inches (20 cm) long and divide it into 6 pieces.

8. Place a morsel of dough cut side down on your work surface. Using your palm, press down to flatten it into a disc. With a rolling pin, roll from the outer edge in, rotating the disc as you go, so that the edges are thinner than the center. The disc should be 4 to 5 inches (10 to 12.5 cm) in diameter.

9. With the disc in one hand, scoop a heaping tablespoon of filling onto the center and then begin to pleat the wrapper following the steps below (see photographs on opposite page). Reverse hands if you are left-handed.

   With your right thumb inside and right index finger out, firmly pinch an edge.

   With the tip of your left index finger, push a fold of the dough onto the nail bed of your right index finger, using your right index finger as a guide for consistent width.

   Slide your right index finger out, and then firmly pinch the pleat between your left index finger and right thumb.

   Return your right index finger to its previous position and repeat pushing and pinching the disc until the whole *bao* is pleated, using the palm of your left hand to rotate the *bao* as you pleat.

   When you return to your first pleat, there will be a neat hole in the center. Continue with a second round of small pleats and then pinch sealed, with a tiny steam hole opening at the top.

   If the filling is spilling out, push it down with your left thumb and gently pull the dough upward with your right fingers when pleating, so the dough comes over the filling.

   Repeat with the remaining dough and filling.

10. Place the *baos* on a parchment paper–lined steamer with holes cut in the parchment at least 1½ inches (4 cm) apart. Cover and place over boiled water that has rested for 5 minutes (so that the steam is not too intense) and let them rise in the warm environment for 10 to 15 minutes. I like to do this in the wok so that I can go straight to

steaming (make sure the water does not touch the bottom of the steamer basket). If you have to work in batches due to a small steamer, refrigerate the *baozi* to halt the fermentation as you work.

11. To steam the *baos*, bring the water under the steamer to a boil over high. Once the water boils, immediately reduce the heat to medium and steam for 15 minutes.

12. Remove the lid. Press a fingertip into a *bao*; if the indentation bounces back, the *baos* are ready. If not, let them steam for another 3 to 4 minutes. Serve immediately, or let cool, at which point you can refrigerate or freeze them. If you're not eating them within a few days, freeze and use within several months. To reheat from the fridge, steam for 2 to 3 minutes. To reheat from the freezer, steam for 8 minutes, or microwave with a damp paper towel covering them for 2 to 3 minutes.

GREENS BAO

蔬菜包 | shū cài bāo | *Makes 12 buns*

The counterpart to pork *baozi* is 蔬菜包 *shu cai bao*, "greens bao," with a stunningly fragrant filling of *yu choy*, shiitake, and spiced tofu. The flavor is almost entirely derived from those three ingredients, with a touch of sesame oil to elevate the buns. If available, adding fresh winter bamboo shoots provides a lovely crunchy texture and delicate fragrance.

1 recipe bao dough (page 231)

8 dried shiitake mushrooms, rehydrated in hot water to cover for 1 hour until soft, stems removed

1 square (about 3 ounces/80 g) five-spiced tofu, 五香豆腐干 *wu xiang dou fu gan*

1 teaspoon kosher salt, plus more for blanching

15 to 20 stems (500 g) Chinese spinach, 油菜 *yu choy*

3½ ounces (100 g) fresh winter bamboo shoots (optional)

2 tablespoons neutral cooking oil, such as canola or grapeseed oil

1 teaspoon minced fresh ginger

2 tablespoons granulated sugar, plus more as needed

2 tablespoons pork lard (store-bought or homemade, page 271) or neutral cooking oil, such as canola or grapeseed oil

2 tablespoons sesame oil

1. Prepare the bao dough according to steps 1 through 3 on page 231.

2. To make the filling, squeeze the shiitake caps to wring out any excess liquid. Strain the mushroom stock through a fine-mesh sieve to remove any grit and set aside. Finely dice the mushrooms and tofu. Set aside.

3. In a pot of boiling water with a pinch of salt, blanch the *yu choy* until the stems become a brighter green color. Place in an ice-water bath to stop the cooking. Drain the greens and wring lightly to remove the excess water. Chop finely.

4. If you're using the bamboo, blanch it in boiling water for 3 minutes, then drain and let cool. Dice finely.

5. Heat a well-seasoned wok over medium-high. Add the oil and swirl to coat the pan. Add the ginger and stir-fry for a few seconds. Add the mushrooms, tofu, and bamboo and stir-fry for 2 minutes. Add 2 tablespoons of the reserved mushroom stock. Stir in the sugar and dissolve. Continue to cook over medium-high until most of the liquid has evaporated. Set aside and let cool.

6. Meanwhile, vigorously wring out any excess water from the chopped greens with your hands. In a large bowl, combine the mushroom mixture with the greens. Season with the 1 teaspoon of salt and add the lard. Drizzle with the sesame oil and mix to combine.

7. Cover the filling and refrigerate for at least 2 hours to marinate and set.

8. Proceed with wrapping and cooking the baos as in steps 5 through 12 on pages 232–233.

SCALLION FLOWER BUNS

葱油花卷 | cōng yóu huā juǎn | *Makes 8 buns*

There are two important elements for a perfectly shaped, fluffy *mantou*: kneading and temperature moderation. The kneading time is long but will yield a fluffy texture. Kneading vigorously after the second rise is crucial, as it collapses the air bubbles and results in a smooth texture once steamed. This dough can be delicate, so it's important to increase the temperature slowly. Heating the steaming water from cold allows the buns to rise slowly with the temperature. Make sure to turn the heat to medium after the water boils, as extreme heat will shock the dough, causing it to rise too much and then collapse.

NOTE: I use a mix of cake flour and all-purpose flour to mimic the lower protein flour used in China. You can also use 3¾ cups (500 g) all-purpose flour.

DOUGH
1 teaspoon active dry yeast
1 cup plus 2 tablespoons (270 ml) warm water
1 tablespoon granulated sugar
2¾ cups plus 1 tablespoon (350 g) all-purpose flour, plus more for dusting
1¼ cups (150 g) cake flour
1 teaspoon vegetable oil, plus more for greasing the bowl

SCALLION SPREAD
3 scallions, finely chopped
1 tablespoon scallion oil (see page 167, step 3) or vegetable oil
¼ teaspoon granulated sugar
1 tablespoon sesame oil
1 teaspoon kosher salt

1. **MAKE THE DOUGH:** Mix together the yeast, warm water, and sugar in a medium bowl. Let sit for 5 minutes to bloom, ensuring that the yeast is indeed active. Foamy bubbles should appear on the surface.

2. Mix the flours in a bowl and make a well in the center. Gradually stream in the yeast mixture, mixing with chopsticks with your other hand. Once all the water is in and the dough is loosely mixed, stir in the vegetable oil.

3. Use your hands to knead the dough until it is soft, elastic, and so smooth it can be described as "three shines," 三光 *san guang*, about 10 minutes. Your hands, the dough, and the bowl should be "shiny," without anything sticking to them. If you try to stretch the dough, it should have some resistance and pull back. If the dough is too tight, wet your hands with water and keep kneading. (Alternatively, combine the dry ingredients in the bowl of a stand mixer with a dough hook, and mix on low speed until combined. Slowly stream in the yeast mixture, then when the dough starts to come together, add the oil and increase the speed to medium. Mix until smooth and elastic and the dough pulls away from the sides of the bowl. The dough and bowl should be smooth and shiny—if not, add more flour gradually.) Place the dough in an oiled bowl. Let it rise in a warm place until it has doubled in size, 60 to 90 minutes. Alternatively, let the dough rise in the fridge for up to 24 hours. When ready to work with the dough again, let it come to room temperature.

4. Meanwhile, mix together all the scallion spread ingredients except the salt in a medium bowl and set aside.

5. When you pull the dough from the edge of the bowl and see a honeycomb of air bubbles, the dough is ready. Punch the dough down and knead vigorously for another 5 to 7 minutes, until no large air bubbles remain and the dough is smooth once more.

6. On a lightly floured surface, use a rolling pin to roll the dough into a large rectangle about ¼ inch (6 mm) thick and 12 inches (30.5 cm) wide and 15 inches (38 cm) long. Arrange the dough with the long side facing you. Add the salt to the *(continued)*

scallion spread and mix to combine. Brush the dough with a thin layer of the scallion spread. Fold the top edge into the middle, then fold the bottom edge up to the middle, meeting the upper edge, to make a long rectangle. Pat firmly to remove any air bubbles.

7. Brush more of the scallion spread over the surface of the dough, then fold the top half over the bottom half (at the midline). Use a sharp knife to cut the dough into thin strips, about ¼ inch (6 mm) wide.

8. Grab the top and bottom edges of four of these strips, and place them on top of the next three or four, to form a stack.

9. Using your hands, pinch both ends of the stack, gently pulling the strips until they are doubled in length, and then twist them. Tie into a knot and tuck in the ends (see photographs on opposite page).

10. Repeat steps 8 and 9 with the remaining dough.

11. Place the knots about 1½ inches (4 cm) apart in a bamboo steamer lined with parchment paper with steamer holes. Cover the steamer with the lid and let rise for 15 to 20 minutes. If your steamer is small and you are working in batches, refrigerate the other buns to pause fermentation.

12. Add 2 inches (5 cm) of cold water to the wok, making sure no water touches the bottom of the steamer, and bring to a boil over high, then reduce the heat to medium. Steam the knots over simmering water for 15 minutes.

13. Remove the lid of the steamer. Press a fingertip gently into the bun, and if the indentation bounces back, the buns are ready. Serve immediately, or refrigerate for a few days or freeze the buns for several months to use at another time. You can freeze these buns after you steam them. To reheat from frozen, steam for 7 minutes, then turn off the heat and let the buns sit in the steamer for another 5 minutes. Alternatively, wet a paper towel, wring it out so it's not sopping wet, and place it over a bun on a plate. Microwave for 3 minutes to reheat.

CHINESE FRIED CRULLERS

油条 | yóu tiáo | *Makes 6 to 8 crullers*

Chinese fried crullers are the reliable accompaniment to so many breakfast options, a wonderful sidekick to savory soy milk, tofu flower, glutinous rice rolls, even sweet rice pancakes. My mom told me that before plastic bags were so ubiquitous, you'd approach a *you tiao* hawker with your own chopstick. The chef would skewer the freshly fried crullers, puffed and hollow, with the chopstick, which would be used to transport them back home.

You tiao are one of the famous "Four Warriors" of Shanghai breakfast foods. In folklore, the 四大金刚 Si Da Jin Gang, "Four Warriors," were the legendary gods from the Han dynasty, guards of Buddhism. In a breakfast context, this phrase refers to the four classic breakfast dishes from old Shanghai: 粢饭 *ci fan*, "glutinous rice rolls"; 豆浆 *dou jiang*, "soy milk"; 大饼 *da bing*, "sesame pancakes"; and 油条 *you tiao*, "fried crullers."

To get the right texture, the frying temperature must be hot—up to 375°F to 400°F (190°C to 205°C). I use a candy thermometer to monitor my temperature. Constantly turning the dough with long chopsticks while frying is also crucial to ensure even cooking. If the two halves come apart, then you're either overfrying or the two halves weren't pressed together well enough.

NOTE: Leftovers freeze wonderfully. They can be crisped up by reheating in a toaster oven or a 375°F (190°C) oven for just a few minutes.

2 cups (250 g) all-purpose flour, plus more for dusting
¾ teaspoon salt
½ teaspoon baking soda
½ teaspoon baking powder
²/₃ cup (144 ml) warm water
1 tablespoon vegetable oil, plus more for brushing and deep-frying

1. Whisk the flour with the salt, baking soda, and baking powder in a bowl. Make a well in the center of the flour and stream in the warm water. Mix until just combined, then add 1 tablespoon of vegetable oil. Knead vigorously with your hands for 10 to 15 minutes, until the dough is soft, smooth, and elastic. Alternatively, mix in a stand mixer fitted with a dough hook on the lowest setting for 7 minutes.

2. On a lightly floured surface, roll the dough with a rolling pin into a rectangle ⅓ inch (about 1 cm) thick and about 4 inches (10 cm) wide and 16 inches (40 cm) long. Brush lightly with vegetable oil, then cover with plastic wrap and refrigerate for at least 8 hours or overnight.

3. Allow the dough to come to room temperature, about 1 hour.

4. When the dough approaches room temperature, heat enough oil for deep-frying in a wok or tall-sided, heavy-bottomed pot (to prevent splashing) over medium-high until it reaches 375°F to 400°F (190°C to 205°C). Test with a small morsel of dough—when added to the hot oil, it should immediately puff up and float.

5. While the oil heats, cut the rectangle of dough widthwise into 1-inch (2.5-cm) strips. You should have 12 to 16 pieces. Stack one strip on top of another. Use a chopstick to gently press down across the length of the strips, so that the two sides pop up (see center photograph on page 242). Grasp the two ends of the strip and stretch it out to the length of your pot, or about 9 inches (23 cm) long. *(continued)*

6. Gently place the strip in the heated oil to cook for a few minutes. It should immediately float to the top and start puffing. (If not, your oil is not hot enough.) After 3 to 5 seconds, use long chopsticks to start turning the strip constantly, until it is deeply golden brown on both sides, 1 to 2 minutes.

7. Remove the cruller to a wire rack to drain. Repeat with the remaining strips in batches as needed, allowing the oil to return to temperature between batches.

8. Serve hot and fresh—a slice into it should reveal large air holes.

SOY MILK

豆浆 | dòu jiāng | *Makes about 4 cups (960 ml)*

In China, soy milk is a staple morning drink, much like coffee in the United States. In fact, when I am in China, I rarely get coffee in the morning. Instead, I get a cup of hot, slightly sweetened soy milk. Conveniently, the places that sell soy milk also sell breakfast items like *bao zi* and *you tiao*—they are one-stop shops.

Making soy milk is very easy to do at home and is similar to making nut milks. Soaking the soybeans helps to soften the legume and make the end result creamy. There are many variations in the order of when to blend or cook the beans. If you have a soy milk machine at home, like my parents do, that will make your life easier. I live in a small apartment with too many kitchen appliances already, so I make it on the stovetop. I've tried all the combinations, and the method I've included below results in the best, most aromatic soy milk. I prefer to sweeten it with a touch of rock sugar, and it pairs wonderfully with Chinese Fried Crullers (page 240).

Unsweetened soy milk is used in a quintessential Shanghainese breakfast dish, 咸豆浆 *xian dou jiang*, "savory soy milk," hot soy milk poured into a bowl with pickled vegetables, tiny dried shrimp, scallions, and a touch of soy sauce and vinegar. The process for preparing *xian dou jiang* is called 冲豆浆 *chong dou jiang*, "flushing" or "rinsing" soy milk: hot soy milk is ladled, from a height of about one foot, into a bowl with the seasonings. The rush of soy milk, combined with the acidity of vinegar, "blooms" the soy milk.

NOTE: I buy high-quality organic soybeans when making soy milk, as the quality of the ingredient really does dictate the flavor, particularly so in this recipe.

3 ounces (80 g) dried soybeans, soaked in enough water to cover overnight

1. Drain and rinse the soybeans.

2. Place the beans and 4 cups (960 ml) of water in a blender and blend on high speed until silky smooth. Strain through a cheesecloth, fine-mesh sieve, or nut-milk bag into a deep, large pot, squeezing out as much liquid as you can.

3. Bring the soy milk mixture to a boil—watch this step carefully, as it can foam up dramatically in the blink of an eye. When it bubbles and foams, remove briefly from the heat to allow the foam to subside (you can even use a sieve to scoop out additional foam), then continue to boil over medium-high for 5 minutes.

4. Reduce the heat to low and simmer for another 10 minutes. Remove from the heat. Proceed to make either savory or sweet soy milk with the recipes that follow on page 244.

SAVORY SOY MILK 咸豆浆 | xián dòu jiāng | *Makes 2 servings*

2 large eggs
pinch of kosher salt
2 teaspoons neutral cooking
   oil, such as canola or
   grapeseed oil
1 teaspoon black vinegar
2 teaspoons light soy sauce
½ teaspoon sesame oil
1 to 2 teaspoons pickled
   vegetables, 榨菜 *zha cai*
   (see page 29)
1 tablespoon dried seaweed
   strips
1 scallion, finely chopped
1 teaspoon tiny dried shrimp,
   虾皮 *xia pi*
4 cups (960 ml) plain soy milk
   (page 243)
half of a Chinese Fried Cruller,
   油条 *you tiao* (page 240),
   torn into chunks

1. **PREPARE EGG RIBBONS,** 蛋皮丝 *dan pi si*: Beat the eggs thoroughly and add the salt, then strain them to make a silky mixture. Heat the oil in a large nonstick pan over medium-low. Add about half of the egg mixture and immediately spread it to cover the pan in a thin layer. Cook, undisturbed, until set, about 2 minutes, then remove to a cutting board and set aside. Repeat with the remaining egg mixture. Once cool, cut the omelets into thin strips.

2. Combine the vinegar, soy sauce, sesame oil, pickled vegetables, seaweed, scallion, dried shrimp, and egg ribbons, and then divide into two bowls. Bring the soy milk to a boil, then pour the milk over the ingredients in each bowl.

3. Serve with chunks of fried cruller on the side or dunked in the soy milk.

SWEET SOY MILK 甜豆浆 | tián dòu jiāng | *Makes 2 servings*

4 cups (960 ml) plain soy milk
   (page 243)
rock sugar, crushed coarsely
   with a mortar and pestle
Chinese Fried Cruller, 油条 *you*
   tiao (page 240)

1. Bring the soy milk to a boil over high, then reduce the heat to low and simmer. Add the rock sugar to taste (start with 1 tablespoon) and dissolve.

2. Serve steaming hot with a side of Chinese fried cruller.

SHANGHAI SHAOMAI

上海烧卖 | *shàng hǎi shāo mài* | *Makes 32 dumplings*

My mom would make *zongzi* and *shaomai*, then freeze them neatly stacked in plastic bags, to be packed away in my check-in luggage for me to bring to college. They held up surprisingly well on the flight from California to Saint Louis. When I moved into my freshman dormitory, my parents came along and helped me transform my room into one that felt like home: an electric kettle and a jar of loose leaf tea in a corner, a mini fridge filled with those precious treats, bedsheets from Ikea in a cheerful daisy pattern. Then I was on my own to meet my floor mates, who would be my neighbors for the next year.

Awkward introductions and small talk fell to the wayside as I prepared a plate of *shaomai* in the communal kitchen. Back at my room, I left the door ajar as an open invitation, and soon there were a bunch of us, drawn in by the delicious smell, sitting around the small coffee table provided by the university eating *shaomai*. I tried my best to explain what they were: open-faced dumplings filled with soy sauce–flavored sticky rice and minced pork. In the same family as pork *shumai*, this treat is one of my favorite snacks. I loved introducing my new neighbors to my mom's cooking. (Thank you, Mom!)

From then on, my mom always prepared a few bags of *shaomai* for me to take to college—a tangible, edible comfort of home away from home.

This dumpling is often sold at breakfast in Shanghai in the outdoor markets. Vendors can buy freshly made *shaomai* skin, but it's harder to find in the United States. I often make these at home with my family, as the Asian supermarkets on the West Coast are more likely to sell *shaomai* skin than those on the East Coast. You can substitute wonton skins.

NOTE: If you don't want to make the *shaomai* wrappers from scratch, substitute one 14-ounce (398-g) package of eggless *shaomai* wrappers.

FILLING

3 cups (600 g) glutinous (sweet) rice, soaked in cold water overnight

10 dried shiitake mushrooms, rehydrated in hot water to cover for 1 hour until soft, stems discarded

2 tablespoons neutral cooking oil, such as canola or grapeseed oil

1 teaspoon minced fresh ginger

4 scallions, white and green parts kept separate, minced

(continued)

1. **MAKE THE FILLING:** Drain and rinse the sweet sticky rice. Cook by steaming over high in a heatproof shallow bowl for 15 to 20 minutes, until translucent, plump, and soft. Set aside, covered with a damp towel to prevent the rice from drying out.

2. Strain the mushroom soaking liquid through a fine-mesh sieve to remove any grit and set aside. Finely dice the mushrooms.

3. Heat the oil in a well-seasoned wok over medium-high. Add the ginger and the white parts of the scallions and cook until they explode into fragrance, 爆香 *bao xiang*. Add the mushrooms and cook until browned, about 2 minutes. Add the pork and cook until browned. Add the sticky rice and immediately add the light and dark soy sauces, wine, salt, pepper, sugar, and 1/3 cup (80 ml) of the mushroom soaking liquid (or water). Stir-fry until well combined and all of the liquid has been absorbed. Taste for seasoning and adjust to your preference—it's okay for the filling to be on the salty side.

4. Remove the wok from the heat and drizzle in the sesame oil. Fold in the green parts of the scallions. Set aside and let cool, covered with a damp towel to prevent the filling from drying out.

5. **MAKE THE *SHAOMAI* WRAPPERS:** Pile the flour in a large mixing bowl and make a well in the center. Stream in the just-boiled *(continued)*

8 ¾ ounces (250 g) ground pork
   or hand-minced pork (page 270)
¼ cup (60 ml) light soy sauce
1 tablespoon dark soy sauce
2 tablespoons Shaoxing wine
1 teaspoon kosher salt
pinch of ground white pepper
2 tablespoons granulated sugar
½ teaspoon sesame oil

SHAOMAI WRAPPERS (see Note)
2 cups plus 2 tablespoons (275 g)
   all-purpose flour, plus more
   for dusting
⅓ cup plus 1 tablespoon (95 g)
   just-boiled water
⅓ cup (75 g) cold water

water while stirring with chopsticks, then stream in the cold water, mixing as you go. Continue to mix with chopsticks until a workable dough forms. When cool enough to handle, knead the dough on a lightly floured surface until it is smooth and elastic but not sticky, 5 to 10 minutes. Wrap in plastic and let rest for 20 minutes at room temperature.

6. Divide the dumpling dough in half. Place one half, wrapped in plastic, in the fridge. Dough will keep in the fridge overnight but should be used the next day. Divide the remaining dough in two. Work with one of these halves (a quarter of the total dough) at a time, taking care to cover the other half with a damp kitchen towel or sheet of plastic wrap to prevent the dough from drying out.

7. With your hands, roll a quarter of the dough into a log and cut it crosswise into 8 pieces. Place one piece cut side down on a lightly floured surface and flatten it with your palm. Use a rolling pin to roll it into a paper-thin (about 1 mm thick) circle.

8. Use your nondominant hand to hold the edge of the circle half off the work surface. Use your other hand to flatten the portion of the wrapper on the board with the rolling pin. Rotate the dough as you go so that you flatten the entire circumference to a 4-inch (10-cm) disc. This creates a wrapper that is thinner on the edges and thicker in the center. (See top left photograph on page 233.)

9. Repeat with the remaining dough, including the chilled one, remembering to flour the work surface and rolling pin regularly to prevent sticking. You should have 32 wrappers.

10. When you're done rolling out all the dumpling wrappers, hold a stack (about 8) of well-floured wrappers together and, with one hand at the 10 o'clock position and the other at 2 o'clock, stretch the skins out slightly, working your way around the circumference of the circle, resulting in a wavy border (see top left photograph on opposite page).

HOW TO ASSEMBLE AND STEAM THE *SHAOMAI*

1. Place about 1 heaping tablespoon of filling in the center of a wrapper.

2. Start loosely gathering and pleating the edges. Pinch the pleats together and plump the filling down in the *shaomai*, forming a small pouch.

3. Gently un-pleat and spread out the wrapper, then stuff another tablespoon of filling on top. Use your hands to press the filling in, scrunching at the top to form an opening. The more packed and tightly pressed, the more likely it will hold together when steaming. Repeat with the rest of the wrappers and filling.

4. Steam in a single layer, 1 inch apart, for 10 minutes.

5. To store, let the steamed *shaomai* cool to room temperature. Place them on a lined baking sheet and freeze. Once frozen, store in plastic bags. They will keep in the freezer for several months.

PAN-FRIED PORK BAO

生煎包 | *shēng jiān bāo* | *Makes 20 buns*

When in Shanghai, you eat 生煎包 *sheng jian bao*, "pan-fried pork dumplings." They're found in the famous restaurant Yang's Dumpling or in the breakfast wet markets. Often, they are cooked nestled next to pot stickers in large, flat-bottomed cast-iron pans. *Sheng jian bao* are like small *baozi*, with a delicious pork filling and soup (similar to Soup Dumplings, page 255), encased in a yeasted, fluffy dough. These *bao* are pan-fried and steamed simultaneously to create a fluffy wrapper and a crusted shell. The resulting contrast in textures (crunch from the pan-fried bit, pillowy softness from the steamed parts) is utterly delightful, and it soaks up all the flavors in the filling.

Pan-fried pork bao are often served on small paper trays and look like no other dumplings you've seen before: a rounded top sprinkled with sesame seeds and the occasional scallion slice and a dark, crusty bottom. If you go to the right place, these dumplings are freshly fried and hot. My tongue has been scalded many times when eating these Shanghainese gems, but I can never stop myself from going back for more.

NOTE: The size of your pan is essential in holding the baos' shape and character. The baos will be nestled next to one another in a circle. With extra space, the buns can flatten and spread out, but you want tall, almost cube-like shapes. Plus, water will fill those empty spaces and saturate the dough and prevent proper steaming. For this recipe of 20 baos, I've found my skillet with a flat bottom measuring 8½ inches (21.5 cm) in diameter (not rim to rim, but the flat part where the baos will touch) to be perfect. The pork filling by itself is juicy and tender, but if you want stock in the buns, add Jellied Stock *(Pi Dong)*, (page 257). I've included two recipes for *bao* dough—the traditional one is leavened with yeast, for a little bit of fluffiness. The street-food version is very popular and relies only on baking powder for its rise.

(continued)

1. **MAKE THE TRADITIONAL DOUGH:** Combine the yeast, sugar, and warm water. Let sit for 5 minutes to bloom to ensure that the yeast is indeed active. Foamy bubbles should appear on the surface.

2. In a large mixing bowl, make a well in the center of the flour. Sprinkle the baking powder along the outer edge of the flour so that it is incorporated last. Gradually stream in the yeast mixture while stirring with chopsticks. Once all the dough loosely comes together, add the oil.

3. Use your hands to form the dough and knead for about 10 minutes, until the dough is soft, elastic, and so smooth it can be described as "three shines," 三光 *san guang*. Your hands, the dough, and the bowl should be "shiny," without anything sticking to them. If you try to stretch the dough, it should offer some resistance and pull back. If the dough is too tight, wet your hands with water and keep kneading.

4. Place the dough in an oiled bowl. Let rise in a warm place, covered, for 10 to 15 minutes, until soft and easily stretchable. Do not let your dough rise beyond this—it is important that the dough be half-proofed for proper formation of the pan-fried bao. An indentation with a finger will not see the usual instant bounce back, but a slow rebound. Let sit in the fridge for 15 minutes to bring the temperature down, so that the dough won't rise as quickly while you are wrapping.

1. **MAKE THE STREET-FOOD DOUGH:** In a large bowl, mix the flour with the sugar and make a well in the center of the flour. Sprinkle the baking powder along the outer edge of the flour so that it is incorporated last. *(continued)*

TRADITIONAL DOUGH, LEAVENED

1 teaspoon active dry yeast
1 teaspoon granulated sugar
½ cup (120 ml) warm water
1²/₃ cups (200 g) all-purpose flour
1 teaspoon baking powder
1 teaspoon neutral cooking oil,
    such as canola or grapeseed oil,
    plus more for greasing the bowl

STREET-FOOD DOUGH, UNLEAVENED

1²/₃ cups (200 g) all-purpose flour
½ teaspoon granulated sugar
2 teaspoons baking powder
½ cup (120 ml) warm water
1 teaspoon neutral cooking oil,
    such as canola or grapeseed oil,
    plus more for greasing bowl

FILLING

7 ounces (200 g) ground pork
1½ teaspoons light soy sauce
1½ teaspoons dark soy sauce
1 tablespoon Shaoxing wine
1½ teaspoons granulated sugar
pinch of white pepper
½ teaspoon sesame oil
½ teaspoon minced fresh ginger
6 tablespoons (90 ml) Ginger-
    Scallion Water (page 257)
½ teaspoon kosher salt
3 tablespoons Jellied Stock
    (Pi Dong) (optional; page 257),
    chopped
1 tablespoon neutral cooking oil
    such as canola or grapeseed oil,
    plus more to grease pan
1 scallion, green part finely
    chopped
black sesame seeds

Gradually stream in the water while stirring with chopsticks. Once all the water is in and the dough is loose, add in the oil.

2. Use your hands to form the dough and knead for about 10 minutes, until the dough is soft, elastic, and so smooth it can be described as "three shines," 三光 *san guang*. Your hands, the dough, and the bowl should be "shiny," without anything sticking to them. If you try to stretch the dough, it should offer some resistance and pull back. If the dough is too tight, wet your hands with water and keep kneading.

3. Place the dough in an oiled bowl. Let rise in a warm place, covered, for 20 minutes, until soft and easily stretchable.

4. **MAKE THE FILLING:** Combine the pork, light and dark soy sauces, wine, sugar, white pepper, sesame oil, and ginger. Use a spatula and mix in a circular motion, in one direction (see page 133, step 1). Add the ginger-scallion water in two batches, incorporating the water completely after each addition. The motion with the spatula is almost like whipping to incorporate air into the filling. Mix until the filling resembles a paste. Add the salt. The texture should be tacky and paste-like, with no residual liquid.

5. Fold in the chopped jellied stock, if using. If the mixture is too wet from the *pi dong*, place the mixture in the freezer for 5 to 10 minutes. Otherwise, refrigerate the filling until you're ready to assemble the bun.

6. **ASSEMBLE THE BUNS:** The dough should be super soft and easy to stretch at this point. Punch the dough down and knead vigorously until smooth and shiny once more, about 3 minutes.

7. On a clean work surface, with your hands roll out the dough into a log and divide it into two portions. You can lightly dust the surface with flour if you want, but you shouldn't need to. Cover one portion with plastic wrap while working with the other half.

8. Roll the dough into a longer log and divide it into 10 portions, about 1 tablespoon (16 g) each. Place a morsel of dough cut side down and, using your palm, press down and flatten it into a disc. With a rolling pin, roll from the outer edge in toward the center, rotating as you go, so that the edges are thinner than the center. The disc should be 3 to 3½ inches (7.5 to 9 cm) in diameter.

9. With the skin in your nondominant hand, scoop 1 tablespoon of filling onto the center, or measure out about ²/₃ ounce (18 g). Pleat the dumpling skin closed, using the method described in step 9 of Morning Pork Bao, page 232.

10. Place the dumpling in a greased 8- to 9-inch (20- to 23-cm) flat-bottomed skillet. Repeat with the remaining dough and filling, placing the dumplings in the skillet in a circle. Drizzle 1 tablespoon of oil lightly over the *baos*, aiming for the cracks between them.

11. Heat the skillet over medium-low. Fry the dumpling for 3 minutes, until the sizzling has somewhat subsided and the bottoms are deeply golden, then add just enough hot water to reach halfway up the *baos*, leaving the tops exposed. Cover the skillet, increase

the heat to medium-high, and let come to a boil. Shake the skillet periodically to make sure the dumplings don't stick to it. Once the water comes to a boil, reduce the heat to medium-low. You are looking for a gentle, not rolling, boil. Let the *baos* steam until the water has mostly evaporated and you can hear the oil sizzle, 7 to 9 minutes. Remove the lid and let the water finish evaporating, another minute or so. The *baos* should be puffed and springy with very crisp, golden bottoms, not doughy or wet-looking.

12. Sprinkle the *baos* with the scallion greens and a scattering of black sesame seeds. Remove the skillet from the heat, place a plate over the top, and let sit, covered, for 1 minute. Then, using oven mitts to prevent burns, gently flip the dumplings onto the plate.

SOUP DUMPLINGS

小笼包 | xiǎo lóng bāo | *Makes about 42 dumplings (20 to 22 at a time)*

I remember my parents casually ordering three baskets of soup dumplings in a crowded little eatery in a residential neighborhood in Shanghai, as we kids prepared ourselves for a delicious, tongue-scalding experience. When I met Alex, whose family is from Suzhou, and learned that he also grew up eating these, I realized they were more than just a tasty treat, they're a truly special dumpling. Supposedly native to the Jiangsu region (though this is all hearsay by locals), each region of the province has its own version: 无锡小笼 *Wuxi xiao long* is famous for its large size, thicker skin, and sweetness; Suzhou has both *xiao long bao* and 汤包 *tang bao*, "soup dumplings," which are steamed with the pleats facedown and hold more stock than meat; Shanghai's are smaller, thinner skinned, and more mild in flavor. Even Taiwan has claims to the dumpling, where the popular Din Tai Fung restaurant boosted soup dumplings to international renown.

Freshness is key, for the texture of the filling and skin will change as the dumpling sits, plumping up the skin in an undesirable way.

I purposefully listed the dough as one-half batch at a time, so you wrap one-half of the filling at a time. A key part to the dough is thin, elastic skin, requiring a fine balance in hydration. If you are not used to pleating and will take more time to roll and pleat, I recommend working maybe even with one-quarter of the dough (so half of the specified amount), working with 10 to 12 dumplings at a given time so your dough does not overhydrate. The longer it sits waiting to be wrapped, the more it will be hydrated. After one batch is made, you can cook it for immediate consumption before making another batch, or immediately freeze it for storage for several months.

NOTE: Roll out the wrapper so thin you can see the shadow of your fingers behind the disc.

FILLING

7½ ounces (250 g) ground pork (on the fatty side, 4:6 fat to lean meat ratio)

1 tablespoon Shaoxing wine

1½ teaspoons light soy sauce

1 tablespoon dark soy sauce

1 tablespoon and 1 teaspoon granulated sugar

½ teaspoon sesame oil

pinch of ground white pepper

1 tablespoon cornstarch

6 tablespoons (90 ml) Ginger-Scallion Water (page 257)

1 teaspoon kosher salt

½ cup plus 1 tablespoon (250 g) Jellied Stock (*Pi Dong*) (page 257), chopped

(continued)

1. **MAKE THE FILLING:** Combine the ground pork with the wine, light and dark soy sauces, sugar, sesame oil, and white pepper and whip in one direction (see page 133, step 1) until it becomes paste-like. Add the cornstarch.

2. Add the ginger-scallion water in two to three batches, mixing thoroughly after each addition. The water should be completely absorbed and the filling should be almost sticky. You can even blend the filling or process it in a food processor for a super-paste-like texture. Add the salt.

3. Fold the chopped *pi dong* into the mixture gently—do not overmix. You should still be able to see dots of *pi dong* in the filling. Let chill in the fridge while you prepare the dough.

4. **MAKE THE DOUGH** (for half of the filling): Mix together the flours and salt in a large bowl. Make a well in the center and stream in the water while stirring with chopsticks.

5. Knead vigorously until smooth and elastic—try to refrain from adding more water until you've kneaded for 3 to 5 minutes (additional water at this stage will make the dough too soft, changing the texture). The more you knead, the smoother the dough will become. Once there is no more loose flour left in the bowl, invert the dough onto a clean surface and knead until smooth and *(continued)*

DOUGH (½ batch)

¾ cup plus 1½ teaspoons (100 g)
   all-purpose flour

½ cup (58 g) cake flour

pinch of salt

5 tablespoons (75 ml) warm water,
   plus more if needed

elastic, about 10 minutes. Cover with plastic wrap and let rest for 20 minutes.

6. Work with one-half of the dough at a time, leaving the remainder covered so it does not dry out. With your hands, roll the dough into a thin log, almost 1 inch (2.5 cm) in diameter. Using a kitchen scale for the most accurate measurements, divide the dough into pieces, each 10 or 11 grams (2 teaspoons), about ½ inch (12 mm) thick. Each half of the dough will yield 10 or 11 pieces. Working with one piece of dough at a time, flatten the dough with your hand and with a rolling pin, roll it into a disc. Roll it from out to in (see the top left photograph on page 233) as thin as you possibly can into a 3-inch (7.5-cm) disc. The disc should be so thin it starts to become translucent, but elastic enough to hold together without breaking. If the dough tears when being stretched, it may not have rested enough—let it rest 10 more minutes.

7. Place 16 grams (about 1 heaping teaspoon) of the filling in the middle of the disc. Using your nondominant thumb to press the meat down, begin to pleat the dough (see page 233) with your dominant hand. With every pleat, pull up slightly while gently pressing the meat down, so that a purse begins to form. Pleat 18 to 20 times, then pinch shut (no need to leave a steamer hole) and give the dough a final twist. Repeat with the rest of the pieces of dough from the first half.

8. In a steamer lined with parchment paper cut with holes, place the dumplings about 1 inch (2.5 cm) apart (or freeze the dumplings at this point). Steam them over 2 inches (5 cm) of simmering water on high for 7 minutes. Prepare the rest of the dumplings from the second half of the dough in the same way until all the dough has been used.

9. Make another batch of dough (starting at step 4) to use the remaining half of the filling, or refrigerate the filling for up to 2 days before continuing.

10. To heat frozen dumplings, steam over high for 10 to 12 minutes.

GINGER-SCALLION WATER

2 thin slices (about ½ ounce/
15 g) fresh ginger
2 scallions

In a blender, combine the ginger, scallions, and ½ cup (120 ml) of water and blend on high until pureed. Strain through a fine-mesh sieve and reserve the flavored water.

JELLIED STOCK (*PI DONG*)

½ pound (225 g) pig skin,
cut into 1 x 3-inch (2.5 x
7.5-cm) strips
½ pound (225 g) pig trotters,
including skin, joints, and
tendons
6 cups (1.4 L) chicken stock
or High Stock (page 277)
2 scallions, chopped into
1½-inch (4-cm) segments
2 dried bay leaves
2 slices fresh ginger
2 whole star anise
2 tablespoons Shaoxing wine
½ teaspoon ground white
pepper
2 teaspoons salt

1. Place the pig skin and bones in a large pot. Add enough water to cover. Bring to a boil and cook until the skin curls up, about 5 minutes. Strain and reserve the trotters and skin.

2. When cool enough to handle, cut the pig skin into ½-inch (12-mm) dice.

3. In a clean pot, combine the trotters and diced pig skin with the chicken stock, scallions, bay leaves, ginger, star anise, and wine. Bring to a boil over high, then reduce the heat to low, cover, and simmer for 2 hours. Add the white pepper and salt and adjust to taste.

4. Strain the stock into a heatproof container with a lid. Let cool to room temperature, then refrigerate to chill and set overnight. The stock can be made in advance and will keep in the fridge for a few days.

THRICE-FRESH SMALL WONTONS

三鲜小馄饨 | sān xiān xiǎo hún tun | *Makes 80 to 90 wontons*

Small wontons are often served for breakfast. The Shanghainese (and anyone from Jiangsu) order these when they're in the mood for something comforting but not too substantial. More wrapper than meat, small wontons were perplexing to the non-Shanghainese friends I once served them to. "What's the point?" they asked.

The point is the 口感 *kou gan*, "mouthfeel." These wontons are made lightning quick, with just a smear of pork in the center of the wrapper, then scrunched up to form a loose dumpling, closed with a pinch. I believe the smear of pork is only present for that touch of meaty flavor and not meant to be a specific filling. Because of this, the filling is made especially salty, as a small amount needs to flavor an entire mouthful of wonton. In China, a thinner skin is used specifically for these smaller wontons, which is another reason there can't be too much pork filling; the thinner skin would be overcooked by the time the pork filling was done. You can make many small wontons with a small batch of pork.

三鲜 *san zian*, "three fresh," refers not to the filling, but to what the wontons are served with: egg silk, seaweed, and tiny dried shrimp. Together with piping-hot soup and a touch of pork in the thin wonton skin, the *kou gan* is perfect and fragrant. It's a dish that's meant to be slurped down, a wonderfully warming way to start the day.

¼ pound (115 g) ground pork
½ teaspoon grated fresh ginger
½ teaspoon light soy sauce
1 teaspoon Shaoxing wine
pinch of ground white pepper
2 tablespoons Ginger-Scallion Water (page 257)
¼ teaspoon salt
1 (14-ounce/398-g) package thin eggless wonton wrappers
3 cups (720 ml) High Stock (page 277) or chicken stock, plus more as needed for 2 servings

TOPPINGS
egg ribbons (see page 244)
dried seaweed
dried shrimp, 虾皮 *xia pi*
thinly sliced scallions
kosher salt
ground white pepper

1. Combine the pork, ginger, soy sauce, wine, and white pepper in a bowl and whip in one direction (see page 133, step 1) to combine. Add the ginger-scallion water 1 tablespoon at a time and whip until a paste forms. Add the salt and mix to combine.

2. Using a small spatula, scoop about ¼ teaspoon of filling onto a wonton wrapper and smear it across the center. The filling must be smeared instead of dolloped for the right texture. Use the spatula to press the wonton skin into your hand and begin to scrunch the wrapper around the spatula. Remove the spatula and seal the wonton by pressing the scrunched edges together tightly. Set aside on a parchment paper–lined baking sheet, and keep covered with plastic wrap or a damp towel to prevent drying out. Repeat with the remaining filling and wrappers. To eat immediately, proceed to the next step. To store, freeze on the baking sheet and, once frozen, transfer to a freezer-safe container.

3. Bring a large pot of water to a boil over high. Add the wontons, return to a boil, add 1 cup (240 ml) of cold water, then return to a boil again. Remove the wontons with a slotted spoon and divide them between two bowls.

4. Meanwhile, heat the stock.

5. Serve the wontons in the heated stock, topped with egg ribbons, seaweed, dried shrimp, and scallions. Season to taste with salt and white pepper.

SCALLION PANCAKES

葱油饼 ｜ cōng yóu bǐng ｜ *Makes 4 (8-inch/20-cm) pancakes*

Everyone has a favorite version of scallion pancakes—it's one of those popular treats that people get into arguments about because there are so many versions out there. But I'm not here to argue. Instead, I will share my favorite scallion pancake, modeled on the street-style scallion pancakes I've had in Shanghai, and I'd love for you to give them a try. Shanghai street-style scallion pancakes are famous and beloved. The little, thicker rounds are assembled in real time with amazing efficiency and grace, often with pork lard or shrimp, and then pressed onto a hot, fired surface. Because of recent crackdowns on street-food vendors in Shanghai, only a few traditional vendors are left. There are always long lines of locals and tourists waiting for their happy pancakes. I love them, too, but sometimes after eating them, I feel as if I'm covered in grease. This recipe is my happy in-between: it has all the scallion flavor but less of the grease.

The secret is 油酥 *you su*, "oil paste," which holds all the flavor. In Shanghai, you'll see chefs spread a thick layer of yellow *you su* across the surface of the supple dough, dot it with lard and scallions, and then roll it up. I use scallion oil as the base of my *you su*, so the scallion flavor is doubled without doubling the number of scallions in the pancake. Too many raw scallions can expel too much water, causing the pancake to be soggy. This way, both the flavor and the texture are optimized.

This pancake is crispy on the outside but has a chewy, multilayered interior. It's not so crispy that it's brittle, though, like so many scallion pancakes end up being. This is achieved by starting and finishing the pancake on relatively high heat (but not so high as to burn the pancake).

DOUGH

2⅓ cups plus 1 tablespoon (300 g) all-purpose flour

1 teaspoon salt

¾ cup plus 1 tablespoon (195 ml) warm water

油酥 *YOU SU* (OIL PASTE)

5 tablespoons (35 g) all-purpose flour

1½ teaspoons salt

4 tablespoons vegetable oil, plus more for the work surface

2 scallions, chopped into 2-inch (5-cm) segments

DIPPING SAUCE

1 tablespoon black vinegar

1 tablespoon light soy sauce

1 teaspoon granulated sugar

1 clove garlic, minced

1 (1-inch/2.5-cm) piece fresh ginger, peeled and julienned

(continued)

1. **MAKE THE DOUGH:** Mix together the flour and salt in a large bowl. Slowly stream in the water while stirring with chopsticks. Continue to mix until a workable dough forms.

2. Knead by hand for 15 minutes, or in a stand mixer fitted with a dough hook for 7 to 10 minutes on medium speed, until the dough is "smooth and shiny," 光滑 *guang hua*, and begins to pull away from the sides of the bowl. If the dough feels too sticky to knead, very lightly flour your hands. If the dough is too dry, add more water, a teaspoon at a time, and work it into the dough completely before adding more.

3. Wrap the dough in plastic and let it rest for 1 hour at room temperature, or in the fridge for up to 1 day.

4. **MAKE THE OIL PASTE:** Combine the flour and salt in a small heatproof bowl and set aside. Heat the vegetable oil in a small saucepan over medium. Use the side of your cleaver to smash the scallion segments. Add the scallion to the oil and cook until the scallions begin to turn golden, 5 to 7 minutes. Remove and discard the scallions. Pour the hot oil into the heatproof bowl to toast the flour mixture. Mix until a paste is formed.

5. **MAKE THE DIPPING SAUCE:** Whisk together all of the dipping sauce ingredients and set aside. *(continued)*

FILLING

neutral cooking oil, such as canola or grapeseed oil, for greasing and frying

2 teaspoons pork lard (optional; store-bought or homemade, page 271)

3 scallions, finely chopped

6. **ASSEMBLE AND COOK:** Preheat the oven to 200°F (90°C). Set a wire rack onto a baking sheet and place this in the oven. Divide the dough into four equal parts. Work with one quarter at a time, keeping the other parts covered with plastic wrap or a damp dish towel. Use your hands to shape a piece of dough into a log. On a lightly greased work surface, use a rolling pin to roll out the log into a rectangle that is approximately 12 x 4 inches (30.5 x 10 cm). The precise dimensions don't matter too much; the important thing is to roll the dough into a thin rectangle, with a long side nearest you.

7. Thinly spread one-quarter of the oil paste on the surface of the dough, avoiding clumps. It's okay if you have some spots without oil paste. If using, place ½ teaspoon of the lard in the center of the rectangle. Evenly sprinkle one-quarter of the scallions over the dough in an even layer.

8. Fold the rectangle into thirds as if you were folding a letter. Starting from one of the short sides, roll up the dough into a short log. Stand the log vertically so that the spiral faces up. Place your palm over the spiral edge and press down to flatten it into a circle.

9. Use your rolling pin to gently roll the dough into a 7- to 8-inch (17- to 20-cm) round, about ¼ inch (6 mm) thick. If the dough springs back, reverting to its original size before you fry the pancakes, let it sit, covered, for 5 minutes, then roll it out again. Repeat with the remaining dough to create 4 discs.

10. In a skillet large enough to comfortably hold an 8-inch (20-cm) pancake, heat 2 tablespoons of oil over medium-high. It's important not to have the heat too high, as you don't want to burn the pancake or create scalded spots. When the oil shimmers, gently slide in a disc of dough. Cook for 1 minute, then reduce the heat to medium-low and cook, now with the lid on, for 2 minutes more. The bottom should be golden and slightly puffed.

11. Carefully flip the pancake using a spatula and cook for 2 minutes with the lid on. Remove the lid, increase the heat to medium-high, and cook for a final 1½ to 2 minutes, until crispy on the bottom. Use tongs or two spatulas on opposite sides of the pancake to expose more layers. Remove the pancake to the rack in the oven to keep warm. Repeat with the remaining discs of dough.

12. Serve the pancakes hot, cut in wedges—or simply ripped apart—with the dipping sauce.

13. Keep leftovers in the fridge. Reheat in the oven or on the stovetop.

STUFFED STICKY RICE ROLL

粢饭团 | cí fàn tuán | *Makes 1 roll; 2 servings*

A bold breakfast item, 粢饭团 *ci fan tuan* is extremely popular in Shanghai and the surrounding provinces because it is portable and filling. Freshly cooked glutinous rice is rolled into a ball or log, cradling a mix of 油条 *you tiao*, "fried cruller"; pickled vegetables; savory pork floss; and, if you're feeling decadent, a hard-boiled egg. The rolls are packaged in plastic wrap, making them handy for travel. I often see people on their way to work munching on them. There are two kinds you can get: sweet, 甜饭团 *tian fan tuan*, and salty, 咸饭团 *xian fan tuan*.

My favorite is the sweet kind, with black sesame and sugar filling, instead of the savory kind with pickled vegetables and pork floss. I had a particularly delightful *fan tuan* one morning before Alex and I headed off to hike 灵岩山 Ling Yan Mountain, which inspired this recipe. As we made our way to the bus stop in the early hours of the morning, we passed by a lone wooden cart selling glutinous rice rolls. The vendor rolled out a sticky rice mix of purple and white glutinous rice, sprinkled on a light bed of black sesame and sugar mix and crushed peanuts, and crowned it with a freshly fried *you tiao*. She deftly wrapped it into a fat log, then handed it to me. The first thing that struck me was how heavy it was! This would take care of breakfast and then some.

NOTE: If you have a sushi roller, place that underneath the plastic wrap for easier wrapping!

NOTE: When handling sticky rice, slightly dampen your hands with water to prevent sticking. To make a savory version of this recipe, simply omit the black sesame–sugar mixture and add in a sprinkling of pickled vegetables, pork floss, and perhaps even a hard-boiled egg. The Chinese fried cruller is delicious with both sweet and savory versions.

¾ cup (150 g) glutinous sticky rice
¼ cup plus 2 tablespoons (75 g) white rice
½ cup (60 g) toasted black sesame seeds
3 tablespoons granulated sugar
half of a Chinese Fried Cruller, 油条 *you tiao* (page 240)

1. Soak the sticky rice and white rice together with enough water to cover for at least 2 hours but preferably overnight.

2. Drain the rice and cook in an electric rice cooker with a little less water than the manual instructs (I use about 1 cup of water).

3. Place the toasted sesame seeds in a food processor and pulse to coarsely grind. Add the sugar and pulse to combine.

4. Lay out a sheet of plastic wrap on a bamboo sushi mat. Sprinkle some black sesame–sugar mixture on the surface.

5. Dip a wooden spoon in water, then use the spoon to scoop the rice and spread it across the plastic wrap to form an 8 x 6-inch (20 x 15-cm) rectangle. Tightly pack the rice by pressing on it with the back of the spoon.

6. Sprinkle a layer of the black sesame–sugar mixture over the rice. If using, sprinkle a layer of pork floss across the rice.

7. Place a half stick of fried cruller horizontally across the rice.

8. Roll up using the sushi mat. In China, they use a towel and their hand to form more of a closed ball, but at home a sushi mat does the job—the difference is the ends will be open.

9. Squeeze the sushi roller to make sure everything is packed tightly. Cut in half and serve immediately. This transportable treat is eaten slowly from the cut ends, peeling back the plastic wrap as you go!

YEASTED SCALLION AND SESAME BING

羌饼 | qiāng bǐng | *Makes 1 bing; 8 servings*

羌饼 *qiang bing* is a treat from Shanghai's past that lives on through memories. It's hard to find on the streets today, but it used to be sold on many street corners and in wet markets. Sold in wedges sliced from a round circle of bread for as little as 1.5 yuan, they're a bit like yeasted scallion pancakes. This bread wonderfully juxtaposes textures—it's the Chinese equivalent of the French baguette, fluffy and chewy on the inside with a wonderful, crispy crust on the outside. Like a baguette, when testing the doneness of this bread, you tap it to hear that hollow sound. The anticipation builds as you cut into it for the first time—hearing that crackle, seeing steam wisp up—until you get to have that first warm bite, fragrant with green onions.

You can eat this bread whenever you want—as breakfast, with meals, or as a snack—but my favorite way is to have a wedge with a bowl of soup. It's delicious soaked in the soup broth, and handy to wipe up any leftovers.

NOTE: Make sure the scallions used in the filling are very dry; moisture can hinder the cooking of the bread and cause the edges to be soggy.

BREAD DOUGH

¾ cup (180 ml) warm water
2 teaspoons granulated sugar
1½ teaspoons active dry yeast
2 cups (250 g) all-purpose flour, plus more for dusting
pinch of kosher salt
2 tablespoons pork lard (store-bought or homemade, page 271) or vegetable oil

SCALLION FILLING

2 tablespoons vegetable oil, plus more for brushing
8 scallions, finely chopped and patted dry (see Note)
about ½ cup (75 g) white sesame seeds

1. In a small bowl, combine the warm water, sugar, and yeast. Let sit for 5 minutes to bloom to ensure that the yeast is indeed active. Foamy bubbles should appear on the surface.

2. Stream the yeast mixture into the dry ingredients slowly while stirring with a pair of chopsticks. When the dough just comes together, add the lard. Mix until a workable dough forms.

3. Use your hands to knead the dough in the bowl until it is smooth and elastic, about 10 minutes. Cover with plastic wrap and let rise, or until the dough has doubled in size, 1½ to 2 hours.

4. Punch down the dough and, on a lightly floured surface, knead again for 5 to 7 minutes. Cover with plastic wrap and let rise for 20 minutes more.

5. Turn the dough out onto a lightly floured surface, and with a rolling pin, roll it into a large ¼ inch (6 mm) thick rectangle, about 20 inches (51 cm) long and 15 inches (38 cm) wide. Brush the dough with vegetable oil and sprinkle with salt to taste and the chopped, dry scallions.

6. Roll the dough into a log, starting on one of the long edges. Let rest for 5 minutes. Then, starting with one end of the log, roll it up to form a spiral. Using your hands or a rolling pin, flatten the entire spiral to about 1 inch (2.5 cm) thick. Sprinkle some water over the surface and use your hands to spread the moisture. Sprinkle the sesame seeds over the top to cover.

7. Heat 2 tablespoons of vegetable oil in a flat-bottomed nonstick skillet with a lid over medium-high, and then carefully transfer the dough to the skillet with the sesame seed side up. Turn the heat to low, and cover the skillet. Slowly cook the bread for 15 minutes. Carefully flip the bread and cook, covered, for another 10 minutes.

Remove the lid and flip so the sesame seed side is up again and cook for another 5 minutes.

8. Tap the surface of the bread with the tips of your fingers—the sound should be hollow. Remove the bread from the pan and slice into 8 wedges. Serve hot!

CORE RECIPES

WIND-CURED SALT PORK 咸肉 | xián ròu | *Makes 4 pounds (1.8 kg)*

A good salt pork is a treasure of umami, something to be added to any stock, stir-fry, or stew. It's one of the star ingredients for Double Pork Soup (page 102), but it can also be eaten alone, steamed until translucent (one of my dad's favorite ways to eat it). Making salt pork at home is a time-honored tradition that's usually done during the winter season, when the temperature is just right. A mix of salt and Sichuan peppercorns gives it a wonderful aroma. You can certainly find salt pork prepackaged in the store, but making it yourself allows you to control the level of saltiness. If you are using store-bought salt pork, you can decrease the saltiness by soaking it in cold water and then rinsing before using. The amount of salt should be about 10 percent of the pork's weight.

I make my salt pork in big batches and store it in the freezer until needed. Because it's salt-cured, the pork belly doesn't freeze completely, so you can take a block out of the freezer and cut right into it with no need to defrost.

The ideal conditions for making salt pork are cool temperatures, 40°F to 50°F (5°C to 10°C), with good airflow. If it's too hot or humid to safely make salt pork, you can always dry it in the fridge—simply place it on a rack, uncovered, for three days.

NOTE: Traditionally, salt pork is cured in a big ceramic fermentation crock, which used to be a standard item in all Shanghai households. A large, heavy rock is used to press the meat down. Because I use the fridge method, I just use a ceramic or glass pan large enough to fit the pork belly in a single layer. I then place a piece of parchment paper over the meat, then top it with anything heavy I have on hand, such as my cast-iron skillet. This recipe does take some time: 5 days of salt-curing, then another 4 to 5 days of wind-drying.

4½ pounds (2 kg) pork belly
½ pound (225 g) coarse sea salt
½ cup plus 1 tablespoon (1¼ ounces/35 g) whole Sichuan peppercorns
2 tablespoons white Chinese liquor, 白酒 *bai jiu* (page 27)

1. Pat the pork belly dry with paper towels. Let air-dry for 5 minutes.

2. Heat a well-seasoned wok over medium-low, then add the salt and Sichuan peppercorns and toast until the salt becomes golden and aromatic, about 20 minutes. Stir periodically to ensure even toasting. Let cool completely.

3. Place the pork belly in a rimmed pan and rub two-thirds of the cooled salt mixture into the meat to coat on all sides.

4. Drizzle 1 tablespoon of the white liquor over the meat. Cover with a piece of parchment paper, then press down the pork belly with something heavy—I use a cast-iron skillet—and refrigerate to cure for 24 hours.

5. Pour off any liquid that has collected in the pan. Rub the remaining third of the salt mixture on the pork and drizzle with the remaining tablespoon of white liquor. Cover with parchment and the weight again, and refrigerate for an additional 96 hours, pouring off any collected liquid after 48 hours. *(continued)*

6. Remove the pork from the fridge and rinse under cold water to wash away all the salt.

7. Pat the pork belly dry with paper towels. String up the slab with kitchen twine, and hang it in a place that is cool and dry with good airflow, to wind-dry for 4 to 5 days, until dry to the touch but not rock-hard. A slice will reveal a luminous, almost translucent interior.

8. Store in a sealed plastic bag in the freezer for up to 6 months.

HAND-MINCED MEAT 手工剁肉 | *shǒu gōng duò ròu* | *Amount will vary*

NOTE: You will need a heavy, sharp meat cleaver for this recipe.

1 piece of pork (choose pork belly for a fattier mince; otherwise pork butt, shoulder, or any boneless piece works well, too), amount depends on how much you want to mince

1. Place the pork in the freezer for 30 minutes to an hour, until it is half frozen for easier cutting. Alternatively, let the frozen pork thaw in the fridge or in a sealed bag soaked in cold water until half-thawed.

2. Using a meat cleaver, cut the pork into 3-inch (7.5-cm) portions.

3. Working in batches, slice one portion of the pork into very thin (1/16-inch/2-mm) slices.

4. Stack 3 or 4 of these slices together and cut them into very thin (1/16-inch/2-mm) strips. Continue with the remaining slices.

5. Rotate the strips to be perpendicular to your knife, then cut the strips into a tiny dice; do your best to make these cubes uniform in size and shape (in French cooking, this is called a fine brunoise). Continue with the remaining strips.

6. Repeat steps 2 through 5 with the remaining portions of pork until all the meat is cut into a tiny dice.

7. Now you are ready to mince the meat. I like to place a kitchen towel under my cutting board to keep it from sliding around as I chop. Do your best to spread the dice out into a single layer on your cutting board. Utilizing the heaviness of your meat cleaver, repeatedly chop across the layer of meat. I chop in a crisscross pattern: first with my knife oriented vertically to the board, then oriented 45 degrees to the left, 45 degrees to the right, and horizontal. This method of rapidly, repeatedly chopping breaks the tiny cubes of meat into a proper mince.

PORK LARD 猪油 | zhū yóu | *Makes about 1 cup (240 ml)*

NOTE: Be careful not to burn yourself when working with hot fat or grease.

1½ pounds (680 g) pork fat
½ cup (120 ml) cold water

1. Cut the pork fat into ½-inch (12-mm) slices.

2. Place the chunks of fat and water in a wok. Bring the water to a boil over medium-high, then reduce the heat to medium-low and simmer, uncovered, until the fat becomes transparent.

3. Keep simmering, allowing the water to slowly evaporate. When almost all the water has evaporated, reduce the heat to the lowest setting and let the water cook off completely. The pork fat will begin to render. The transition is so smooth I usually don't catch the exact moment it begins. I just notice clear yellow grease starting to build up.

4. As the fat renders, spoon out the grease and strain it through a fine-mesh sieve into a bowl. The whole process will take 45 to 60 minutes, depending on the heat of your stove.

5. When you have rendered and strained all the fat, let it cool to room temperature. Discard the leftover cracklings (or keep as a snack, mix with salt to make pork crackling–flavored salt, or toss them into whatever you are cooking that day for some flavor and crunch). Pour the fat into a sterilized glass or nonreactive metal container and store in the fridge, where it will solidify into creamy white lard. Lard is incredibly shelf-stable and will keep in the fridge for up to a year. Alternatively, freeze the lard and scoop off portions as you need them.

SNOW VEGETABLE 雪菜 | xuě cài | *Makes about 3 cups (300 g)*

1 pound (455 g) fresh small
  mustard greens
2 tablespoons coarse sea salt

1. Wash the mustard greens thoroughly in a large bowl filled with cold water, making sure to wash between the leaves and discarding any silt that sinks in the bowl.

2. Let the greens air-dry completely, 20 to 30 minutes. Alternatively, string them up with kitchen twine and hang overnight in a cool place to dry.

3. Spread the greens out on a baking sheet and sprinkle evenly with the salt. Use your hands to massage the salt all over the stems and leaves. Let stand for 15 minutes.

4. Reserve the liquid that has collected in the pan and set aside. Place the mustard greens in a large plastic bag. Continue to massage the leaves and stems through the bag until the greens are dark colored and moist.

5. Transfer the greens to a sterilized jar or fermentation crock and press them down with a spoon to the bottom of the jar. Place a heavy weight on top to press down the greens even farther to submerge them in the liquid that will seep out, which may take some time. If after an hour the greens are still not submerged, add the reserved liquid to completely submerge them. Close with an airtight lid.

6. Let the mustard greens ferment at room temperature, opening the jar once a day to allow any gases to escape and pressing the greens down to ensure they are covered by liquid. Let sit for 3 to 5 days, depending on your preference for tang as well as the fermentation temperature. When pickled to your liking, store in the jar or crock in the fridge for up to 2 months.

RED CHILI OIL 红油 | hóng yóu | *Makes about 2 cups (480 ml)*

My parents joke that they fed me hot pepper when I was a baby, and that's why I can tolerate heat in food. While my father grew up in Shanghai, his side of the family has deep roots in 成都 Chengdu in Sichuan, so along with Shanghainese food, my dad has always loved adding heat to his cooking, and I've adopted this practice in my own cooking. Chili oil, peppers, and Sichuan peppercorns are always in my pantry.

Give this a try. It's slightly different from other oils because the first step includes infusing a variety of aromatics, which adds depth and fragrance to the oil.

There are two important components of this recipe: choosing quality ingredients and not burning the spices. Unfortunately, the best chili flakes and peppercorns are usually sourced directly from China. If all else fails, try to find Korean pepper flakes (*gochugaru*) in an Asian supermarket, which will give a different flavor profile but still a good amount of heat. You can omit the peppercorns in infusing at the end, but I find they add that wonderful hint of 麻辣 *ma la*, "numbing spice," and fragrance.

NOTE: To avoid burning the spices, use a candy or deep-frying thermometer to help you keep an eye on the oil's temperature. Be careful when working with hot oil.

AROMATICS

2 cups (480 ml) vegetable oil (rapeseed/canola or grapeseed work well)
2 thin (1-inch/2.5-cm) slices of ginger, smashed
3 scallions, trimmed to fit in pan
2 whole star anise
1 piece cassia bark or cinnamon stick
5 dried bay leaves
3 tablespoons whole Sichuan red peppercorns, slightly crushed
2 dried tangerine peels
1 teaspoon fennel seeds
6 to 7 dried chilis

CHILI OIL

½ cup (50 g) crushed red pepper flakes (or freshly crushed dried Sichuan chili peppers)
¼ cup white sesame seeds
1 teaspoon Sichuan red peppercorns, freshly ground
½ teaspoon green peppercorns, freshly ground
2 cloves garlic, grated (optional)

1. **INFUSE THE AROMATICS:** Place the oil and the aromatics in a medium heavy-bottomed saucepan and heat over medium.

2. When the oil begins to bubble and sizzle, reduce the heat to low and heat the oil until it reaches 300°F to 305°F (150°C to 152°C).

3. Simmer very gently at that temperature for 15 minutes, adjusting the flame as necessary to keep the oil at 300°F (150°C) to prevent the aromatics from burning.

4. **MAKE THE CHILI FLAKE MIX:** Meanwhile, in a heatproof bowl, mix the crushed red pepper flakes, white sesame seeds, and ground red and green peppercorns. Add the garlic, if using.

5. Bring the temperature of the oil up to 325°F (163°C).

6. Stream ¼ cup of the hot oil into the bowl with the chili flake mix. I do this a few spoonfuls at a time—be careful of splashing.

7. Turn off the heat and gently stream the remaining oil through a fine-mesh sieve into the chili flake mix, being careful to avoid splashes. If the spices bubble up too vigorously, the oil might be too hot. If this happens, stop adding in the oil and let it cool down for 1 minute before proceeding with pouring it into the bowl. Discard the aromatics.

8. Let cool, then store in a sterilized jar at room temperature for up to 6 months. For best results, let the oil sit for 48 hours before using. If you added fresh garlic, keep in the fridge for up to 1 month.

STOVETOP RICE 白米饭 | bái mǐ fàn | *Makes 2¾ to 3 cups*

1 cup (180 ml) dried medium-grain rice

1. Rinse the rice thoroughly in the same pot you will be cooking it in, until the water runs clear.

2. Add fresh water to the rice until the water level is about ½ inch to ¾ inch (12 mm, or about the length of your middle fingernail) above the rice.

3. Bring to a boil over medium-high and cook until enough water has been absorbed that the water level and rice level are the same, about 5 minutes. Stir to distribute the water and dislodge any rice that may have stuck to the bottom of the pot.

4. Cover the pot, reduce the heat to low, and cook for an additional 20 minutes, until the rice is tender. Fluff the rice with a spatula before serving.

CONGEE 粥／稀饭 | zhōu / xī fàn | *Makes 4 servings*

Congee—called 粥 *zhou*, if thicker like a porridge, or 稀饭 *xi fan*, if thinner in consistency—is a fool-proof breakfast food. White rice is cooked in water until it disintegrates, blooming and thickening up the congee.

Congee is a universal Chinese breakfast, shared across many regional cuisines. It's light yet nourishing, gently "coating your stomach" for comfort, or so my mom says. In the Jiangnan region, the preference is for *xi fan*. In fact, my parents often serve large bowls, saying it's basically "just water."

If you are looking for a basic congee, a trick I've learned to speed up the cooking is to rinse and freeze the rice overnight. The next morning, simply combine it with water and reduce the cooking time to 15 to 20 minutes, adjusting for consistency as needed.

7 to 8 cups (1¾ to 2 L) water, chicken stock, or High Stock (page 277)

¾ cup (150 g) short- or medium-grain rice

OPTIONAL ADDITIONS
dried lily bulb
dried gorgon fruit, soaked in water overnight
dried mung bean, soaked in water overnight

SUGGESTED TOPPINGS
pickled vegetables
thousand-year egg (page 29)
salted duck egg
chili-fermented tofu

1. Bring the water to a boil over medium-high. Add the rice as well as any optional additions of your choosing and bring back to a boil.

2. Reduce the heat to low and simmer, covered, for about 1 hour, stirring periodically to prevent the rice from sticking, until the rice grains have "blossomed" and the congee has a thick, porridge-like consistency.

3. Check to see if the consistency matches your preference. If you want it thicker, cook longer without the lid. If you want it thinner, add some room-temperature water.

4. Serve with your choice of toppings. I recommend placing a few pickled vegetables in your bowl, then swirling them around with your chopsticks to flavor the congee.

FRIED RICE 炒饭 | chǎo fàn | *Makes 4 servings*

This is a leftovers, blank-canvas pantry dish. It's not fancy—in fact, it's not really a recipe, more a method to throw rice, eggs, and whatever you have on hand into a wok. The dish typically progresses like this: start with a hot wok with oil (pork lard, olive oil, or butter), cook some eggs, aromatics (scallion), then add the variables (chicken, beef, tofu, peas, greens), followed by rice (leftover or freshly cooked on the dry side). In true Shanghainese fashion, I utilize the toasty aroma of cooked scallions. After frying the eggs, I toast the white parts of the scallion in oil, drawing out that nutty fragrance that will serve as the foundation for this dish. I season primarily with salt and sometimes add a tiny touch of soy sauce. The main flavor is not soy sauce, though—it can overwhelm and add too much moisture. I finish with the remaining green parts of the scallions sprinkled on top, stir-fried two to three times to incorporate. Some tips for successful fried rice: use day-old rice or undercooked rice to prevent having too much moisture. A hot wok is imperative for developing the flavor and texture of this dish. Have all your ingredients ready.

2 tablespoons vegetable oil, plus more if needed

4 large eggs, beaten until the yolk and whites are just combined

4 scallions, white and green parts separated and sliced thinly

salt

ground white pepper

2 cups (360 ml) cooked rice, preferably kept overnight in the fridge

1 teaspoon light soy sauce

OPTIONAL ADDITIONS

chicken, beef, firm tofu, ham, Chinese sausage, bacon, mushrooms, peas, other vegetables

1. Heat a well-seasoned wok over medium. When the wok is hot, add the oil and swirl to coat.

2. Add in the beaten eggs—they should bloom and sizzle. Scramble quickly so generous curds form. When almost cooked through (but still moist), remove and set aside.

3. Add more oil if needed, and toast the white parts of the scallion for 5 to 10 minutes until aromatic.

4. At this point, add in any other optional ingredients (protein or vegetables) you want and stir-fry to cook or reheat (if using leftovers). Season with salt and white pepper.

5. Once all of your proteins and vegetables are cooked or warmed through, add the rice to the wok and break it apart with your spatula. Stir to coat the rice with the oil. No clumps should remain.

6. Add the eggs back into the wok and gently mix without breaking up the curds too much.

7. Adjust the seasonings to taste and add the soy sauce for depth.

HIGH STOCK 高汤 | gāo tāng | *Makes about 3 quarts (3 L)*

If pork lard is the secret flavor bomb, this is the flavor elixir. Use this stock as a base for any noodle or wonton soups, or as additional flavoring in stir-fries or braises. It's not so different from any other stock you'd make. According to my mother, the trick is to cook it for as long as you can—the longer, the better—until the chicken or pork meat very easily flakes off the bone, or even detaches on its own. In the winter, with frozen wontons and stock ready in my freezer, I can put together wonton soup, a satisfying, warming meal, with minimal effort.

Other umami ingredients, such as dried scallops, squid, ham, or salt pork, can also be added, as desired. In fact, dried scallops are a favorite addition!

To make plain chicken stock, just omit the pork.

1 (3- to 4-pound/1.4- to 1.8-kg) whole chicken

1 pound (455 g) pork bones (back, neck, trotter, or other)

5 (1-inch/2.5-cm) pieces fresh ginger

5 scallions

¼ cup Shaoxing wine

1. In a large pot, combine the chicken, pork bones, and 4 quarts (4 L) water, or enough water to cover the chicken. Bring to a boil over high, and boil for 1 to 2 minutes.

2. Drain and rinse the chicken and pork, discarding the liquid—this step will make for a cleaner stock. Rinse and clean the pot, or else use a new stockpot, and place the chicken and pork in the pot.

3. Smack the ginger and scallions with the flat side of a cleaver to release the aromatics. Add the ginger and scallions to the pot along with 4 quarts (4 L) fresh water, or enough to cover.

4. Bring to a boil over high, then reduce the heat to low. Add the wine, cover, and simmer very gently for 4 to 5 hours.

5. Strain the stock, discarding the chicken, pork bones, ginger, and scallions. Let cool and then transfer the stock to airtight containers and refrigerate for up to 3 days or freeze for up to 3 months.

6. While the stock chills in the refrigerator, a layer of fat will collect on the surface—simply scoop it out with a spoon. Be sure to reserve that fat and use it as you would lard to flavor any dish!

ACKNOWLEDGMENTS

What I love about this book is not just the final product, but everything and everyone who made this come to life. Thank you to all.

Alexander Xu, thank you for being there for me on my trips to Shanghai, including forages into the bamboo forest, ventures out to the middle of a lake to peer at hairy crabs, trekking to rural Jiangnan to see where river shrimp is harvested. We ate way too much in the name of research, and you were with me every step of the way. You are my partner. Thank you so much for your support, cheering, guidance, and expert eye in photography and postprocessing.

My parents, Yaqin Zhou and Dongtai Liu, this book would not exist without you. The food you cooked for me growing up is like a warm blanket of home for me today, and the inspiration behind this book. This book is an homage to you both. Thank you for teaching me and sharing this with the world. Even if I can make my own *zongzi* or *shaomai*, I will still request it when I come visit, and I know my future children will beg me for their grandparents' food!

To my other parents, Nu Xu and Fei Xu, as well as my sisters Aimee and Angelina Xu. From the start of the book, you all have been so incredibly kind and supportive. Nu Xu, your recipe for saltwater duck is legend, and I'm so thrilled to be sharing it with the world. I now associate all celebrations and holidays with it, because of you!

Berta Treitl, my wonderful agent and friend, you have believed in me since 2015. I remember I had the seed of an idea, and then when we talked on the phone, you not only expressed support but also helped me grow this seed.

Cristina Garces, I will never forget your investment in me. Your cheerleading, support, and understanding were crucial, and I don't think I would be here without you.

Harper Design, you are the dream team that made this book what it is. From the very start you saw my vision and stood behind it. I am so filled with gratitude for your support and efforts. Tricia Levi, I will never forget how much you listened and welcomed my opinions with patience. My thoughts on layout, typography, cover, and even small things such as the weight of the paper stock were taken seriously. I appreciated every question and note you sent my way, because that detail orientation and meticulousness is what made this book what it is today. Claudia Wu, thank you for your stunning, magical vision. For listening to my numerous design inputs and requests for variations. From the beginning, it was obvious that you clearly understood what my book was about because your design is just perfect. To Soyolmaa Lkhagvadorj, Lynne Yeamans, Marta Schooler, and Suzette Lam. Thank you.

Lucy Liu, my dear twin. Your cheerleading is unparalleled and I will always appreciate seeing a text from you telling me that you have found more fans for me who plan to preorder my book. I love you.

Caroline Ricard, George Munger, and Sullivan: you are my best friends. Thank you for always cheering me on and patiently listening as I blathered on and on about this book. Love you all.

To Mr. and Mrs. Zhou, thank you for showing me your hairy crab farm. To Dai Jianjun of Dragon Well Manor and Mr. Zhou, thank you for introducing me to the farming community in

Hangzhou. I learned SO much. Also, Betty Richardson, it was so much fun walking around with you in Shanghai and hearing your experience with Shanghainese food as an ex-pat.

Jenny Huang, you are a constant inspiration and role model to me. Your words of support and thoughts on photography, design, and basically input on every part of the book were so necessary and had a huge influence on the final outcome. You were with me every step of the way and not shy about telling me when something was off. I needed that. Please don't ever stop being yourself. Here's to so many more years of friendship.

Alana Kysar, you are a gem and I am so thankful for your friendship. I feel like we were talking about this book two years before I got my book deal. You've always believed in this book and its longevity. Thank you so much for your cheerleading, for being there, and for giving me honest and necessary insight into all parts of the process.

Hetty Lui McKinnon, you get me. You were one of the first to believe in my book. Thank you so much for always being there.

Michelle Lopez, you lent me your ear every step of the way. I ranted to you about every struggle, sheer frustration, and small wins, and you always shared a wise word that got me through it all. Thank you.

To my wonderful community of recipe developers, prior cookbook authors, and food photographers, I don't think I could've made it through without your sage wisdom and conversations. Thank you to Michelle Lopez, Alana Kysar, Skye McAlpine, Valentina Sofrini, Lily Diamond, Andrea Gentl, Martin Hyers, Carey Nershi, Jessie Snyder, Mandy Lee, Summer Min, Mythy Huynh, Alanna Taylor-Tobin, Sarah Menanix, Amanda Paa, Michael Piazza, and many others.

Caroline Lange, this cookbook could not have been done without you. Thank you so much for meticulously cooking through my cookbook, testing my recipes with an eagle eye and taste, expert editing, and just making this process fun. One of my favorite memories was coming over to your home in Brooklyn and making a meal together with friends.

Mimi Chau, you cooked through so many of my recipes, providing honest feedback, and the photographs you've shared with me of your family eating the food has brought tears to my eyes. You reminded me many times why I was writing this book. Thank you.

Sam Merlin and Emily Geldwert, you two have been stalwart supporters since before the cookbook was born. Sam, I am honored you cooked my recipes and gave me honest, much needed feedback. Emily, thank you for tasting what Sam cooked. We love you both (and your little ones).

Lainey Fink Scott, your ceramics are breathtaking, and I will forever cherish the pieces and the role they play in my book. It was a deliberate and meaningful choice to style my food on non-traditional ceramics, beloved pieces I use in my everyday life.

A huge thanks and endless hugs to my recipe testers, who dealt with my nitpicky comments and questions and provided invaluable feedback: Caroline Lange, Lucy Liu, Sam Merlin, Mythy Huynh, Lily Cheng, Summer Min, Alana Kysar, Soe Thein, Johnny Wang, Lucia Lee, Sheri Chun, Max Walker, Alina Gatowski, Emily Abdinor, Kevin Masse, Linh Pham, Allison, Marsha Ungchusri, Yishian, Yeesheen Yang, Maria Mei, Yakira, Connie Jew, and Mireia Roura.

To my fellow Chinese Americans who grew up eating home-cooked Chinese meals, thank you for writing to me and sharing your own experiences with food—you are an inspiration and I hope this brings some nostalgic joy to your table. To all my readers at bettysliu.com, thank you for your never-ending support. You made my dream come true.

INDEX

ABOUT THE AUTHOR

Betty Liu is a Chinese-American home cook who resides in Boston with her husband, Alexander Xu, and their dog, Annie. Her whole family is from Shanghai, and her husband's family is from Suzhou and Wuxi, so she grew up eating homecooked food from the region, both in the US and in China. She started writing about Chinese food in 2015 on her award-winning blog *bettysliu.com* and found joy in talking about the food that reminded her of home. Since then, her writing, photography, and recipes have been featured on sites such as *Bon Appétit* and *Saveur*, and she has taught food photography workshops around the world. She is a doctor training to be a surgeon, but in her spare time she continues to cook.

My Shanghai.
Copyright © 2020 Betty Liu.

All rights reserved. No part of this book may be used or reproduced in any manner whatsoever without written permission except in the case of brief quotations embodied in critical articles and reviews. For information address Harper Design, 195 Broadway, New York, NY 10007.

HarperCollins books may be purchased for educational, business, or sales promotional use. For information please email the Special Markets Department at SPsales@harpercollins.com.

First published in 2020 by
Harper Design
An Imprint of HarperCollins*Publishers*
195 Broadway, New York, NY 10007
Tel: (212) 207-7000
Fax: (855) 746-6023
harperdesign@harpercollins.com
www.hc.com

Distributed throughout the world by
HarperCollins*Publishers*
195 Broadway, New York, NY 10007

Book designed by Claudia Wu

ISBN 978-0-06-285472-8
Library of Congress Control Number:
2020039142

Printed in China
First Printing, 2020